The Lynching of Peter Wheeler

THE
LYNCHING
OF PETER WHEELER

DEBRA KOMAR

Edited by Paula Sarson.
Cover image by Thomas Maxwell Rodger (www.thomasmaxwellrodger.com).
Cover and page design by Chris Tompkins.
Printed in Canada.
10 9 8 7 6 5 4 3 2 1

Library and Archives Canada Cataloguing in Publication

Komar, Debra, 1965-, author
The lynching of Peter Wheeler / Debra Komar.

Includes bibliographical references and index.
Issued in print and electronic formats.
ISBN 978-0-86492-417-9 (pbk.). — ISBN 978-0-86492-603-6 (epub)

1. Wheeler, Peter, 1869-1896 — Trials, litigation, etc. 2. Kempton, Annie, 1881-1896. 3. Lynching — Nova Scotia — History — 19th century. 4. Trials (Murder) — Nova Scotia. 5. Criminal justice, Administration of — Nova Scotia — History — 19th century. I. Title.

HV6471.C32N6 2014   364.1'34   C2013-907609-3
                           C2013-907610-7

Goose Lane Editions acknowledges the generous support of the Canada Council for the Arts, the Government of Canada through the Canada Book Fund (CBF), and the Government of New Brunswick through the Department of Tourism, Heritage and Culture.

Goose Lane Editions
500 Beaverbrook Court, Suite 330
Fredericton, New Brunswick
CANADA E3B 5X4
www.gooselane.com

To my brother Mark,
who can't understand why all books
aren't dedicated to him.

*[T]he newspapers of a town are its looking glasses...
it is here you see yourself as others see you.*

Bridgetown Monitor, March 4, 1896

Contents

Preface

Violent crime renders us myopic. In the immediate aftermath of a murder, it can be impossible to see things clearly; emotions run high and the desire for vengeance often trumps reason. When the crime has racial overtones, justice is rarely colour-blind, and for cases that capture the media spotlight, the wave of punditry and prognostication that inevitably follows sweeps away all hope of ever separating fact from fiction. That is why crimes pulled from the annals of history have such value — with distance comes clarity. The lessons are readily learned once the passion has dimmed, much like failed relationships. We even have the benefit of knowing how the story ends, or at least thinking we do. And it is through the benefit of the cold, clear lens of hindsight that we can finally raise questions for which there were no good answers in the heat of the moment.

One of the telltale symptoms of our crime-induced myopia is wrongful conviction. The need for swift justice easily morphs into a race to convict, and in our haste, the innocent are sometimes mistaken for the guilty. It can be nigh on impossible to recognize a false conviction while it is happening: the victim's family demand closure and the wounded community wants nothing more than to once again feel safe and secure. The presumption of innocence that is at the heart of our justice system is a noble ideal, but it is no guarantee that we know an innocent man when we see one, particularly when we are blinded by the need to find a guilty one. And so, if proximity to the crime blinds us to our mistakes, it stands to reason that a little distance may bring the truth into focus.

This book began with a simple question: is it possible to recognize a wrongful conviction buried deep in our nation's past and, in so doing, identify how and why the mistake occurred? The erroneous judgment could cut either way: an innocent person falsely accused or the guilty party set free. Since a wrongful conviction inherently implies error, I would need to apply modern forensic science and investigational standards to a crime in antiquity in order to establish a credible basis for an erroneous verdict. To that end, I began searching through past criminal cases, looking for files with extensive surviving documentation, including trial transcripts, autopsy records, and police reports. In addition, the outcome of the case had to rely in some measure on physical evidence — fingerprints, blood, footprints, or tool marks to name just a few — and the vestiges of that evidence had to be retained in the archives, at least in the form of testimony and reports from the original expert witnesses or investigators. It was a tall order; the historical archives relating to crime are notoriously spotty or even entirely absent. Furthermore, forensic science was not recognized as a discipline until the early part of the twentieth century and its precursors rarely made an appearance in nineteenth-century courtrooms. After months of searching, I found what I was looking for in my backyard: the murder of Annie Kempton in Bear River, Nova Scotia, in the winter of 1896. Peter Wheeler was later convicted and hanged for the crime.

Although Annie's death was front-page news in its day, the case has largely been forgotten outside of Bear River. It has been the subject of a single work of fiction: Arthur Thurston's 1987 self-published novel, *Poor Annie Kempton: She's in Heaven Above*, in which the author imagines having conversations with the saga's key players. In the past decade an original play based on the crime was produced but this, too, was a creative work loosely founded on fact. While there have always been doubters and rumblings about Peter's innocence over the years, this is the first factual public examination of the case since his trial and the first credible attempt to challenge his conviction. Initially, I briefly toyed with the idea of trying to identify "the real killer" but as I began to research Wheeler in earnest, the mechanics of how and why he came to be falsely accused and convicted were far more compelling. Those interested in pursuing alternative suspects will be heartened to learn that, in the course of laying out the case for Wheeler's innocence, all the collected evidence is carefully detailed. Hidden within is the identity of the actual killer and your guess is as good as mine.

For more than twenty years as a practicing forensic scientist, I frequently testified as an expert witness but it was never my job to tell the jury who was innocent and who was guilty. My role was to identify, collect, and analyze all the available evidence; develop a cohesive narrative that explained that evidence; present it in a clear manner; and help the triers of fact to understand the science and technical aspects of the testing process. It then fell to the jurors to add that information to the other testimony they heard and reach their verdict. The same methodology follows here. My goal was to collect and analyze the information; call your attention to the evidence or testimony that warrants your consideration; develop a cohesive narrative; and guide you through the technical aspects of the research. After that, it falls to you, the reader as the thirteenth juror, to reach your own conclusions as to what really happened in Bear River in 1896.

This re-examination of Wheeler's conviction began as an intellectual exercise and so it remains. This is not an impassioned quest for belated justice and the results of this inquiry have no impact on the historical verdict in the case. The window for altering Wheeler's fate closed the day he was hanged; the introduction of new exculpatory evidence will not change the fact that in the case of *Crown v. Wheeler* history and the Canadian justice system record Peter Wheeler as a guilty man. Rewriting history was never the point. This book looks back so we can see ourselves more clearly now.

❨

This is a true story. The text in quotations draws from original sources: court records, newspapers, and other historical documentation.

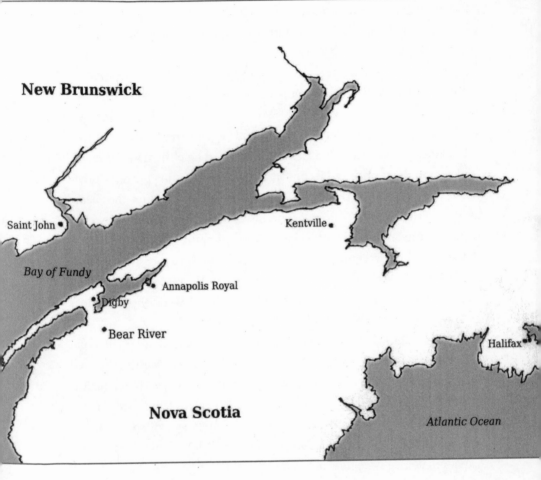

New Brunswick

Saint John •

Bay of Fundy

Kentville •

Annapolis Royal •
• Digby
• Bear River

Halifax •

Nova Scotia

Atlantic Ocean

one

And So It Begins

The killer was long gone but the violence lingered, casting a pall over the house. Her body lay broken in the sitting room. Its awkward position — on her knees, arms to her side, face to the ground — seemed staged, an unnatural end to an unspeakable act. She was cold to the touch. Blood pooled thick and glutinous around her head, matting her hair. Tiny flecks of gore speckled the walls and floor, castoff from the blunt instrument used to obliterate any semblance of her once-winsome face. She was half-dressed, her underclothes an assault on Victorian modesty. A man's coat had been draped over her in a last desperate measure of dignity.

Her body, like the house that enshrouded her, bore signs of the fatal struggle. Her limbs were bruised and bloodied. The carpet was torn, chairs overturned. Upstairs, her bed was in disarray, as if she had been pulled from its safe, warm confines. A framed sampler mounted on the wall above her head listed at a precarious angle. A cruel cosmic joke, its embroidered message read "Do right and fear not."[1]

It was not the only jarringly inappropriate artifact in the room. A container of homemade preserves lay half-eaten beside her, a spoon still cradled inside. The bloody fingerprints on the handle beckoned a sickening thought: her assailant had paused to eat the jam after killing her.

Her cause of death was painfully obvious. A short cut of stove wood rested on the rug, painted with her blood. Its dimensions perfectly mirrored those of the jagged wounds across her face, but the log was not what killed her. Three deep gashes across her throat were the fatal injuries, stigmata of her killer's uncontrollable rage. Two silver case knives lay near her head. Lest anyone doubt their significance, they were coated in blood. One, however, did not look sharp enough to cut butter. The far more formidable blade of a well-honed butcher's knife lay in wait on the only standing table in the room, yet it bore no trace of her blood. It was a curious anomaly, one that escaped all notice.

Like a shadow box, her blood had captured the outline of her killer. Bloody handprints were plastered on the cutlery and the window ledge. Bloody footprints faded in the snow, flagging his escape route through the back door. The assault had been quick but he had not been careful. He made no effort to mask his crime or destroy the telltale traces of it. There was little question her assailant had left soaked in her blood, a marked man.

Her name was Annie Kempton. She was fourteen years old, just two weeks shy of her fifteenth year. She had spent the evening alone in her family home; it was her first and only night of independence. She had not lived to see the dawn.

In her short life, Annie had known her fair share of heartaches. As she entered her teens, Annie took her maiden voyage to the United States under less than ideal circumstances. Her cleft palate resulted in a noticeable speech impediment, and to ease the social stigma such afflictions carried, her parents had sent her south in search of a corrective operation. The procedure was not successful. Once puberty had had its way with her, Annie was left with a pretty face but was cursed with a large awkward frame and an incorrigible lisp.

As if that were not a sufficient cross to bear, Annie had already fallen victim to crime, although mercifully not of the violent sort. Some months prior, a small cache of money she had saved working odd jobs was stolen. The thief was quickly apprehended and sentenced to two years in jail. For those possessed of a prescient mind, the incident struck a tocsin note in her otherwise sheltered existence.

The Kemptons lived in a sturdy if modest frame house in a village full of the same: Bear River, Nova Scotia. History records that, "Although socially not occupying an exalted position, the family [was] generally respected for their clean name and industry."[2] Clean and industrious to a fault, the Kemptons found themselves scattered far and wide in the dawning days of 1896. Annie's father and brother spent weeks at a stretch in the surrounding forests, cutting lumber. Her mother and three sisters had all fled south, across the border to the Boston area — a consequence of marriage for Annie's siblings, a matter of financial necessity for the family matriarch.

In absentia, parents and siblings alike agreed that Annie was too young, too naive, to be left home alone. There were plans in place, arrangements made with several local women to stay with the teen and fill the parental void. Even the best-laid plans sometimes go awry.

Whether Annie found herself alone that night by choice, by accident, or by malicious design would be a question much debated in the press, in the meeting houses and local taverns, and at no less than four public inquiries over the next six months. By then, everyone felt certain they knew the answer, knew who was to blame. That's the problem with rumour masquerading as certainty: the "facts" seem more absolute than they actually are.

Annie had been alone that night — Monday, January 27, 1896 — but she was not alone the next morning. Her body was discovered by a neighbour, a young man by the name of Peter Wheeler. Peter's landlady, Tillie Comeau, had sent him to the Kempton house to buy milk. On a frigid pewter Maritime morning, just after eight, Peter had walked into the Kempton home, calling a greeting to announce his arrival. As he made his way from the kitchen to the parlour, searching for the youngest lady of the house, he saw Annie crumpled and exposed on the sitting-room floor. What happened next came under harsh scrutiny, repeatedly called into question by those fostering their own agendas. At some point, all could at least agree that Wheeler ran and raised the alarm in the village.

Within seconds, the room began to fill with onlookers: doctors, police, neighbours, and friends — the concerned, the curious, and the morbid alike. Many people saw Annie as she lay on the floor, broken and lifeless. Far too many trampled through the crime scene: touching things, moving things, trying to "help." Some in the village took it upon themselves to play detective, collecting evidence and documenting what they saw as material to the case. Others simply pointed fingers and demanded instant justice.

Word of the murder spread quickly. Urgent cryptic messages were sent, pleading for the hasty return of the girl's parents and siblings. A call went out to Halifax requesting the assistance of a seasoned detective to head the investigation. A coroner was named and an autopsy arranged. The local funeral home was put on notice. Those without a defined role did the one thing they could: they disseminated the tragic news. Neighbour told neighbour. Distant relatives were contacted. And, in the midst of it all, a lone reporter began taking notes.

In the coming days, the number of journalists jockeying for position would grow exponentially, like parasites on an accommodating host. The headlines they generated repulsed and captivated an audience hungry for every repugnant morsel. The melodrama they choreographed became a guilty pleasure for those blessed by distance. For those who knew and loved Annie, the glare of the media spotlight cauterized the still-gaping wound, dulling their pain.

Annie Kempton was no longer alone. Her tantalizing glimpse of privacy was gone, snuffed out by a momentary flash of violence and the opportunistic scavenging of a press corps drawn by the chum of senseless tragedy. Her life had been cloistered, bucolic, and unremarkable. Her death now belonged to the masses.

two

"Nearer Brute Than Human"

Since such things matter, the credit for breaking the news of Annie's murder goes to the *Digby Weekly Courier*, even if such things mattered only to the *Courier* and its less expeditious competitors. On Tuesday afternoon, less than five hours after Annie's body was discovered, the *Courier* went to press with a special edition: a single handbill dedicated to the "Murder at Bear River."[1]

The *Courier* paid a price for its haste. Though scant in detail, the tabloid still managed to get wrong the few facts they had. Annie was reported to be sixteen years old, two years more than her true age. The paper claimed Annie was last seen alive in the town at nine o'clock on Monday night, a full four hours later than was actually the case. In an age before bylines, the reporter — identified only as "the COURIER man"[2] — asserted that the perpetrator or perpetrators hid in the home prior to the girl's return, awaiting the opportunity to strike. Such speculation was later revealed to be false.

The report was quick to identify potential suspects: "two suspicious characters"[3] allegedly seen near the Kempton home the night before. The two men were arrested and jailed in nearby Annapolis Royal. They were said to be "railway employees"[4] and "Italians."[5] In its rush to beat its rivals to the punch, the *Digby Courier* was clearly drafting the edition on the fly. In the space of a single article, the *Courier* labelled the pair as prime suspects, then strangely backpedalled. The report claimed "they tell a straight story, however, and are not thought to be implicated,"[6] a mere two paragraphs after being the lone voice implicating them. In its regular edition three days later, the *Courier* was forced to recant even further, noting the two men "were clearly innocent."[7]

In retrospect, the special edition stands as a testament to hyperbolic fatuity, designed to incite panic and outrage in a community that needed no such goading. Although specifics of the killing remained scarce, the *Digby Courier* did not shrink from declaring the murder to be one of the most "revolting crimes in all Canada,"[8] committed by a fiend "nearer brute than human."[9] Clearly conflicted with his new agenda, the paper's editor declared that the details of the case were "sickening,"[10] even as he rushed to produce sufficient copies to nauseate the entire eastern seaboard.

☾

The next morning, Wednesday, January 29, one of the major Halifax dailies, the *Morning Chronicle*, waded into the fray, a tad more cautious and circumspect that its laurel-hoarding challenger, the *Digby Weekly Courier*. The *Chronicle* took great delight in correcting many of the *Courier*'s more egregious errors before outlining its own theory of the crime: the assailant had intended to rape Annie Kempton but she had fought back, prompting the craven villain to kill her to shield his identity.

This theory was echoed by the *Bridgetown Monitor*, although it, too, fell prey to much of the same erroneous reporting as the *Digby Courier*. The *Monitor* also made some gaffes all its own. The weekly reported that Annie's mother was away receiving medical treatment in Boston, a claim it was obligated to retract in its next edition. The most offensive media blunder, however, belonged to a New Brunswick paper. The *Saint John Daily Record* inflamed the community when it mistakenly announced "that the victim had been outraged before the murder was committed."[11] The *Toronto Evening Star* repeated the unsubstantiated claim,[12] giving it credence and a nationwide audience.

With the release of the two Italian railway workers, the hunt for a viable suspect began in earnest. The local constabulary was hamstrung, forced to cool its heels awaiting the arrival of the Halifax detective. That

Illustration of Annie Kempton based on the only known
photograph of her, taken when she was twelve.

left a killer still at large, still unnamed. The media pundits filled the suspect void with speculation and semantic gymnastics. Unwilling to wait for facts, the *Bridgetown Monitor* went to press with a cryptic tease, saying only that "rumors are afloat as to the identity of the dastardly wretch but no positive clue has yet been discovered,"[13] a tantalizingly vague bit of reporting that combined the zest of gossip with the safeguard of equivocation.

Having interviewed every last county official and village resident, the *Chronicle* reporter had clearly heard the same rumours. Less than twelve hours into the criminal investigation, the whispers carried a single name: Peter Wheeler. As a twenty-six-year-old foreigner, Wheeler made a feasible if unlikely suspect. He was a neighbour of the Kemptons, renting a room just down the road for the past twelve years. Wheeler also had the misfortune of discovering Annie's body. Despite the grumblings about Wheeler, the *Chronicle* showed remarkable restraint, stating only that "some suspicion rests on a certain individual, but with very little as yet to warrant it."[14] It would be the last time a provincial newspaper gave Peter Wheeler the benefit of the doubt.

☾

The village of Bear River — then home to a thousand intrepid souls, give or take — sits nestled on the banks of its eponymous tributary. The river forms the boundary between two counties: Digby to the west and Annapolis to the east. The town's divided loyalties were (and remain) an administrative headache for its populace, a geopolitical quirk that would prove a point of contention in the criminal proceedings to come.

In a well-intentioned if somewhat misguided bid for tourism, Bear River dubbed itself "the Switzerland of Nova Scotia,"[15] a slogan proposed by a town council that had obviously never set foot in the Swiss Alps. Buttressed by its gently undulating hills, village fortunes rose and fell with the tides. Fishing, shipping, and lumber were the primary industries, attracting a never-ending stream of itinerant labourers, single, often

A view of Bear River, Digby County side, circa 1900.

Bear River, Annapolis County side, circa 1900.

foreign-born men in search of a day's work. Though many of the rovers drifted through with little notice, a few elected to stay and join the permanent residents, setting down shallow roots in the boarding houses and company shacks that dotted the town's landscape. One such man was Peter Wheeler.

While the rest of polite Victorian society marched headlong into a brave new world that embraced technological marvels and urban blight in equal measure, Wheeler turned and ran in the other direction. Peter steadfastly refused to settle down, master newfangled gizmos, or kowtow to the mores of the genteel class. He followed his own lodestar, circumnavigating the globe as a hired hand aboard a catena of merchant ships. During his brief landlocked moments, Wheeler did odd jobs, off-loading the fishing boats or cutting lumber to make his rather modest ends meet.

Peter Wheeler was a native of Mauritius, a series of tiny islands off the southeast coast of Africa. He came into the world early and unannounced in 1869, reportedly taking his mother by surprise as she travelled near the capital city of Port Louis. As a boy, his formative years seemed idyllic and were spent exploring his carefree island paradise. His father Louis and mother Emily were both English. Louis was a decorated soldier in the British army, stationed in what was then a French colony. Wheeler's Arcadian childhood came to an abrupt and violent end when his father was beaten to death one night by his fellow soldiers. It is not clear what became of Peter's mother.[16]

At the tender age of eight, Wheeler left Mauritius, boarding the barquentine *Lochiel* under the command of his uncle, Captain David Stevenson Wheeler. Peter's recollections of his teen years were vague. He recalled travels through London, France, and Scotland. Indeed, Scotland proved particularly memorable; while there, he was hospitalized for almost nine months, suffering from an undisclosed ailment. Once released, Peter continued his vagabond ways on the high seas, always paddling his own canoe as he later told one reporter. As the years passed, Wheeler grew into his inquisitive mind, along with a rather unfortunate eggplant-shaped physique that called unwanted attention to his short stout stature and narrow shoulders. Possessed of a world-class analytical brain — an asset of little merit on the loading docks — he yearned for the physical prowess so prized by his fellows, hoping to call a halt to the endless mocking he endured at the hands of his burlier bunkmates. What he lacked in mettle, however, he made up for in bonhomie. Wheeler was a true hale and hearty fellow, well-met.

After a stint in the West Indies, Wheeler signed on to the brigantine *Edmund*, bound for Digby. Many of the crew were natives of Nova Scotia, and when the vessel docked on October 9, 1884, Wheeler followed a shipmate, Charles Jeffrey, to nearby Bear River.

Affable and easygoing to a fault, if Peter had a boiling point, he rarely reached it. He also had a surprising penchant for domestic chores, winning him a place in the heart of many a harried housekeeper. As Peter scrubbed floors to earn his keep, Charles's mother took a shine to the industrious young lad and he stayed with the Jeffreys for several weeks. To net some much-needed pocket money, Wheeler approached the locals in search of day labour. One of the first to hire him was Annie's father, Isaac Kempton. Kempton was pleased with Wheeler's work ethic, and with the promise of steady wages, Wheeler decided to call Bear River home, at least for the foreseeable future. Much to the dismay of Charles Jeffrey's mother, Peter found lodging with the Kemptons' neighbour, Tillie Comeau. From that day forward, Peter occupied the same cramped room off the kitchen.

Rough-hewn but courteous and polite if not terribly refined, Peter Wheeler's peripatetic upbringing left him without social graces. He was not a gentleman by any stretch of the imagination, but he was every bit a man, despite his diminutive size and odd shape. He displayed a caustic wit and enjoyed saucy exchanges with his fellow working men. He also maintained a firm grasp of his true place in the world, exhibiting none of the usual immigrant striving. More interested in living than earning a living, Peter answered to no one but usually deferred to those above his social station.

Solitary and untethered, with no special lady laying claim to his heart, Wheeler's long-standing and ill-defined relationship with the equally unmarried Tillie Comeau led many in town to speculate as to which room Peter slept in at night. The Comeau boarding house was an unconventional bohemian enclave in a town that did not cotton to those who fell out of lockstep. And, as the luck of geography would have it, Tillie's house was just down the road from the Kemptons', making Wheeler a potential suspect by virtue of nothing more than proximity.

three

Blame It on Saucy Jack

As with most aspects of nineteenth-century life in Canada, the nation's newspapers had their deepest roots in England. Colonial standards of decency, content, and tone — as well as stylistic and marketing traditions — all hailed from the British media. On both sides of the Atlantic, Victorian mores demanded that all manner of social discourse adhere to quintessential English values: formality, decorum, modesty, and restraint. While the tabloids paid lip service to such ethos and aspired to civility, there was one realm in which public morality gave way to society's baser instincts: crime reporting. There, the public's thirst for the salacious details of the latest gruesome murder overrode all societal constraints.

It was not always thus. From their very inception, newspapers were bastions of propriety and gentility, reflective pools of the tranquil (if somewhat narcissistic) society that created them. All the news that was fit to print tended toward the mundane: price lists, reports of past weather (with little effort to forecasting future conditions), shipping news, agricultural concerns, and just a smattering of polite local gossip. A subject as distasteful as death was confined to the obituaries, where the elite were venerated with the appropriate taste and hyperbole. The front pages were reserved for such fare as prolonged travelogues of foreign adventures or a rapturous audit of a society maven's spoon collection. Reportage and editorials were safe, dull, and as far removed from controversy as was humanly possible. All that changed on August 31, 1888, when, in a London slum known as Whitechapel, a thoroughly modern invention came into being: the serial killer. His name was Jack the Ripper.

The Ripper saga began on Buck's Row in the heart of London's notorious East End. Long touted as a dumping ground for the country's huddled masses, Whitechapel had a well-earned reputation as a blight on the world's most cosmopolitan city. Overflowing with prostitutes, petty thieves, and destitute immigrants, murder was nothing new in Whitechapel. Yet even the most world-weary detectives were visibly shaken at the sight of the mutilated body of Mary "Polly" Nichols, a bargain-basement hooker whose throat was slashed from ear to ear. Stripped of her tattered layers of clothing during her autopsy, the coroner uncovered deep stab wounds to her stomach and genitals, all rendered post-mortem.

The macabre nature of the crime garnered some notice in the London tabloids, but it was not until the discovery of the second victim — Annie Chapman, another local prostitute — that the news media took notice. Chapman's body was found a half-mile from Buck's Row. Like Polly, her throat had been cut. This time the post-mortem mutilations were far more extensive: Annie had been disembowelled and her intestines tossed callously over her shoulder. Her reproductive organs had been removed with almost surgical precision and were not recovered at the scene. At autopsy, the medical examiner Dr. Bagster Philips remarked: "Obviously, the work was that of an expert — or one, at least, who had some knowledge of anatomical or pathological examinations as to be enabled to secure the pelvic organs with one sweep of the knife."[1]

With a madman on the loose, the city's papers — highbrow and low, broadsheet and tabloid — abandoned all prior decorum. Many rushed to produce special editions that sold faster than the presses could churn them out. News agents employed street urchins to run through the cobbled avenues, their arms draped with the latest edition, shouting "'orrible murder."[2]

In Whitechapel police had few leads but an avalanche of suspects. No fewer than eighteen men were named by the media, sparking hysteria and a wave of vigilante justice. Yet, for all the names carelessly bandied about, the unknown assailant remained just that — an "unknown assailant"

— until September 28, 1888. On that morning, a plain white envelope addressed in red ink arrived at the offices of London's Central News Agency. The missive, purportedly written by the killer, was signed "Jack the Ripper." The pithy moniker caught on and soon news organs across the globe dedicated front-page coverage to every flick of the Ripper's blade.

Two days later, Jack obliged their interest and struck again. This time, to taunt police and bait the media, he claimed two victims in a single evening. The first, Elizabeth Stride, was found just after midnight in a small courtyard off Berner Street. Her throat was slashed but it seemed as though the killer had been interrupted before he could perform any of his trademark mutilations. Less than one hour later, a constable on routine patrol in Mitre Square came upon the second victim, Catherine Eddows. She was "gutted like a pig in the market," the officer told reporters, her entrails "flung in a heap about her neck."[3] In a final indignity, one of her kidneys had been removed. Just above the body, someone had scrawled a cryptic message: "The Juwes [sic] are not the men that will be blamed for nothing."[4]

The self-anointed Ripper appeared to relish his new-found fame. As police combed the streets, he mailed another letter to the Central News Agency, boasting of "Saucy Jack's work" on a "double event."[5]

The tabloids printed each sadistic letter verbatim, accompanied by graphic line-art renderings of the victims and crime scenes; the lower the tabloid, the more tasteless the images. Many illustrators took considerable artistic license, depicting Jack as a top-hatted dandy who seduced his victims before dispatching them. The least reputable rags referred to the murders as "the romance of Whitechapel,"[6] equating the killings with the bodice-ripping seductions of the boudoir novels so popular among delicate Victorian ladies.

The Ripper tale reached new levels of depravity when a third communiqué was sent to George Lusk, director of the newly formed Whitechapel Vigilance Committee. The envelope bore the return address "from hell"[7] and the package contained a small section of what later proved to be human kidney. The author claimed to have "fried and ate"[8] the rest of it. The grisly tidbit arrived on October 16, sparking another media furor, but by Halloween, interest in the murders began to wane. With no arrests or further letters from the killer, public obsession with the case faded. Life in Whitechapel returned to its baseline degenerate normalcy, but behind the scenes, Jack the Ripper was scripting his swan song.

On the morning of November 9, an errand boy was sent to the home of Mary Kelly, a slattern who plied her wares from the bed in her squalid flat. The boy had been dispatched by the landlord to collect some long overdue rent. Pushing open the front door, the lad stumbled upon what was left of Mary, ghoulishly arranged on the bed that had been her stock-in-trade. Her throat was cut as usual but this time the wound ran so deep she was almost decapitated. The only victim killed indoors, Jack had made the most of the privacy afforded to create his masterpiece. He had flensed the skin from her forehead, nose, and ears. Her left arm dangled by a thin strip of flesh and both legs were flayed open from her thighs to her ankles. She was disembowelled and the killer had placed her hand inside her own gaping stomach, casually draping her liver across one of her legs. Her breasts, heart, and kidneys were dissected out and ghoulishly arranged on the nightstand. Strips of her flesh hung from nails once used for picture frames. Blood had been broadcast on every surface, a clear mockery of a priest wielding an aspergillum, dispensing holy water on the faithful. Most repugnant of all, Mary was three months pregnant when she died, and Jack had claimed her uterus and fetus as trophies.

Police officers investigating Kelly's murder made ample use of the latest innovation in crime scene work: photography. The killing ground was captured in a series of starkly graphic images, copies of which somehow ended up in the hands of the local media, who plastered them across every newsstand in the country.

Mary Kelly was the last of the Ripper's official victims. Some experts include the murders of two other prostitutes — Alice Mackenzie on July

17, 1889, and Frances Cole on February 13, 1891 — in Jack's final tally. A merchant seaman, James Sadler, was arrested for Mackenzie's murder but never formally charged. He remains among the favoured suspects of Ripperologists to this day.

☾

There is a fitting symmetry to the Ripper's involvement in the Annie Kempton story, even if he is only relegated to the cameo role of catalyst. For Saucy Jack remains the standard by which all killers are measured. There have been countless pretenders to the crown since — killers with higher body counts or greater savagery — but few have evaded capture as effectively or retained the stranglehold on our collective imaginations quite like the Ripper. Compared to Jack, Annie's killer was a rank amateur; yet, thanks to Jack, his single act of depravity garnered all the attention any criminal could want and no innocent man could survive.

The legend of Jack the Ripper also gave birth to a new kind of journalism — graphic, provocative, titillating, vulgar, and speculative. It introduced the notion of murder as entertainment and marked the start of a bold new experiment that stretched the boundaries of what polite society would tolerate and even come to enjoy. The Ripper's arrival signalled a new wave in the fourth estate: a tectonic shift from nationally syndicated news agencies pedalling innocuous human interest puff pieces to locally based news bureaus covering stories relevant to their own communities. As with all seismic fluctuations, the ripples forever altered the landscape of the Canadian press. Wire services were out and homespun stringers were the new world order. The local papers finally spoke in the voice of the people they served. A hierarchy soon developed in the media food chain: tiny regional rags, unable to sustain a reporting staff, scavenged furtively on the questionable tripe of their larger, more evolved competitors, always putting their unique regional spin on the story.

☾

The legacy of Jack the Ripper lives to this day: if it bleeds, it leads. Murder sells newspapers, a sanguinary lesson writ worldwide in the wake of Saucy Jack's killing spree. The Ripper's fingerprints can be seen throughout the news coverage of Annie Kempton's murder.

A brutal slaying was an oddly liberating act, at least as far as the Victorian media were concerned. Murder allowed even the most conservative paper to abandon its normal reserve and delve headfirst into a morbid world populated by the criminal element it once so studiously ignored.

For at least one tabloid, such an abrupt deviation from standard operating procedure caused an internal conflict that spawned some truly schizophrenic reportage. In the haze of the Kempton murder and the gathering thunderhead of suspicion over Peter Wheeler, the editor of the *Digby Weekly Courier* laid bare his moral struggle for all to see: "Criminal reporting is not in our line and to 'kick a man when he is down' is not our practice but the most lenient and sympathetic of men cannot but recognize now in Wheeler a human sunk to the lowest level."[9]

Yet for all the feigned indignation at being forced to plumb such depths, the *Courier* was quick to draw parallels between Annie's murder and the antics of Jack the Ripper, lest any of its readers failed to make the connection: "The details are sickening, even in the short mention we make herewith. It ranks with the worst of London slum scandals."[10] The *Courier*'s feeble protestations continued throughout its coverage of the murder and the subsequent trial, which — despite the editor's vehement objections — monopolized every issue for the next nine months.

❰

Jack the Ripper was not the media's lone invention. If Saucy Jack represented a new breed of criminal, it was only a matter of time before a new species of law enforcement rose to combat him. It was no coincidence that the era of the Ripper was also the era of the supersleuths, eagle-eyed detectives capable of running their venomous arch rivals to ground.

Although entirely a figment of Sir Arthur Conan Doyle's fevered imagination, the fictional Sherlock Holmes exemplified this new genus of investigator: tenacious, brilliant, and genteel, the perfect foil for the newly mutated strain of miscreants and blackguards. Doyle's creation was all the rage thanks to a phenomenally successful serial in *Strand Magazine*. For a populace besieged by crime at every turn, the allure of an infallible detective who solved every case was obvious. Holmes's popularity spawned countless knock-offs, including Agatha Christie's crack detectives Miss Marple and Hercule Poirot, who collectively ushered in the golden age of detective fiction.

Commerce abhors a vacuum and the press is first and foremost a business. There was money to be made in murder, and ruffling the feathers of a few society dandies seemed a small price to pay for such bountiful riches. The London tabloids had inadvertently stumbled on a winning formula — one readily translated across the globe — and their Canadian counterparts wanted in on the action. England had the Ripper and Holmes; it now fell to the colonies to find their equal. The roles were already scripted: all the media needed were the right actors to fill them. With perfect dramatic timing, Annie's horrific death had given the Maritime press their Ripper — all they lacked was their Holmes.

On the picturesque peninsula island of Nova Scotia, in a country barely two decades old, a star sat waiting to be born. Life would imitate art in a way that left the local press breathless with admiration and scrambling for superlatives. For on that tiny spit of land lived a detective of legendary prowess, a worthy successor to Doyle's masterpiece. His name was Nicholas Power.

Detective Nicholas Power, ready for his close-up,
taken on his seventy-fifth birthday, two years after he retired.

four

The Ineffable Detective Power

Policing in the age of Victoria Regina was in shambles, a tossed salad of do-gooders, cops on the take, and brutal dictators drunk on too much power and insufficient oversight. As went England, so went Canada, and the nation's fledgling system of law and order was no exception. England's paragon of crime busting, New Scotland Yard, was still cutting its teeth and Canada had yet to conceive of its equal.

The crime-fighting ethos at the turn of the nineteenth century was one of prevention rather than solution. The cop on the beat spent his days enforcing bylaws, not collaring the city's riff-raff. As a consequence, corruption was rampant and almost any offence could be overlooked for the right price. A series of comedically inept attempts at altering public perception of law enforcement failed miserably. By mid-century, the image of the uniformed officer patrolling the street, keeping harm at bay, had become a cynical joke. As one astute observer wrote, the force was nothing more than "burly policemen, hunting in couples and used to decorate the entrances to the theatres."[1]

As the century waned, Halifax waxed. The port city, willing to turn a blind eye to more than most, grew in leaps and bounds, bloated with waves of immigrants and groaning under the weight of its accumulated urban blight. The Halifax Police Department was established in 1864 to instill some sense of order in the lawless metropolis. One of its first recruits was an earnest mountain of a man named Nicholas Power. The day he reported for duty, he was all of twenty-four, full of piss and vinegar

The Halifax Police Department, September 15, 1894. Detective Nick Power, sporting his annually allotted suit, stands on the far right.

and unearned swagger. Before joining the nascent force, Power had spent four years in the Royal Navy, serving aboard the HMS *Nile* as a butcher's boy.

As criminals ran riot through the steep streets of "The Big Smoke," Nick Power quickly learned that sporting the uniform afforded little cachet. By that time, fighting crime was largely confined to corralling drunks. Public intoxication was public enemy number one for the Halifax PD, followed closely by such mundane offences as common assault, theft, disorderly houses, profane language, and cattle-at-large.[2] Young Mr. Power soon distinguished himself despite such banal adversaries, boasting an impressive arrest rate and a keen eye for spotting the criminal element.

It was this latter trait that garnered Power his first promotion. In November 1882 Power was named the department's sole detective. With his new rank came a number of perks, including an annual salary of five hundred dollars and a clothing allowance of one suit per year. Nattily attired and released from the burden of herding cattle and rummies,

Power was free to focus on a new avenue of police work: identifying and apprehending the unknown perpetrators of crimes already committed.

One of his earliest cases set the tone for the career that followed. Nick Power was dispatched to a robbery on Morris Street, the tony home of the affluent Albro family. That night, the Albros had attended Mass with their two servant girls, leaving the house unattended. They returned to discover more than a thousand dollars' worth of jewellery and silver plate missing. The newly minted detective quickly surmised that the burglars must have entered through the front door and exited from the back, leaving the door ajar. Marks on the backyard fence indicated their escape route. Wax stains throughout the home hinted that the robbers had used candles to light their way. Power even found a candle stub near the backyard fence, buried in the grass.[3]

Power examined the candle with great interest, much to the bemusement of his fellow officers. He thought it stubbier than most, yet it bore no identifying marks. After a restless night pondering this lone elusive clue, Power sprang into action. He sent out a team of constables to query the city's shops, looking for a match to his wax specimen. His instructions were met with derision by the junior officers, who saw it as a fool's errand, but their diligence eventually paid off. Thomas Lahey, a shopkeeper at the head of the market wharf, claimed to be the only merchant in the entire city to carry that particular make of candle. As luck would have it, it was brand new stock and he had only sold one allotment to date: two boxes to the Royal Artillery canteen.

It was Power's first real lead and he made a meal of it. While interrogating the homeowners, Power discovered that the Albros' two servant girls were keeping company with some artillerymen. The detective then paid an unannounced visit to the canteen, where he learned the girls' beaus had access to the candles. Based on this rather anemic chain of circumstantial evidence, the soldiers were arrested and convicted, along with their servant girl paramours.

The detective's powers of deduction soon caught the eye of the city's newshounds. Reporters pestered him for the intricate details of his cases and Power was only too willing to oblige. The Halifax tabloids overflowed almost daily with the detective's latest exploits. Without fail and no matter how daunting the crime, Power somehow found the missing piece of the puzzle and brought the slippery villain to justice.

The press often likened Power to Sherlock Holmes but only because Power asked them to, though the detective then feigned discomfort at the comparison. Nick Power — a man imbued with media savvy decades before the ailment was formally recognized — played the part of the humble public servant to perfection, an act that took considerable pretense given his love of the spotlight and his insistence that his every move be reported to his adoring public. Never had the media met a more accommodating lawman.

Power was not only cunning, he was photogenic. The detective cut a dashing figure, straight out of Central Casting. Tall, regal and "endowed with a strong physique and rugged constitution,"[4] Power was every inch the equal of his fictitious contemporaries.

His leading man looks may have landed him on the front page but his exploits kept him there. Of all Power's high-profile, and highly profiled, cases, one stands head and shoulders above the rest. The detective's magnum opus was a perfect media storm: Power was in rare form, the perpetrators were American, and the victim was no less than a crown prince and future king. It was all too good to be true (and would eventually be revealed as such) but the caper forever cemented Power's reputation as Canada's greatest detective, if only in the Halifax press.

The legendary caper unfolded in the final days of October 1883. Power, still the city's lone detective, was playing a hunch. He spent the day checking out the latest arrivals in some of the downtown's less reputable hotels, searching for anything that made his nose twitch. He noticed two young Americans whose nervous demeanour set off his finely honed criminal radar. As the two men left the hotel, Power took the opportunity to search their room, as was his prerogative in the days before warrants and the mandated protections of civil liberties. Power soon found a forty-eight-pound bag of dynamite underneath one of the beds. When the pair returned to their lodging, Power promptly placed them under arrest. Rummaging through their pockets, the detective came upon some luggage tags for the local depot. With tags in hand, Power raced to the terminal and claimed the waiting baggage. As he forced open the suitcase, Power's hunch was vindicated. The trunk contained two diving suits and what Power later claimed was a terrorist's kit, complete with all the necessary paraphernalia to detonate dynamite underwater.

Back at police headquarters, Power grilled the men for hours alone in a room with no windows or witnesses. When the detective emerged, he had a fantastical story to tell. According to Power, the men intended to blow up the HMS *Canada*, presently lying at anchor in Halifax Harbour. Aboard the vessel was none other than Prince George, who was later crowned King George V, sovereign of the British Empire. The two conspirators — James Holmes and William Breckton — were supposedly outraged by the settlement of the Irish land question and claimed to be part of an international conspiracy looking to strike a blow against the English nobility. Headlines across the country trumpeted the foiled plot, heaping laurels and platitudes on the quick-witted gumshoe who had brought the would-be assassins to heel. Although Power told every pundit who would listen that he had ferreted out the treacherous cabal, exactly how much of the plot and so-called confession were true remains an open question. One clear indicator of the case's dubious merit was the verdict. The two putative terrorists were convicted of a single relatively minor offence — the illegal possession of dynamite — and were sentenced to a mere six months, an almost imperceptible slap on the wrist for allegedly plotting to kill a member of the royal family.

The court's ruling, however, did little to dampen the newspaper's ardour for the detective. In the immediate afterglow of the arrest, nestled in the media's warm embrace, Power cultivated a reputation for being able to see around corners and into the souls of men. Power's fame soon spread beyond

Halifax, propelled by tales of his much-lauded eagle's eye, sharp wits, and deductive reasoning. As the province's only detective, he quickly found himself in high demand, dispatched to wherever wrongdoing occurred.

And so it was that on January 28, 1896, as he closed the book on yet another headline-grabbing case in New Glasgow, Power received an urgent cable from the Solicitor General, instructing him to proceed with due haste to the tiny village of Bear River, to see what he could make of the horrific murder of a fourteen-year-old girl.

five

The Inquest

Like the great Detective Power, Dr. Lewis Johnstone Lovett cut a dashing, if slightly more earthbound, figure. Lovett was resplendent in his foul-weather costume of high celluloid collar, rakish business suit, pince-nez, and full-length fur coat, unquestionably a man of breeding and refinement. His dignified countenance seemed at odds with the unkempt masses inhabiting the shores of Bear River: lumbermen, crofters, dorymen, and rovers whose notion of business attire extended only as far as dungarees and rain slickers. Lovett was a dandy among drones, highly educated in a land where the academy took a backseat to apprenticeships and sons following in their father's seafaring footsteps.

Yet for all his lofty ways, Lovett was a man of the people. He was a true Maritimer by virtue of birth and temperament. Born on August 28, 1867, Lovett was raised in Kentville, one of countless villages vying for the title of "the heart of the Annapolis Valley." The son of Henry Lovett and Anne Johnstone, young Lewis was a dutiful son and model student. He matriculated first at Acadia University in neighbouring Wolfville, then made quick work of New York University's prestigious School of Medicine. Upon graduation, Lovett returned to the Valley intent on setting up practice in Bear River.[1]

Those who questioned his choice of location soon learned he was simply following his heart. Lovett had fallen hard for a local girl, Josephine Marshall. By the fall of 1896, the couple were engaged to be married. Josephine was the favoured daughter of a respected family and every bit Lovett's intellectual equal. She fancied herself a big-game hunter, a crack shot who had proven her mettle time and again tracking moose and bear through the steep hills of her native land. Indeed, it was their mutual love of hunting that first brought Lewis and Josephine together. They were a handsome couple, well-suited to each other and destined for great things.

There was only one problem. Bear River already had a beloved town doctor. Robert J. Ellison, MD, was thirty-five years Lovett's senior and an elder statesman of the medical profession, who had faithfully served Bear River and its occupants for decades. Although he was getting on in years, Ellison had no immediate plans to retire and no intention of relinquishing his stranglehold on the welfare of the town. If Lovett felt the town needed another physician, Dr. Ellison was not inclined to agree.

Still, for all Ellison's reticence, the two doctors developed a grudging respect, which eventually grew into a friendship that endured until Ellison's death on February 13, 1907. In 1896, however, the uneasy truce between the two medical men was tenuous at best, forged of little more than feigned professional courtesy.

To house his new wife and budding practice, Lovett built a striking Empire-style home on a particularly scenic slope overlooking the river. Actually, it was his future father-in-law — Alpheus Marshall, a prominent village merchant — who built the house, but Lovett bought it at a favourable rate and claimed it as his own. Lewis stocked his ground-floor surgery with the latest in medical accoutrements, hung out his shingle, and waited. The response was immediate and positive. Spryer than his competitor, Lewis soon found himself in constant demand. The image of Lovett atop a horse-drawn sleigh, battling his way through the debilitating winter snows to aid his outlying patients became a permanent fixture of village life. In short order, there was a discernible spike in the number of children christened "Lewis" or "Lovett," in homage to the man who had braved the elements to shepherd them into the world.

Lovett's glory days were legion and legendary but on January 28, 1896, as Annie Kempton's body lay cooling on her father's sitting-room floor, Lovett's polished facade barely concealed the timid novice lurking beneath.

Dr. Lewis Johnstone Lovett in his Bear River surgery, circa 1900.

Lewis was still wet behind the ears and struggling to find his footing. He was well-educated and brilliant but such qualities were no substitute for real-world experience. Lovett's high-priced education had not prepared him for the task now at hand: to convene a formal inquiry into the death of Bear River's beloved daughter, Annie Kempton.

Lovett's legal mandate stemmed from his first official appointment to public office, that of county coroner. There would be other, more prestigious posts in his future — including serving 1,423 days as a Liberal Party member in the Canadian House of Commons[2] — but for the moment, Lovett's role as coroner was the pinnacle of his nascent career.

The timing of Lovett's appointment proved unfortunate and left him balancing precariously on the cusp of a fundamental shift in the paradigm of medico-legal death investigation. Less than one year prior, Dr. William D. Finn had been appointed as the province's first medical examiner for Halifax and Dartmouth. Finn's tenure would be a chronicle of the region's darkest hours. He oversaw mortuary operations for victims of the *Titanic* and the 1917 Halifax Explosion, and necessity being the true mother of invention, he pioneered revolutionary methods still in use today for dealing with mass casualties.[3]

Finn's arrival heralded the beginning of the end for the coroner system in Nova Scotia. Originating from the 1194 Articles of Eyre, a precursor of British Common Law, the position of coroner arose from Article 20, which empowered its holder "to keep the pleas of the Crown."[4] From this nebulous and all-encompassing mandate, the duties of the coroner grew to include the keeping of the Rolls (an early form of birth and death registration) and the investigation of all sudden deaths. While historians agree that the earliest coroners were "not particularly concerned about discovering the culprit in a homicide,"[5] focused as they were on record keeping and taxation, later appointees expanded the scope of their authority to include the powers of subpoena, bail, and arrest in criminal proceedings.

Such unchecked power grabs soon derailed the wheels of justice. Coroners were not doctors or lawyers, nor did they receive any specialized training; the right political connections sufficed to hold the position. That these unregulated benighted overseers had the power to pronounce guilt, only to then tax the accused without recourse, created a system rife with abuse and injustice. As the separate but symbiotic spheres of jurisprudence and policing advanced, the purview of coroners to adjudicate criminal matters was sharply curtailed. The final step in the system's evolution was the introduction of medical examiners: licensed physicians specifically trained to evaluate suspicious or violent deaths. Unlike their coroner brethren, medical examiners fulfilled only two prescribed functions: to offer a medical opinion as to the cause and manner of death and the issuance of death certificates. Questions of culpability, criminality, or the Crown's right to compensation were entirely outside their scope.

It was into this rapidly changing new world order that the untested Dr. Lovett stepped headfirst and guileless, oblivious to the pitfalls that lay ahead. He possessed the qualifications of a medical examiner but the title of coroner. As for the actual parameters of his duties at that moment, no one could say for certain. Indeed, the exact powers of a coroner in

Nova Scotia had never been set down in law and the jurisdictional authority of a medical examiner would not be codified by legislation for more than six decades. Lovett was working blind in uncharted territory, untethered by statutes and unguided by experience.

However murky the waters he found himself in, Dr. Lewis Lovett had a pressing yet grim function to perform. Lovett, suspecting that the proceedings would be standing-room only, elected to hold his inquest in the Oakdene Academy, a recently constructed schoolhouse and town hall that came with the then-exorbitant price tag of eight thousand dollars.[6] Rising like a tombstone out of the valley floor, the academy was the town centre in more than just the geographic sense. Word of the inquest spread through the village like tentacles of kudzu, and as Lovett called the hearing to order at precisely 2:00 p.m. on Tuesday, January 28, it seemed as if every resident of Bear River stood at the ready, awaiting their chance to be heard.

Inquests carry the full force of law but are not technically trials, merely fact-finding missions. As no one stands accused of a crime, there is no need for defence counsel and no judge to oversee the proceeding, although the coroner fills that role for all intents and purposes. There is a jury, sworn and empanelled, to hear the evidence and render a verdict. As murder is a crime against the state, the interests of the Crown are represented by a prosecutor. When it came time to address the Queen's matter touching the death of Annie Kempton, the region's lead Crown Attorney — Mr. A.J. Copp — was unavailable. In his stead, his alternate Mr. J.M. Owen presided.

Lovett, new to both the town and the role of coroner, saw the proceedings as an opportunity to establish himself in the community. He ran the hearing with a quiet dignity and firm hand, demanding courtesy and decorum from the excited crowd and returning them in kind. Yet Lovett's calm demeanour masked some deep-seated insecurities. News of Annie's death had come only hours before. With no detective as yet on scene and the autopsy still not underway, Lovett was unmoored and forced to cast a wide net. The doctor had yet to formulate a plan, although the crowd could not tell to look at him. Driven by instinct if not expertise, Lovett decided the right course of action was to begin by questioning those who lived closest to the Kempton house: Tillie Comeau and her older children (Hattie and Herbert), who lived just down the road, and their lodger, Peter Wheeler, who had found the body. Tillie's youngest child Walter was also sworn and told a chilling tale. Just days before the murder, as Annie worked alone in the kitchen preparing her midday meal, she looked up to see a strange man standing on the kitchen step, staring at her through the window. As their eyes met, he turned and ran.[7] Annie told Walter that she did not recognize the man but the incident had frightened her enough to tell others. Clearly, someone with questionable intent had discovered Annie was often home alone.

With his tentative witness list compiled and an auditorium packed to the rafters with townsfolk anxious to testify, Lovett gavelled his inaugural inquest to order. The first to take the stand was Peter D. Wheeler.

six

The "Lie"

In the days and months to follow, all sources could agree on only one thing: Peter Wheeler became the prime suspect because of a single simple statement, a story he told that was perceived by many to be a lie. Wheeler first told the story to his landlady on the night Annie was killed, and not recognizing the trouble it might cause him, he repeated it again during the coroner's inquest.

Wheeler's supposed deceit centred on how Annie came to be alone in the house on the night she died. According to Peter, he met Annie in passing earlier that day, at which time she told him there was no need for Tillie Comeau to come by the house that evening as a local girl named Grace Morine would be staying with her. Wheeler relayed Annie's message to Tillie, who followed the girl's directive and did not spend the night in the Kempton house as previously arranged.

During the inquest, Wheeler's story initially passed without comment. He gave his account without hesitation, his brain draining into his mouth at an alarming rate, unchecked by guilt, awareness, or defence counsel. Tillie Comeau later took the stand and confirmed that Peter had told her there was no need to stay with Annie because the Morine girl would be there.

Wheeler's private road to hell was paved with the good intentions of Grace Morine. Grace was a schoolmate of Annie's who lived about a half mile from the Kempton house. Grace was precocious — some might say exasperating — but she offered the most exacting testimony of the proceedings. Under oath, Grace said she had seen Annie between 3:30 and

4:30 that afternoon on the road between the Brook house and where the Millers lived. So precise was her recall that she recounted their conversation as though reading from a transcript. The Morine girl swore Annie never asked her to stay that evening or any other. Under questioning, Grace was defiant, wielding all the petulance and indignation afforded a teenage girl accused of something she did not do. Morine emphatically told the court she was not in the habit of stopping with Annie in the evenings and that Annie made no mention of needing a companion that night. Asked to clarify one last time, Grace claimed Annie had no conversation with her about it and that Wheeler was mistaken.

The packed hall fell silent. As if mounted in a single head, all eyes turned to Wheeler. Whispers eddied throughout the hall, swelling to howls of undignified pother as the news sunk in. The realization whipped through the academy like a cut power line. In an instant, every man, woman, and child in Bear River leapt to the same damning conclusion: Wheeler had lied to get Annie alone that night.

Within seconds, the tenor of the inquest changed from sombre inquiry to vengeful wrath. Several men in the crowd had to be restrained as they lunged for Peter Wheeler, who sat bewildered but mercifully sequestered with the other witnesses. He seemed genuinely unaware of the shift in winds that enveloped him, absorbing the abuse like a tree in a storm. To Peter, the din was unintelligible, strange yet familiar, like a word repeated endlessly until its syllables lost all meaning. That word was his name, hissed time and again in rage.

Although lost on Wheeler, the emotional fluctuation was palpable to all others assembled. Standing at the back of the hall, the *Saint John Daily Record* correspondent noted that in the blink of an eye, "every incensed resident mentally appointed himself or herself as duty-bound to do all in their power to run the perpetrator to earth."[1]

Lovett, calling for calm, slowly harnessed the room back to order. Fearing violence, he suspended the inquest for the day, declaring that testimony would resume the next morning. The town constables were called in, and as the crowd was forcibly dispersed, accusations continued to fly. Based solely on the peevish word of a confused teen, Wheeler had gone from co-operative eyewitness to ruthless murderer.

The press gaggle hovering on the fringes of the inquest were quick to turn the misunderstanding into conclusive evidence of guilt. The *Morning Chronicle* was first out of the gate, announcing that "suspicion now rests solely upon Wheeler and with good circumstantial evidence to back it. The facts are these: Wheeler prevented Tillie Comeau from going to Kempton's."[2] The *Digby Weekly Courier* also claimed Wheeler had "prevented"[3] his landlady from staying with Annie as part of his nefarious plan. Although Peter was not yet charged with any crime and was in no way behaving in a guilty manner, the *Courier* held forth on his character and culpability ad hominem: "Wheeler has kept up his bold front through all the investigation. If he is guilty, as certainly is very probable, he is a remarkably cool and an audacious villain."[4] Wheeler's inattention in the witness dock, borne of a clear conscience, was now being posited as proof of his cold-blooded nature.

The papers were not alone in their hasty assessment of Wheeler. Detective Nicholas Power was newly arrived in Bear River and was less than one hour into his investigation when he held an impromptu press conference on the academy steps. According to the *Courier*, "Detective Power said outside that he had no doubt himself that Wheeler was guilty."[5] If experience had taught Power anything, it was to follow the path of least resistance. Gaining a conviction — even a wrongful conviction — was far easier if the victimized community were already convinced of the accused man's guilt.

❨

What no one — Lovett, Power, the jurors, or the media — was willing to consider was the possibility Wheeler was telling the truth. The lone contingency no one entertained was that the "lie" had been Annie's, not Peter's.

Before her body was even cold, Annie Kempton had been lionized, even canonized, by the townsfolk and in the press. Deemed innocent *in excelsis* and virtuous beyond measure, Annie had become purity personified. In death, she was perfect, she was faultless, she was divine.

In reality, Annie Kempton was a teenage girl, possessed of the same angels and demons as every other pubescent lass of the era, or indeed, any era. Just shy of her fifteenth birthday and "well-developed for her age,"[6] Annie likely resented being saddled with a nightly babysitter as she blossomed into womanhood. She had finally caught the fancy of a boy but was surrounded on all sides — and at all times — by parents, siblings, and the prying eyes of the town busybodies. Yoked with the burden of managing a household in her mother's absence, Annie may have told a harmless fib in order to gain a moment's peace. Wanting her first taste of privacy did not make her rebellious or wanton — it made her a typical teen.

Yet the idea that events had played out as Wheeler claimed — that the deception had originated with Annie — was summarily dismissed. By naively repeating what he had been told, Wheeler was not simply a pawn or gullible dupe. He was now a sadistic killer.

seven

The Parker Brothers

Obadiah Parker was not a man to be trifled with. A machinist by trade, Obadiah was exacting in business, imposing in stature, and dictatorial in nature. He ran a very tight ship, a conspicuous absence of nautical experience notwithstanding. He demanded no less of his wife Harriet (née Rice) and his children, including elder son Bernard and his youngest Herbert. Devout Adventists, the Parkers brooked no frivolity and tolerated no fools. The family was admired by their neighbours in Bear River, if not particularly liked.

Bernard Parker — just shy of his thirty-fifth birthday as the Kempton drama unfolded — was as unerring and precise as his father and soon found gainful employment as a government surveyor. Having gone in search of a stable, obedient spouse, Bernard settled on Christine Milner (who bore the necessary requirements in abundance) and the couple had two children: son Chauncey and daughter Millie. Bernard Parker, who was only slightly less autocratic than his father, did little to counter the family's reputation for earnestness and a decided lack of humour.

With Herbert, the apple fell a little farther from the tree. All of eighteen and bristling with the first flush of manhood, young Herbert was in the employ of the lumbermen who harvested the teeming woodlands of the Annapolis Valley. Herbert possessed a certain witless charm but was far coarser in tongue and spirit than his elders; by unanimous consent, he still had some growing up to do.

The Parker brothers were lifelong denizens of Bear River, well-acquainted with the Kemptons and with Peter Wheeler. Herbert had occasionally worked alongside Wheeler in the lumber mills. Prior to January 28, 1896, Herbert and Peter had been friendly, if not exactly friends. They shared a love of bawdy jokes and earthy conversation, long-time staples in Wheeler's hardscrabble life but still novelties for nihilists like Herbert Parker. Brother Bernard knew Wheeler only by reputation and by sight, having encountered him in passing over the years. If either Parker bore Wheeler a grudge, it was well-hidden from those around them.

Through a convoluted series of circumstances, the Parkers found themselves in the hot seat alongside Wheeler, although unlike the accused, the brothers had voluntarily taken their seats. The strange chain of events that bound their fates together began when Annie's body was discovered. As Lovett asked for any and all witnesses to come forward just six hours later, the Parker boys were among the throng who stepped up. Bernard, the elder, went first.

Earlier that day, while others stood huddled and horrified around the tangled remains of the murdered girl, Bernard Parker sprang into action, accompanied by a few of the younger local men. Parker as amateur sleuth and his self-deputized posse searched the grounds surrounding the Kempton home. According to Bernard's testimony, he quickly discovered a set of tracks in the snow near the family's barn. Ever the surveyor, Bernard unrolled a map he had drawn to illustrate his findings.[1] On the schematic Parker had made a series of dashed lines in red to indicate the footprints.

It was compelling evidence. Although the tracks did not identify the assailant, they gave some hint as to how the killer made his way to the house. Lovett admitted the map into evidence, thanked Bernard for his efforts, and that seemed to be the end of it. Other witnesses came and went as the coroner continued his inquiry. By the end of the first day, Wheeler's so-called lie had been exposed and the inquest had taken on a far more malodorous stench.

Before Lovett called the second day's session to order, Bernard Parker approached the coroner for a quiet word. Bernard told the young doctor that, in light of Wheeler's obvious involvement in the crime, he had

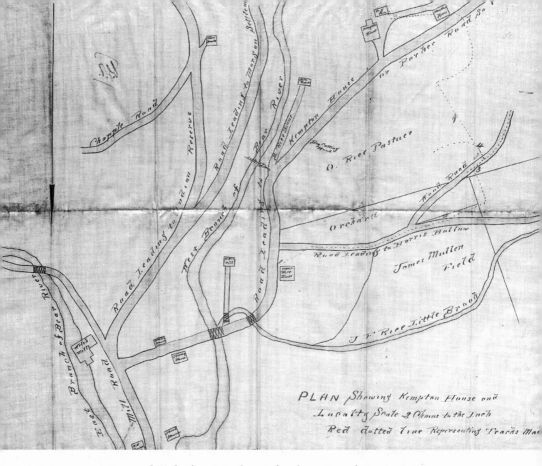

Bernard Parker's original map for the coroner's inquest,
the dashed line indicating the path of the footprints (upper right).

returned to the hillside near the Kempton home and discovered some
additional evidence. Parker asked Lovett to recall him to the stand so
that he might reveal his new findings.

As the morning session began, Bernard Parker once again raised his
hand to God. He unfurled a new hastily rendered map and told the
enthralled audience he had discovered yet another set of tracks, also
shown in red.[2] In addition to the footprints near the barn, the newly
found tracks ran from the back door of the house to the street, veered
across a field and continued toward the road where Wheeler lived. Parker
was resolute: there was only one set of tracks in the snow and they led
straight from the crime scene to Wheeler's front door.

To further bolster his case against Wheeler, Parker took the time to make a few additions to his latest map. Parker drew in key features not evident on his first map, including the locations where children in the village claimed to have seen Peter in the hours before Annie died. Viewed today, the differences between the two maps are subtle, disturbing, and unquestionably damning, both for Wheeler and for Parker. The first map was a simplified schematic of some suspicious footprints. The second map was a blueprint for murder in which all roads led to Peter Wheeler. The latest revisions to Parker's map and his testimony left little doubt as to the surveyor's intentions. Bernard Parker was no longer bearing witness in generalities. He was now spearheading the effort to convict Peter Wheeler on the spot.

Still acting as a self-appointed lawman, Parker had — over the course of the prior evening — examined the suspect footprints in far greater detail. He claimed each impression measured exactly ten inches in length, a tad on the small side for a man's shod foot. Parker was certain the tracks were made by someone sporting larrigans — a traditional knee-high oiled-skin moccasin, typically fringed and laced up the front. Larrigans were readily available from the merchants in town; favoured by working men, a pair could be had for $1.75.[3] Using the length as a guide, Parker had deduced the size of the larrigans responsible for the prints: the boots were, he announced confidently, a size six.

Parker's detective work drew admiring murmurs from the crowd. The whispers — the new coin of the realm — decreed that the footprints proved Peter Wheeler was the killer, even though no one had yet ascertained the size of Wheeler's feet. As rampant speculation ricocheted about the hall, Lovett took Parker's second map into evidence and thanked him for his testimony.

The Parkers were not yet finished with Peter Wheeler. Later that same day young Herbert Parker supplanted his brother in the witness chair but with an entirely different tale to tell. Herbert had no maps on offer, but what he wielded was far more incriminating. He told the people of

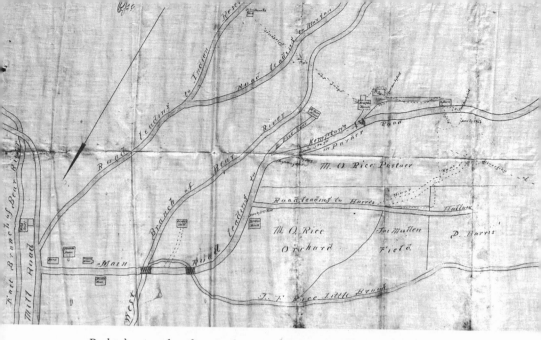

Parker's second and revised map, with the telltale footprints again illustrated by a dashed line (faintly visible on the right side of the image).

Bear River that on several occasions, he had heard Peter Wheeler "speak of Annie with immoral threatenings."[4] As the predicted gasps subsided, Lovett pressed Herbert to elaborate. Herbert, showing uncharacteristic restraint, recounted how Peter often boasted that he would have his way with Annie, whether she obliged or not. Herbert then stepped down, having planted the knife squarely in Wheeler's back.

As this was an inquest and not a court of law, little could be done to repair the damage wrought by Herbert Parker. Parker's testimony was hearsay, and during a trial, would have been deemed inadmissible, as any opposition was a simple case of "he said — he said." In a coroner's inquest, however, the rules of evidence are loosened. If it came down to a question of credibility, Herbert Parker was not under suspicion and his word automatically carried more weight. The constraints of a coroner's hearing may be relaxed, but such flexibility did not favour Peter Wheeler. He was still prohibited from speaking in his own defence and had no counsel representing him to object to the hearsay. As such, Parker's accusation went unchallenged.

Like an Atlantic-born blizzard, the Parkers had swept in and buried Peter Wheeler. They were, after all, only preaching to a dangerously hostile choir. The crowded academy was already predisposed to think the worst of Wheeler and eagerly accepted the brothers' jaundiced testimony as fact. So, too, did the coroner's jurymen.

Between the brothers, Bernard's testimony may have seemed far more reasoned and objective, at least at first glance, but it was in reality hopelessly flawed. Much of Parker's evidence would have been called into question had opposing counsel been permitted, but Wheeler sat defenceless and undefended as Bernard's unsubstantiated theories were admitted as facts. The first fly in Parker's ointment was the footprint medium itself: that most malleable and unpredictable bane of Canadian winters — snow.

Of all the scientific advances of the late nineteenth century, arguably the most utilitarian was the emergence of relatively precise meteorology. Victorian houses, hotels, and marinas filled their vestibules with a dazzling array of barometers, thermometers, gauges, and all things atmospheric. Almost overnight, the weather had gone from a banal topic of conversation to a full-fledged science, complete with its own governmental agency generating mountains of data.

According to that agency — Environment Canada and its National Climate Data Archives — the week surrounding Annie's death was a rough one for Bear River. On Saturday, January 25, five and three quarter inches of snow fell on the town, lending some small credence to their stake as the "Switzerland of Nova Scotia." This deluge was followed by three quarters of an inch on Sunday the twenty-sixth, a light dusting on the twenty-seventh, another inch on the twenty-eighth — the day Bernard and his gang searched for prints — and just shy of another inch on Wednesday the twenty-ninth, the occasion of Parker's second search.

As if the serial snowfall were not enough, temperatures fluctuated wildly throughout the week, with daytime highs well above freezing and nighttime lows in the single digits. Accordingly, the accumulating snow melted and settled and each new fall obliterated all prior prints. Any impressions made in the ever-shifting blanket of white were significantly modified in the process. This meteorological roller coaster left any and all tracks indistinct, unstable, and therefore unreliable. Indeed, the notion that accurate measurements were possible under such conditions was as suspect as Parker's motives.

Bernard's second problem was his stubborn stance regarding the number of prints. According to his statement, there was a lone set of tracks leading from the house to the barn. It was a straightforward declaration that sounded convincing. The problem was that the heaviest snowfall, in which the prints were made, came on Saturday when both Isaac Kempton and his son Earnest were still in the house with Annie. Isaac would later testify that the two men did not leave the home until 8:30 a.m. on Monday the twenty-seventh. The weekend of the blizzard, Isaac, Earnest, or Annie each made several daily trips to the barn to milk and tend to the family cow, yet Parker claimed to see no evidence of such traffic recorded in the snow — just a lone set of prints that he argued could only have been made by the killer on Monday night.

Problem number three: Bernard Parker's unflinching identification of the make and size of the footwear responsible for the prints. Such an unprecedented act of sleuthing bordered on the incredible, elevating Parker to the rarefied air normally reserved for Holmes and Poirot. How Parker reached his astonishing conclusions was not stipulated — hardly surprising, given there was no defence counsel present to obligate him to reveal his methodology.

In the end, Bernard Parker's testimony was a classic case of smoke and mirrors, a triumph of flash over substance. Parker spoke with his characteristic certainty, a model of gravitas and sombre reflection. His manner was one of staunch conviction, and barring any defence queries to invoke doubt, the audience and jurors embraced his testimony without question. That it was, at best, the grasping of a novice detective escaped the uncritical eyes of those assembled. What also evaded detection was the nuanced yet unmistakable way Bernard changed his testimony between his first and second appearance, revisions clearly recorded on the maps Parker admitted into evidence. The first map shows a set of footprints. The second might as well have been a photograph of Wheeler committing the act.

Why Bernard Parker took it upon himself to play both detective and prosecutor in the case evaded the historic record. In all likelihood, his initial search of the area and his documentation of the footprints were altruistic. A beloved member of his community had been murdered, and he, along with his fellow residents, wanted to do all they could to help. But something clearly shifted in Bernard Parker on the night of January 28, 1896, and, as suspicion fell on Peter Wheeler, so, too, did the heavy hand of Bernard Parker.

The Parker brothers would go on to repeat their accusations and testimony for a second time in a makeshift courtroom of Bear River and twice more in a courthouse in Kentville as Wheeler sat on trial for his life. Herbert's testimony never wavered. Bernard's continued to morph in artful but telling ways. At every juncture, the media was there to contort Parker's words even further to fit their prescribed apologue. If ever a man needed a lawyer, it was Wheeler and it was now. That there was none to be had proved, quite literally, to be the death of him.

eight

The Mortis Sisters

Establishing an exact time of death remains the holy grail of forensic science. It is a critical step in assessing the alibi of any given suspect and establishing a peri-mortem timeline. Yet even today, the best methods produce estimates with disturbingly broad confidence intervals — the "plus or minus" wiggle room scientists add to make the result statistically valid. Early critics of time-of-death estimation argued that the results were so flawed and wide-ranging as to allow for "the farcical possibility of the person still being alive"[1] and that all results must be seen as a matter of guesstimation rather than determination.

Keeping in mind that such estimates remain more art than science, it is not surprising the methods themselves have changed little in the past century. The techniques available in 1896, as today, rely on three key elements: temperature, lividity, and muscle rigidity. In scientific circles, these elements are known as "the triad," although they are often jokingly referred to as the Mortis Sisters — Algor Mortis, Livor Mortis, and Rigor Mortis.

The pretty, popular sister is Algor Mortis — the predictable cooling of the body after death — which ranks among the oldest of forensic methods and was widely used in death investigations as early as 1850.[2] Like all town tramps, Algor is simple and easy. The corpse cools at a rate of 2°F per hour, slowing to 1.5°F per hour at twelve hours, until the body reaches ambient temperature. A murder victim with a normal body temperature (98.6°F) reaches typical room temperature (72°F) within fourteen hours after death.

Lividity, or Livor Mortis, is the ugly stepsister. Lividity is the purplish discoloration that manifests as blood pools in patterns dictated by gravity. Accordingly, livor develops in the dependent parts of the body, for example, on the back of a decedent prone on the floor. Livor arrives about twenty minutes after death and never leaves. It is a progressive process, with the purple staining becoming more marked as time goes on, and after eight to twelve hours, lividity becomes "fixed" or permanent as the blood congeals. Livor may be unsightly but she is a godsend at crime scenes, telegraphing to investigators that a body has been moved after death, as the staining faithfully records the original position of the remains.

If Algor is cheap and Livor is hard on the eyes, the middle sister, Rigor Mortis, is an inflexible harridan. After death, the muscles of the body are flaccid and easily moved. That flabbiness is soon replaced by increasing rigidity, known as rigor. With time, rigor becomes stronger, eventually reaching a maximum during which the body becomes stiff as a plank. Rigor develops in all muscles at the same rate; however, because of their relative masses, smaller muscles (such as those of the face) display rigor first, followed by larger muscle groups such as the thighs. Once rigor reaches its peak, it recedes in the same order it first appeared, releasing the smaller muscles first before relinquishing its grip on the major muscle masses, usually twenty-four hours after death. Rigor's lone lingering effect is a stiffness of the major joints, which "freeze" at the peak of Rigor's powers. Like her sisters, Rigor is progressive, reaching her full expression in temperate environments twelve to eighteen hours after death.

The Mortis girls collectively reveal that twelve hours post-mortem is a major benchmark, a period in which all three sisters are at their best and most developed. This brief primer in determining the time of death paves the way for evaluating the testimony of the inquest's next witness: Dr. Robert Ellison, the physician who performed Annie Kempton's autopsy.

❬

As the afternoon session of the inquest's second day gathered steam, Dr. Ellison — a physician respected and trusted by all in attendance — reluctantly took the stand. Ellison had the unenviable task of relating the mechanics of how Annie died. He had cared for the victim since her birth, and the doctor's face bore the ravages of what he had just done and what he must now do. Like most trained physicians, he found solace in clinical detachment. He also knew his audience, simultaneously translating his medical jargon into lay terms all could comprehend.

Ellison began by describing Annie's injuries. He found five distinct wounds to the head: two blunt force defects to the scalp and three incised wounds to the throat. The blunt injuries had torn the skin clear through to the bone. In his expert opinion, the blows to the head had stunned her but it was the deep cuts to the throat that killed her. For the sake of thoroughness, Ellison then catalogued the other bruises and abrasions to Annie's body, each a silent testament to her last desperate minutes.[3] Ellison, in deference to the family, avoided any gratuitously graphic details.

Then came the question few dared ask aloud: had Annie been sexually assaulted? The *Saint John Daily Record* had reported as much that very morning. Ellison announced, to the audible relief of those assembled, that Annie had retained her virtue throughout her ordeal. Relief soon turned to chagrin as the discussion took an anatomical turn. Women blushed crimson and men looked askance as the doctor stated matter-of-factly that "he found the vagina all right."[4] If the unknown assailant's intent was to rape her, he had not succeeded. Not once did Ellison mention Peter Wheeler by name.

After documenting the fatal wounds and addressing the question of sexual assault, Ellison made a bold pronouncement. He had estimated Annie's time of death. Based on his assessment of the triad — temperature, lividity, and rigor — Ellison stated with confidence that when he examined the body at 3:00 p.m. on Tuesday, January 28, Annie had been dead approximately thirteen hours. To err on the side of caution, Ellison fixed her time of death as sometime between midnight and 4:00 a.m. on Tuesday the twenty-eighth.

The doctor's estimate was consistent with evidence at the scene, specifically Annie's state of dress and the condition of her bed. The estimate also ruled out another troubling possibility. Given the girl's body temperature and the degree of rigor and livor development, the doctor was positive the murder could not have occurred after 8:00 a.m. on Tuesday, excluding any chance that Wheeler had committed the act when he arrived that morning to buy milk for his landlady. The crime, Ellison concluded, must have occurred in the early morning hours of the twenty-eighth — of that he was certain. The body does not lie, Ellison told the awestruck crowd, although at least one detective in the crowd paid the good doctor precious little heed.

nine

The Verdict

Dr. Ellison's learned testimony notwithstanding, the second day of Lovett's inquest bore little resemblance to the first. Gone was the pretext of reconstructing Annie's final hours. The sole remaining goal of the inquiry was to gather sufficient ammunition to eviscerate Wheeler. The quest for understanding had been shelved; in its stead, the lynching of Peter Wheeler began in earnest. The lone voices of reason — Doctors Lovett and Ellison — were quickly drowned out by a chorus of accusations ringing forth from the Parker brothers and their supporters.

One by one, the citizens of Bear River took the stand and laid waste to Wheeler's name and reputation. Hostile to a man, the tiny hamlet had transformed overnight into a seething mob bent on meting out their notions of justice.

If the mood had changed, so too had much of the previous day's testimony. Everyone in the village suddenly recalled seeing Wheeler near the Kempton home that fateful day. Herbert Comeau, who shared his home with Wheeler, said under oath that he saw Peter on the road leading to Annie's house in the late afternoon. Sadie Morine, Grace's more agreeable younger sister, testified to seeing Peter near the Kemptons' between 5:00 and 6:00 p.m. Elmer Crabbe, who lived across the road from Annie and her kin, also reported seeing the accused in the area as the sun was setting.

Still others offered new testimony suggesting Wheeler had lusted after Annie, making no secret of his immoral designs on her. Herbert Parker's accusations had taken hold and festered in the minds of those who once called Wheeler friend. Bear River became a collective of armchair psychiatrists, parsing Wheeler's every word and deed, looking for signs of his evil intent. At least three people took the stand to tell of Wheeler's seemingly odd behaviour in the hours after Annie's body was discovered, converting simple personality quirks into pathognomonic symptoms of mental derangement. Most damning of all, two more people stepped forward and again accused Wheeler of lying.

The first was Stanley Rice. Rice had testified on the first day of the inquest, offering little of substance. By day two, Rice was rabid, foaming at the mouth to retake the stand and refute some previous testimony. During her statement, Wheeler's landlady Tillie Comeau mentioned that Peter had been at Rice's place around sunset — still considered to be the time of the murder in spite of Dr. Ellison's testimony. On his best days, Stanley Rice was as subtle and humourless as a hatchet but on this particular day he practically levitated out of the witness chair, so certain was he that Wheeler had not been at his home that evening. It was, proclaimed Rice, just another of Wheeler's countless lies to cover his heinous deed.

Had cooler heads prevailed, Rice's histrionics would have flamed out before impact. As is sometimes the case in legal proceedings, everyone was telling the truth — at least as they understood it. The mystery surrounding Wheeler's whereabouts, like the fracas over who was to stay with Annie that night, was a simple misunderstanding blown out of all proportion. Wheeler had been on Rice's property as dusk fell, checking his rabbit snares in the fields. In the heat of the moment, Stanley thought Tillie's testimony implied Wheeler was in the house, rather than just on the land. Neither Tillie nor Wheeler had been mendacious as to his whereabouts, merely imprecise. As for Stanley Rice, he simply overreacted.

Wheeler's second and more damaging accuser was Louis Jeremy, an elder of the local Mi'kmaq band, although in press accounts he was known simply as "the Indian who testified."[1] Jeremy lived on the same road as the Kemptons, and after hearing Annie had been murdered, he went to pay his respects at their house. Jeremy then went down to the Comeau house, where he found Peter Wheeler sitting in the kitchen. According to Jeremy, the two men got into a heated discussion as to the position of Annie's body. The crime scene had been anything but closed and members of the community wandered through at will. By the time Jeremy (and most of Bear River) viewed Annie's remains, she was supine on the sitting-room floor. When Wheeler discovered the body, however, she had been on her knees with her head and torso slumped forward, face to the floor. Jeremy said that, as they debated the issue, Wheeler actually jumped up and demonstrated the awkward pose for him, a scene Jeremy re-enacted in the Oakdene Academy before a mortified audience.

In truth, both Wheeler and Jeremy had accurately reported the position of Annie's body as they had seen it. In the interval between Wheeler's discovery and Jeremy's observations, Lovett and other officials had repositioned the body to protect the girl's dignity. That Annie's body was so easily manipulated indicates that Rigor Mortis had not yet paid her inevitable post-mortem call.

Louis Jeremy's testimony, however, ignited a firestorm on two counts. The first was that it suggested Wheeler was lying about the position of the girl, raising the disturbing possibility he had committed further indignities to Annie's remains in the morning before alerting the neighbours to her death — a shockingly salacious allegation that reverberated within the academy's walls. That a rumour is loud does not make it true, however. Review of the witness statements from the first responders to the scene indicate Annie was still in the prone position described by Wheeler when they arrived. Furthermore, according to Ellison's autopsy findings, the lividity in Annie's body supported Wheeler's version of events. The Mortis sisters once again came to Wheeler's defence, for all the good it would do.

The second rumour spawned by Jeremy's incendiary testimony was as logically inconsistent as it was excoriating for Wheeler. In this particular tale of the tape, Wheeler's account as to the positioning of Annie's body was accepted as true. However, in this version Wheeler added a single pertinent detail — he supposedly told Jeremy the girl's throat was cut several times. When Jeremy viewed the body, Annie was covered with a quilt and the nature of her injuries was not apparent. Within minutes, all of Bear River knew Annie was murdered but few knew the specifics of her wounds. Donning their detective caps, many were led to wonder: if Annie's body were face down, obscuring her neck, how had Wheeler known her throat was slashed? Clearly, the would-be Holmes and Watsons of Bear River reasoned, Wheeler knew the exact cause of Annie's death not because he had seen it when he found the body but because he was her killer. It was a classic *gotcha!* moment, ripped from the pages of a panto crime drama. It was also the sort of faulty reasoning that springs from overactive imaginations. Although prone, Annie's face was turned to the side, leaving her neck exposed, a pallid island in the lake of blood seeping from it. Her wounds were equally evident to officials and onlookers who saw her in the moments following the discovery of the crime, before her body was covered for modesty's sake.

Amidst the turbulent rumours, speculation, and outright fabrications of the inquest's second day, the previous day's uncertainty was mere flotsam, swept to sea by an undercurrent of fear. In its wake, a single absolute conviction bobbed to the surface: Peter Wheeler was guilty. The rules of evidence, at first relaxed, were now abandoned and replaced with mob rule; conscious deliberation and reason gave way to an insatiable, irrational thirst for vengeance.

With the citizenry now squarely against Wheeler, one last witness took the stand to deliver a final emotional wallop. Strangely enough, this most powerful witness never implicated Peter Wheeler or even cast a glance in his direction, a nuance lost on the distraught crowd. By this point, the mob tolerated no dissension in their ranks and saw only what they wanted to see.

As the audience sat spellbound, a lone hunched figure laboured his way to the front of the hall. Silence fell, a conscious show of respect for the witness: Annie's father, Isaac Kempton. Grief alone did not account for his slow progression. Isaac had lost a foot at the ankle in a lumbering accident and made his way through life on an ill-fitting cork prosthesis.

His disability had taken its toll. Isaac's face — doughy and long gone to seed, with loosening skin that threatened to swallow his eyes whole — was never truly handsome and now was a monument to misery. Adrift in a fog of guilt, memory, and regret, Isaac Kempton was a lost and ruined man, kept aloft only by his sense of duty to his surviving family.

Isaac was bereaved yet composed on the stand as he told of his final moments with Annie that Monday morning, when he and his son Earnest left for the logging camp. He also repeated the story that overnight had taken on near-mythic proportions: before he left, Kempton had arranged with Tillie Comeau to come and stay with Annie. If Isaac bore Tillie any ill-will, he kept it to himself and his eyes never found hers in the crowded hall. A normally stoic man, he now wept openly before his grief-stricken neighbours as he recounted how he learned of Annie's murder from a man at the logging camp.

Confronted with a father's unfathomable heartache, the prosecution still had a job to do. Under gentle but persistent questioning, acting prosecutor J.M. Owen coaxed Isaac into describing the condition of his cow upon his return. It seemed an odd, almost callous segue after such an emotionally charged account. Isaac Kempton, numb to such trivial distinctions, told how the cow gave twice its normal supply when milked on Tuesday afternoon. The line of questioning threw many in the audience, who could not imagine why a grieving father was made to recall such mundane details at a time like this.

There was, of course, method in Owen's madness. The prosecutor, under the watchful eye of Detective Power, sought to establish a new timeline of events, one very much at odds with the time-of-death estimate provided by Dr. Robert Ellison. The significance of the cow became clear when it was revealed that one of Annie's daily chores was to milk the animal by 6:00 p.m. Annie had obviously not completed her evening chore on time, as the beast's udder was painfully swollen on Tuesday afternoon.[2] Speaking through his proxy, Prosecutor Owen, Detective Power argued that the cow was proof Annie had been killed before six o'clock on Monday, the only time Power could put Wheeler alone near the Kempton house. To drive home this highly contentious point, Owen offered this brief summation: with all due respect to the good Doctor Ellison and his scientific ponderings, a cow never lies. It was, declared the prosecution, all but certain Annie was killed on Monday between 5:00 and 6:00 p.m.

☾

As Owen ruminated on the cow, the inquest was at long last nearing an end. By the close of the Wednesday evening session, a total of twenty-four witnesses had taken the stand, a few more than once. Most had, in some fashion, implicated Peter Wheeler as the killer. Throughout the tortured course of the hearing, the prosecution's theory of the crime had formed then crystallized: at approximately five o'clock, Wheeler went to the Kempton home, where he knew Annie would be alone. In a lustful frenzy, he tried to ravage the girl but she had fought valiantly for her virtue. Enraged at being denied, Wheeler struck her across the head then cut her throat. There was, at least to Power's and Owen's way of thinking, nothing more to be gained from the inquest.

Dr. Lovett, the nominal head of the proceedings, concurred. The time had come for the coroner and his jury to render a verdict. After receiving their instructions from Owen, the jury was sent to deliberate. Those left behind in the hall did not have long to wait. In short order, Lovett and the twelve jurymen filed back into the academy's main gallery. Absolute silence fell as Lovett returned to the podium. The crowd sat so transfixed, one might have performed surgery on them without the benefit of anaesthesia, if so inclined.

In a clear and steady voice, the coroner read the verdict:

> We do upon oath say that Annie Kempton, between the hours of 5 in the afternoon of Monday, the 27th day of January, and the hour of 8 o'clock in the morning of Tuesday, 28th day of January, aforesaid was violently assaulted and

struck on the forehead and head several heavy blows and had her throat cut in several places, causing her death. And we further say that the said Annie Kempton was thereby feloniously killed and murdered at her father's residence in Bear River.[3]

In deference to both his colleague Ellison and the detective from Halifax, Lovett had wisely built some latitude into his estimate of the time of death, concluding only that it must have occurred between the time she was last seen in town and the time her body was found. It was a judicious compromise that belied Lovett's inexperience as a coroner.

The coroner's verdict thus far was proper and exactly as all expected, but there remained one final codicil that would change everything: "And we suspect Peter Wheeler of Bear River in the county of Digby, yeoman, to be guilty of the said murder of Annie Kempton."[4]

After a shocked moment of silence, the capacity crowd erupted, releasing a paroxysm of fury that threatened to bring the academy down on their very heads. As the cacophony reached fever-pitch, Dr. Lovett calmly affixed his signature to the inquest report and gathered his papers. Seemingly oblivious to the uproar, he paused to thank the men of the jury for their faithful service, had a quick word with Detective Power and Prosecutor Owen, then slipped quietly from the hall and made for home.

As the boisterous throng flowed from the schoolhouse into the frozen streets of Bear River, one man was conspicuous in his absence. Peter Wheeler, the focus of the day's inquisition and the object of such derision among his former acquaintances, was not on hand to hear himself labelled a murderer. Detective Nicholas Power had arrested him hours before, as if already certain of the jury's verdict.

Peter Wheeler in police custody in the Digby jail, 1896.

ten

Out of Bounds

Wheeler's arrest was not actually tied to the outcome of the coroner's inquest, although its timing seemed more than coincidental. In the Venn diagram of Annie Kempton's murder investigation, the spheres representing the coroner and law enforcement never overlapped. The stuttering transition to a medical examiner system had muddied the waters for the province's chief death investigators and curtailed the coroner's scope. Dr. Lovett was empowered to convene an inquest, subpoena witnesses, and hear sworn testimony. He lacked the power of arrest, however, an authority squarely within the realm of police. Nor could Lovett indict — much less try or convict — anyone of a crime, and regardless of the inquest's verdict, the coroner had no direct power to dole out punishment.

Detective Nick Power knew this but gambled the press did not, or rather would not care about such subtle distinctions. The media saw only an appointed official questioning witnesses and rendering a verdict. It was therefore troubling — but not at all surprising — when the following day's headlines declared: "Wheeler is the murderer of Annie Kempton."[1]

There was no hedging or equivocation to the pronouncement. In the decades before enforced libel laws and defamation suits brought the media to heel, there was little incentive to hide behind terms like "alleged" or "reportedly." The headline was a precise, unwavering statement of fact: Wheeler had done it. So said the coroner and his jury. So said Detective Power. So said the people of Bear River. And thus, on February 1, less than seventy-two hours after Annie's body was discovered, so said the *Morning Chronicle*.

In fact, Dr. Lovett and his jury had not declared Wheeler to be the murderer. They only "suspected"[2] him of the crime, but such legal hairsplitting does not sell newspapers. The press members took it upon themselves to turn suspicion into proof, a curious brand of alchemy unique to the media.

In the rush to judgment, however, few noticed that the only evidence against Wheeler was the perception that he had lied to Tillie to get Annie home alone. Such slim speculation was soon crushed under the same wheels that had obliterated the concepts of innocent until proven guilty and due process. The gloves were off and the rules of fair play no longer applied. All agreed Wheeler was the killer and the print media were under no obligation — other than that of simple human decency — to suggest otherwise.

As headlines go, it was a barnburner. The *Chronicle*'s ink-stained muckrakers no doubt soothed whatever qualms they had by claiming they catered to the greater public good. The outraged citizens of Bear River demanded swift and decisive justice and the region's news organs felt compelled to provide it at any cost. There was comfort in having absolute certainty so soon after the tragedy — not for Wheeler, of course, but for the family and community so traumatized by the heinous event.

Canada's newspapers had learned well the lessons of Jack the Ripper. Murder sells, to be sure, but an unsolved murder soon leaves a populace uneasy. Morbid fascination (and sales) quickly waned if all that was on offer was speculation and uncertainty. It was far better to have a clearly identified culprit, a focus for the community's anger and anguish. Public fear was only assuaged once the fiend was safely behind bars; polite society could breathe easier, no longer forced to lock their doors at night against the unknown.

As for Detective Power, the media's response fit perfectly into his scheme of things. Once Wheeler was in custody, there was no need to look for alternative suspects. With blinders firmly in place, the crack gumshoe now set about proving Wheeler's guilt, a decidedly easier task than actually solving Annie's murder.

Power may have been single-minded but he was not working single-handed. He was joined by Mr. Charles Dunn, "who has connections with the American Detective Agency,"[3] although that was later amended to the "Amherst Detective Agency."[4] The hows and whys of Mr. Dunn's involvement are now lost in the mists of time. In all reports on the case — official as well as media — Dunn was the recessive gene of the investigation: present but with no tangible influence. Whatever Dunn's contributions, Power ultimately took, or was given, the credit.

☾

It is heartbreaking to think, given how events unfolded, that it all began with an unrecognized but entirely avoidable error by a novice coroner. Dr. Lovett, conducting his very first homicide investigation, overstepped the bounds of his authority, which was simply to determine the cause and manner of Annie's death. Based on the autopsy findings, the cause of Annie's demise was the knife wounds to her throat. The manner of death — the way in which the cause came into being — was homicide, the actions of another. That was the sum of what Lovett needed to decide. The rest was simply the overreaching of a neophyte, however well-intentioned.

More than just an issue of semantics, the line Lovett crossed is crucial to any system of jurisprudence. Homicide is a medico-legal manner of death, recognizing another person's responsibility for the demise. Murder is a specific legal charge, indicating the perpetrator acted with intent. All murders are homicides but not all homicides are murders. Lovett was within his rights to declare Annie's death a homicide, rather than an accident or a suicide. However, it did not fall to Lovett to rule that it was murder — a legal designation far outside his wheelhouse — nor was it Lovett's place to actually identify a suspect or declare him guilty.

Having exceeded his authority, Lovett became a catalyst, the first tipped domino in a cascade that ultimately ended with a noose around Peter Wheeler's neck. That no one recognized the gravity of Lovett's error suggests incompetence, indifference, or — most worrisome of all — a wanton disregard for the rule of law and Wheeler's civil rights.

Lovett's mistake was the tinder but the ensuing inferno was fed by the media. Allowing every benefit of the doubt, Lovett's rookie mistake can be chalked up to the youthful indiscretion of an inexperienced doctor. It was a blunder, but initially, it was a contained one, known only to those present in the Bear River academy that dark January night. It was not until the press broadcast Lovett's error to the province and beyond that the real damage was done. The media's blatant misrepresentation of the ruling smacked of exploitation and malfeasance and obliterated any possibility of ultimately righting the wrong.

In declaring Wheeler's guilt, the *Chronicle* and its ilk did not merely taint any future jury pool, they poisoned it beyond repair. Theirs was a policy of scorched earth and salted ground. With Lovett's misstep providing ample cover, the media publicly hung Peter Wheeler long before the sheriff finally got around to doing it.

eleven

With Friends Like These

It was open season on the beleaguered prisoner following the *Chronicle*'s unequivocal declaration of Wheeler's guilt. Everyone with an axe to grind or a taste for the limelight staked their claim to the front page. Even those with the most tenuous connection to Wheeler garnered their fifteen minutes of fame by telling incriminating tales to a press pack that had made a religion out of ignoring the teller's dubious agenda. Fact-checking or vetting of any sort was deemed unnecessary. The lone requirement for publication was that the story bathed Peter Wheeler in the worst possible light.

First to vent his spleen was Stanley Rice, who so famously rose at the inquest to call Wheeler a liar — twice. The Rice clan were Digby County royalty and Stanley, a lumberman by trade, was comfortable in his favoured-nation status and prone to voicing his opinions without expecting any challenge or fallout. Rice once employed Wheeler for sixteen days and told all who would listen — most notably the *Morning Chronicle* — that Peter often spoke of Annie and not in the most Christian of manners. Although Rice failed to mention this seemingly pertinent information at the coroner's inquest, he willingly shared the tale with the *Chronicle*.

As the correspondent sat, all ears, Rice pulled out the story like a chit saved for just such an occasion. One day at camp the two men got to swapping stories, as men are wont to do, when Wheeler let slip that he would "commit adultery with Annie the first time he got a chance and was going to."[1] Rice had clearly chosen his words with care, ever mindful of the reader's delicate sensibilities if not the actual meaning of the word adultery.

Stanley was hardly one to talk. There was a warrant out for his arrest for using "obscene language in the Salvation Barracks at Bear River."[2] Seems Rice had some unchristian words of his own for one of the local women, claiming he wanted to "screw"[3] her. Stanley was quick to defend himself, saying it was entirely the woman's fault: "I might have said that about an indecent girl. I never used this expression about a decent girl."[4]

It also bears noting that Rice had a beef with Wheeler long before Annie's death. Wheeler had worked for Rice in the lumber fields and was owed two dollars for his labour. Stanley dragged his feet, refusing to pay, so Peter Wheeler filed a civil suit against Rice to recoup his wages.[5] Such suits were commonplace in the era, the only means of recourse for petty disagreements. Stanley eventually settled his accounts, but the exchange had left a bad taste in his mouth. It is not outside the realm of possibility to think Stanley's accusations were prompted by things that had little to do with the grave matter at hand.

❨

Either Peter Wheeler had a big mouth or his friends did. Herbert Parker, the first to besmirch Wheeler at the inquest, repeated his tale ad nauseam to the men of the fourth estate. Parker's assertion that Wheeler spoke of Annie "in a morally threatening tone"[6] unleashed a mutant strain of pathogen. Within hours, it seemed everyone in Bear River was infected with the same fever, a pandemic of gossip and slander that threatened to lay the entire village low. The first to show symptoms was Myrtle Godfrey, a thirteen-year-old classmate of the victim. With reporter's notebooks poised at the ready, Myrtle recounted the time she was sitting in Tillie Comeau's kitchen when Annie Kempton passed by. Wheeler, sporting a sinner's grin, reportedly said that if he got "that girl alone, she would be no good to herself or anyone else."[7] Unsure as to what Peter was implying,

Myrtle innocently asked why. According to the girl, Wheeler's response was equally cryptic: "That's for me to know and you to find out."[8] At some point, Myrtle (or someone close to her) figured out the meaning—and value—of the conversation.

It bears noting that, irrespective of Myrtle's reasons for sharing her story, the self-serving motivation of another Godfrey is forever preserved in the historical archives. Buried deep in the accumulated detritus of the coroner's inquest records is a handwritten letter addressed to W.B. Stewart, Esquire, an attorney associated with the case. The missive was sent by Richard Godfrey, a fifty-one-year-old shoemaker known to all in Bear River as an ardent Baptist and the domineering father to young Myrtle, although not necessarily in that order. Godfrey wrote to Stewart demanding to be paid a witness fee of $1.60, the stipend granted to those subpoenaed to testify at any court proceeding relating to the death of Annie Kempton. It was an odd request given that Richard's name never appeared on any of the countless witness lists.

Exactly what Richard hoped to accomplish with his letter remains elusive. Perhaps he felt everyone willing to slander Wheeler in any forum was entitled to compensation. That his request was dated April 24, 1897 —more than a year after Annie's death and the legal proceedings that followed—only adds to its cryptic mystique. If Richard intended to turn passing time and fading memories into a tiny windfall, gambling on Stewart issuing the honorarium without first checking his records, he was woefully mistaken. Godfrey's request was simply filed away, unanswered and unpaid, an enduring testament to the greed and chaos that permeated the whole ugly affair.

☾

In a further curious turn of events, the *Acadian Recorder* shifted some of the blame for Annie's death back onto Rice, Parker, and Godfrey, taking them to task for failing to act on Wheeler's threats:

Peter had often admired Annie and had on several occasions made improper remarks concerning her, saying he would like a chance to get her alone. Although several people heard him say this, they thought lightly of it and failed to realize the full significance of the monster's words, and no insinuation of his designs upon the girl was ever wafted to the ears of the Kemptons or else the direful tragedy might have been avoided.[9]

Their collective rush to implicate Wheeler — whether driven by a moral imperative, a thirst for publicity, or some darker rationale — had backfired. In smearing their former friend, his accusers had inadvertently tarred themselves. It was, after all, a fair question: if they knew full well Peter had evil designs on Annie, why had they not warned anyone?

Vicious circles of all sorts abound in the sad tale of Annie Kempton and Peter Wheeler. The public's rabid fascination with the case fuelled newspaper sales, which in turn spurred the editors' demands for daily updates. The finite populace of Bear River eventually ran out of mud to sling and reporters were forced to search further afield for fresh dirt, continually lowering the bar for what was acceptable until it scraped the ground. Out of sheer desperation, anyone was given a voice, a small measure of credence, and as many column inches as they could fill.

As the cycle reached its nadir, one of the major Halifax dailies printed an iffy story of a hotel employee who supposedly worked with Wheeler aboard an unnamed ship some untold years prior. Details were sketchy but one thing was clear: the man claimed Wheeler had tried to murder one of the crew. The story was later revealed to be entirely false but that did not stop the *Digby Weekly Courier* from repeating it one week later. In the interests of journalistic integrity, the *Courier* insisted it only reprinted the story to highlight the reckless reporting of other newspapers, which it accused of floating "groundless rumors" that did little more than kick "a man when he is down."[10] Deftly straddling both sides of the fence, the *Courier* declared: "If Wheeler is innocent, he is a greatly misjudged man and a martyr alive; if he is guilty, he is one of the biggest scoundrels and most plausible hypocrites that ever existed. We hope the truth will be reached, whoever suffers."[11]

All attempts by Wheeler to refute the claims or even place the stories in their proper context were summarily dismissed. No matter what he said or did, Peter merely dug the hole a little deeper. "Wheeler is having only his dues," proclaimed the *Digby Courier*, "he has been interviewed by press men and tells such a story as criminals always do. If it turns out to be true it will all be well; but mean time such a case of brutal butchery needs to be given no leniency."[12]

Any hope that all would be well was long gone. Wheeler's so-called friends — with the help of their newest ally, the media — had made certain of that. "No leniency" had become the rallying cry of the *Digby Weekly Courier*, the people of Bear River, and the justice system of Nova Scotia.

twelve

The Harlot of Bear River

No leniency was certainly the watchword of the *Bridgetown Monitor*, and the paper's editor did not stop with Peter Wheeler. Within hours of the tragedy, the editor passed unflinching judgment on two women who, through no fault of their own, found themselves in the eye of the storm. The *Monitor* first set its intransigent sights on Tillie Comeau, the accused man's landlady, although the paper was keen to imply she was so much more.

More than ten years Wheeler's senior, Tillie seemed hopelessly miscast as the object of Peter's affections. She was generously called handsome by some acquaintances, although more thought her plain. Wheeler was a lad of fourteen when he first approached her to rent a room; she was twenty-five and already a mother twice over. The *Saint John Daily Sun* noted that Tillie still "spoke of Wheeler as if he were a boy,"[1] even as he sat in chains, accused of murder at the age of twenty-six. Despite their feint to Tillie's maternal leanings, the *Sun* added the caustic codicil that "if dame rumor is correct, Mrs. Comeau was more of a wife than a mother to the prisoner."[2]

Their unconventional living arrangement had lasted, off and on, for twelve years. Whenever the need arose, Wheeler took work aboard one of the merchant vessels steaming out of Bear River. Months later, with his pockets replenished and his wanderlust sated, Wheeler would once again wash up on Tillie's doorstep.

Money was tight all around. In addition to taking in boarders to make ends meet, Tillie worked a number of menial jobs about town, including that of chambermaid at the Bear River Hotel. One out-of-province news agency found sources who described Tillie as "a hard-working, industrious woman"[3] that "you can trust without limit."[4] No Nova Scotia paper searched that hard.

Yet, in spite of Comeau's gainful employment and a few kind words from her neighbours, the *Bridgetown Monitor* took issue with her virtue and integrity: "This woman bears an unsavory reputation, and has a number of children, although said to be unmarried."[5] At the time of Annie's death, Tillie still had a small brood at home: her daughter Hattie, aged nineteen, and two sons, Herbert, fifteen, and Walter, eleven. While their paternity remains an open question, none of the children were fathered by Peter Wheeler.

The *Monitor* was not alone in challenging the bond between Wheeler and his landlady. One New Brunswick tabloid reported: "There are strange stories afloat concerning their relationship."[6] The critical difference, of course, was that all other news agencies also acknowledged the whispers as exactly that — unfounded gossip by a fearful and traumatized populace. For example, the *Saint John Daily Sun* noted that "some of the neighbors are uncharitable enough to say that the pair are too intimate from a moral point of view,"[7] placing the shame and blame back on the scandal-mongering neighbours where it belonged.

Tillie's tenure in the spotlight was not solely on account of her nebulous relationship with the accused. She, along with her children, played a far more substantial role in the proceedings, namely that of Wheeler's alibi. From the moment Peter left Annie, still very much alive, at her house just after 8:00 p.m. Monday until 8:00 a.m. the next day — when Comeau sent Peter to the Kemptons' to get milk — Tillie and the kids were with Wheeler every second. It was the one question regarding Peter Wheeler that Tillie was eager to answer. She even paused during her inquest testimony and insisted, in no uncertain terms, that her words be recorded verbatim. The irascible landlady, plain-spoken and possessed of a quicksilver temper, was used to being misunderstood and did not want anyone mistaking her meaning.

Time and again, Tillie was asked whether it was possible for Wheeler to leave the house without her knowledge. On this point, Tillie was adamant: "it was next to impossible for Wheeler to go out without being heard.... He had to pass through three doors... two of which made a desperate creaking noise when opened and would surely have been heard."[8]

Despite Tillie's mottled reputation in the village, even the ever-skeptical Detective Power accepted her story. When asked by a reporter from the *Morning Chronicle* if "Tillie Comeau was trying to shield [Wheeler],"[9] Power replied confidently, "No, not in the least."[10] It is a credit to Power's innate chivalry that, in spite of his own vendetta against Wheeler, he did not feel the need to sully the reputation of Peter's beleaguered landlady. That Power would later argue Tillie's testimony supported his much-maligned timeline of the crime may also have contributed to the detective's magnanimous gallantry.

❆

Having waged its unwarranted yet strangely unresented war on Tillie Comeau, the *Bridgetown Monitor* prepared to do battle on an entirely new front: Mary Kempton, the bereft mother of the innocent victim. It was a risky strategy, one sure to ignite controversy and sales, or so they hoped.

In the days following the murder, the circumstances surrounding Mrs. Kempton's absence from the home were the subject of much speculation, as was the duration of her truancy. With little regard for the facts, several news agencies implied that Mary had been gone from the house for months or even years. The truth made for far less scandalous reading. According to her oldest surviving daughter, Mary Kempton had been in Bear River as recently as Christmas. She enjoyed the holiday with her husband, son, and Annie before returning to Boston on December 27, 1895.[11]

What compelled Mary's departure was further grist for the mill. According to the *Monitor*, Annie's absentee mother "has not been under medical treatment as [was] first reported."[12] That the *Monitor* itself was the source of the erroneous report apparently did not bear mentioning.

The *Digby Weekly Courier* printed this illustration
of Mary Kempton on September 8, 1896.

Rather, the fact-challenged tabloid went on to say that she had spent the previous four months in Boston, "working to relieve the straightened [*sic*] circumstances of the family."[13] The editor then proceeded to berate Mrs. Kempton for abandoning her daughter and putting the family finances ahead of the welfare of her child. Conveniently overlooked was the fact that Mary had not abandoned her daughter but had left her in the care of her father and older brother, an entirely safe and reasonable arrangement.

In defiance of all conventional wisdom, the *Bridgetown Monitor* found fault not only with Mary's prolonged absence from the home but also with the Kemptons' choice of chaperone. Killing two birds with a single libellous stone, the *Monitor* hurled the blame for Annie's death at her grieving parents while simultaneously taking potshots at their neighbour

Tillie Comeau, whose only crime was agreeing to serve as Annie's tutelary in their absence. In a meandering yet pointed editorial, the *Monitor* proclaimed:

> We must express a feeling of surprise and wonderment that intelligent and well-intentioned people, as Mr. and Mrs. Kempton undoubtedly are, should have taken no further precautions for the safety of a girl of their daughter's tender years and supplied no better protector during their absence than a woman of such a character and reputation as that born [*sic*] by Tillie Comeau.[14]

Heaping scorn on the guilt-ridden parents of a murdered child was a curious proposition for a local paper, particularly when the only benefit to such censure was the indirect berating of a woman already held in low regard. Neither the Kemptons nor Tillie did anything to warrant the *Monitor*'s sanctimonious tirade, and they had no avenue of recourse or rebuttal. Unlike their tabloid accuser, the slandered objects of the *Monitor*'s ridicule took the high road, electing to remain silent in the face of meritless derision. The Kemptons were occupied by far greater burdens. As for Tillie Comeau, the so-called wanton trollop of the Annapolis Valley, she bore the slings and arrows of the *Bridgetown Monitor* with a strength of character its editor sorely lacked.

❨

A town that had so boldly compared itself to that bastion of neutrality, Switzerland, was now fractured under the weight of an unspeakable crime. In the shards of their once-placid village, the denizens took no prisoners — save for Peter Wheeler — and cast out all sinners, starting with Tillie Comeau.

thirteen

In Black and White

Canada prides itself on being a nation of tolerance and acceptance. Unlike the great melting pot to the south, the "True North strong and free" is a polyglot, pluralistic mosaic in which all are welcome and differences are to be celebrated and preserved.

It was not always thus. In 1896 Canada was unfathomably, unrecognizably racist. The country, a mere twenty-eight years old, had already weathered a turbulent and troubled history. During their formative years, the Maritime provinces had witnessed the expulsion of the Acadians and the systematic denigration of its First Nations peoples. Many had known slavery to be legal in their lifetime. Halifax, the region's capital and one of the principal gateways to the New World, funnelled an endless stream of cultures, creeds, and languages through its port and expelled them into the less than welcoming arms of those eking out a living in the lands and waters beyond. Clashes verging on race wars were inevitable.

Political correctness is of relatively recent invention. By today's standards, the rhetoric of 1896 seems staggeringly offensive. Aboriginals were consistently identified in the press as "Indians," as though the inaccurate moniker alone was sufficient information. In English-speaking tabloids, the French were simply that — "the French" — deserving of neither surname nor respect.

Stereotypes balanced precariously atop popular notions of phenotypes. Physical features were liberally used to define everything, including one's race, ethnicity, religion, nationality, or class. Xenophobia (mixed with more than a dash of prejudice) dictated that the European somatotype was the de facto pinnacle of beauty and desirability.

Such conceits were so firmly entrenched that a report in the *Bridgetown Monitor* claiming that the "civilizees of Japan" were "straightening their eyes"[1] to appear more White was not met with shock or disbelief but rather the tacit approval of its readership. Indeed, many saw God's guiding hand in the notion that "the Japanese have become so progressive in their ideas and so set in their determination to get a position in the van of Caucasian civilization"[2] that they resorted to surgically mutilating their eyes. With blind faith came blind trust and the paper's myopic subscribers accepted the story as gospel, no matter how preposterous the reporting. The *Monitor* concluded its article by noting that post-op, "the Jap arises from the surgeon's chair a happy man, for his eyes are as straight as those of any white man that walks the earth."[3]

The Maritime broadsheets were striped with endless variations on this theme throughout the late 1800s. The influence of such diatribes was so pervasive it is best characterized as casual racism. Bigotry — and the hatred and fear it fomented — was so ubiquitous and unchallenged, it seemed almost an afterthought, the undetected background hum of daily life. Yet, without question, the hum grew louder and more menacing whenever the subject turned to those of darker pigmentation.

The distinct physiognomy of African-derived populations both fascinated and repelled their Caucasian brethren. Postulating theories as to the origins of "Black" traits became a kind of parlour game, one the local papers were only too happy to play. "It is evident that it is the outdoor exposure of the [African] working classes that makes their skin so black,"[4] argued one armchair anthropologist, who went on to suggest that the phenomenon was not exclusive to humans but was seen in all African "birds, beasts, fish, reptiles and plants."[5] Such exposure, he contended, resulted in "the Negro's curly hair — it is a protection to the brain from the tropical sun,"[6] concluding that "the skull of the African, with its peculiar thickness, affords another feature of protection."[7] Whites who found thick-headedness a mark of African inferiority were a textbook case of the pot calling the kettle black, but there was no denying that such physical traits automatically conveyed second-class citizenship to those who bore them, regardless of their point of origin.

Expressions of racial intolerance were not limited to narrow-minded speculation as to the evolutionary benefits of the afro. Although the abolition of slavery in 1832 had freed them from their literal shackles, Blacks were still viewed as property by their fair-skinned neighbours. This ethos was on full display on February 21, 1896, when the *Digby Weekly Courier* ran a front-page story entitled "Three Popular Blacks: They Belong to the Diamond Family." The "Negroes" in question were damned with the faintest of praise as "blacks we like,"[8] the implication being that all others left something to be desired.

It was truly a different time, with the requisite different mindset. Casual racism was the social norm, the lesser of two evils. Commentary on skin colour and ethnicity was not couched in the language of acceptance or diversity. Stereotypes were embraced, cherished, and freely applied. Straw man arguments — such as chalking up questionable sentiments to unnamed sources, rendered untraceable by disclaimers such as "some think" or "they say" — insulated editors from any charges of overt racism, although such precautions seemed unnecessary. Few in the reading audience were likely to complain.

❨

Into this volatile milieu stepped Peter Wheeler, a dark-skinned man of ambiguous ancestry and indeterminate parentage. When queried during the 1891 census, Wheeler identified his birthplace as Australia, a curious deviation from the correct answer: the island of Mauritius. It may have been an act of self-preservation, as Wheeler, better than anyone, understood the prejudice inherent in being African born. To further his cause, Peter took pains to inform the census taker that his parents were born in England, affording him European heritage by proxy.

Wheeler later repeated his contrived Australian genealogy during the coroner's inquest, much to the open disdain of the media. Run through the tabloid presses, Wheeler's right to revise his own history as a hedge against racism was pummelled into further proof of his murderous nature. In the process, reporters revealed their own ignorance of the world's bountiful ethnicities and phenotypes. The *Morning Chronicle* branded Wheeler a liar, stating: "Peter says he is an Australian but he is more probably a Spaniard or Portuguese."[9] The *Digby Courier* echoed the sentiment, writing: "he is a foreigner, evidently a Spaniard, but claims to be a native of Australia."[10] The *Bridgetown Monitor* dismissed Peter's Australian heritage altogether, declaring: "the man Wheeler has the appearance of a Spaniard or Portuguese and is described as short, thick set and of a mulatto color, with unprepossessing countenance."[11] The *Globe* — the precursor to today's national *Globe and Mail* — cut to the chase, describing Wheeler as "the Portuguese who discovered the remains."[12] That all swarthy men were labelled as Spaniards or Portuguese spoke volumes as to the insular nature of the region. Wading into the shark-infested deep end of the great Wheeler ethnicity debate, the *Saint John Daily Record* somehow managed to simultaneously offend and half-heartedly commend the accused man when the paper reported he was "generally looked upon as a half-breed but in no particular is he thought to be of the animal stamp."[13] Peter spoke with an unplaceable, untraceable accent, which only compounded the problem and rendered him all the more incomprehensible to his homogeneous neighbours.

If the local media were to be believed, not only had Peter Wheeler killed Annie Kempton, he had also committed the unforgivable sin of being dark-skinned, woolly-haired, and foreign-born. To hammer home the point, a number of papers — including the *Digby Courier* and the *Bridgetown Monitor* — commissioned a line-art depiction of Peter Wheeler.

A decidedly "black" Peter Wheeler, courtesy of the
Digby Courier and the *Bridgetown Monitor*.

In an eerie precursor of the infamous O.J. Simpson *Time* magazine cover
that outraged a nation one century later, Wheeler's face and hair were
altered to make him appear much "Blacker" than he actually was.

fourteen

Mr. Payne Takes Exception

To the north of Bear River and Digby County, across the Bay of Fundy, lies the bustling seaport of Saint John. It proudly lays claim to being the first incorporated city in Canada, and in 1896, the Fundy city was home to more than thirty thousand souls, each with a story to tell. Tasked with telling the darkest of those tales was Robert Payne, a married father of three who served as crime reporter for one of the city's most venerated news agencies: the *Daily Sun*. Payne, still spry at fifty-one, boasted an impressive array of war wounds and battle scars, each bearing witness to his two decades on the police beat. Unlike his journalistic contemporaries, Payne focused exclusively on crime, having covered all the biggest murder cases in New Brunswick and beyond. Although he was never afforded his own byline, Payne's distinctive prose and conversational writing style were easily recognizable and much admired by his growing legion of readers.

So great was Payne's reputation that, when he docked in Digby mere hours after Annie's body was discovered, his competitors breathlessly reported his arrival.[1] If Robert Payne was sent to cover the story, the murder of Annie Kempton was indeed big news. Had they known the contrary tone his coverage would take, however, they might have held back the welcome wagon.

Kowtowing to his contemporaries was not Payne's forte. He infiltrated a traumatized community with dispatch if not always discretion, reporting with rhetoric hitherto unheard of in the staid world of Victorian journalism. Naturally inquisitive and doggedly determined, Robert Payne was a pioneer of the investigative method. He landed the interviews no other reporters could and never shied away from asking the tough questions. He strove for accuracy, often at the expense of the sensationalism so favoured by his vocational lessers, delivering journalism bereft of maudlin sympathy. He was more interested in getting the story right than getting it first or drenching the facts in purple prose. His lean, pared-down style was very much the template for the best of today's crime reporting.

On January 28, Robert Payne hit the dock running and soon left his competitors listing in his wake. He secured a number of exclusives in quick succession. The first was a walk-through of the crime scene, during which Payne took the liberty of reading a private letter sent by Mary Kempton to the victim just days before her death. Such a gross invasion of privacy violated all professional ethics, not to mention all sense of human decency, yet it was exactly the level of intimate detail the *Daily Sun*'s readers had come to expect from Mr. Payne.

A second coup came in the form of an impromptu interview with the victim's older sister, Mrs. Jessie Rice.[2] Unlike her gangly sibling, the eldest Kempton daughter entered womanhood with a coltish grace that had long since matured into a quiet poise. Whether by luck or design, the reporter found himself travelling aboard the same train as the bereaved sister. Mrs. Rice spoke tearfully of Annie's lifelong ambition to be a music teacher and shared other family secrets. It remains an open question whether Payne identified himself as a reporter at any point during their conversation.

The most envied of Payne's exclusives was his interview with the accused. The first and only of his kind to have actually met and spoken with Wheeler, Payne soon found himself at odds with his brethren in the fourth estate and running counter to the feeling of the community at large. After spending some time with Wheeler, Payne believed him to be an innocent man, wrongly accused and sorely done by. Payne first encountered Wheeler at the Kempton home, where Annie's remains served as a chilling backdrop. He wrote: "In conversation with your reporter today, and within two feet from the corpse, Wheeler wished to know when he could go home, never expecting to be arrested."[3]

A line-art depiction, ostensibly of Annie Kempton but based on
a photograph of her eldest sister, Jessie. The two girls shared a
strong resemblance during their teen years.

Payne's conviction that Wheeler was being railroaded grew even
stronger as he sat through Wheeler's testimony at the coroner's inquest:
"His evidence was given in a straightforward way and he showed no signs
of being the guilty person. He traced his actions [on the night in question]
in a concise and thorough manner...if guilty, he shows an innocent
countenance."[4]

Robert Payne continued his contrarian stance, even as public resentment
grew, and steadfastly proclaimed Wheeler's innocence in the face of
overwhelming opposition. Following yet another exclusive interview with
the accused, Payne noted: "Wheeler, if guilty, shows wonderful power of
control over himself...and to all appearances seems as much interested
in the capture of the murderer as do the citizens."[5]

Payne's unique take on the case also extended to the victim, and his no-holds-barred approach rubbed many the wrong way. The *Sun* reporter — who once ungenerously and erroneously described Annie as "15 years of age but large and would weigh 140 lbs"[6] — did not share the popular perception of Annie as a defenceless maiden. Wheeler seconded the notion, recounting a prior wrestling match between Annie and him: "[Wheeler] mentioned a 'bout' he had once in fun with the deceased and knows her strength."[7] The story did little to curry public favour but it did succeed in countering a commonly held misconception that "a girl of Annie Kempton's station in life... would not associate with a waif, a nobody"[8] like Peter Wheeler.

Aside from the wrestling misstep, Payne did all he could to portray Wheeler in the best and most sympathetic light. Peter acknowledged the untenable position he found himself in, saying, "he would give all he had had he not been the first to have found her and, friend as he was, he feels the strains of knowing the community believe him guilty."[9]

The *Daily Sun* was also the only paper to give voice to Wheeler's version of events and was the lone tabloid to print in full his statement to the coroner.[10] Wheeler emphatically stated that just after two o'clock on the night Annie was killed, he had seen three men — all staggering and clearly intoxicated — on the road that led to the Kemptons'. Wheeler was able to give a detailed description of the men but neither the local constabulary nor Detective Power had given the matter the slightest attention. Payne pleaded Wheeler's case, writing: "the authorities, before it is too late, should see whether this part of the story is true."[11]

While other regional tabloids opted not to dispatch a correspondent to the scene and pillaged freely from the reportage of others, the *Daily Sun* saw the value of putting Payne on the ground. "Some features of the case," argued Payne, "that seem mysterious to people at a distance are as plain as a pikestaff to those who live on the spot."[12] Payne did not simply scoop the competition with his exclusives, he had his finger on the pulse of the community. When it came to the citizens of Bear River, Payne

Another artist's rendering of Annie, one of the less
flattering efforts published.

limned an accurate if somewhat unflattering portrait, telling his readers
that the villagers kept "to a great extent within themselves and, with
them, it is Bear River first, last and all the time."[13] The Saint John–based
reporter found the community tight-knit, with a well-established grapevine:
"what one knows, the other knows."[14]

In a village with tall fences but no boundaries, there was no hiding
the wellspring of hatred toward Wheeler. The local witnesses "felt so
strongly that they could not conceal their hostility to the accused"[15]
during the inquest. Payne did the math: a community of like mind,
coupled with a media-driven misinformation campaign, created a terrible
equation. Payne had felt the tide turn against Wheeler from day one: "the
feeling of the townsfolk is strongly against the accused, and if he should

be tried for the crime here in the present temper of the people, he would undoubtedly be convicted of the murder of Annie Kempton."[16]

There was no question in Payne's mind that "only a circumstantial case"[17] existed against Wheeler, with evidence certainly "by no means strong enough to secure his conviction,"[18] given "there is no positive testimony that he is the slayer of the unfortunate girl."[19] Yet, in spite of the case's crumbling foundations, Payne was equally certain that Wheeler was already a dead man: "The conviction is firmly settled in the minds of the whole neighbourhood that Peter Wheeler is the murderer of Annie Kempton; indeed, so strongly are some people's impressions with the prisoner's guilt that their feelings have so overcome their better judgment that they desire to see summary punishment inflicted."[20]

In a last-ditch effort at damage control, Payne tried to harness the power of the mob, hoping to use its fringes to sway the centre. He knocked on every door in Bear River and found tiny pockets of resistance willing to throw a few kind words Wheeler's way. Payne implored his readers to ignore the epithets shouted by the masses, reminding them that "those who know [Wheeler] intimately give him a good name,"[21] and that Peter "has always been a sober industrious fellow."[22] When the last of the village rebels had said their peace, Payne decided to tap the mother lode. He clung to the words of Wheeler's last remaining friend, Tillie Comeau (although she was no longer considered an unbiased source), who swore at the inquest that Wheeler "never drank, caroused or kept bad company."[23] Payne's efforts incited outrage in the community. Bear Riverites, thinking little of Tillie herself, thought even less of her full-throated defence of her ersatz husband.

Bear River was clearly a village divided by more than a county line. By the time Payne arrived, those who hated Wheeler vastly outnumbered the few still willing to sing his praises. Payne also learned that the villagers' polemic stance on Wheeler was not of recent origin. From the day his ship had docked in Bear River, Wheeler was a marked man, a dark cloud on the region's snowy white landscape. Adding another notch to his tote board of exclusives, Payne was the first to report there had been bad blood between Wheeler and his neighbours long before the murder of Annie Kempton. According to Peter, he had survived two prior assaults, attacks that had left him bloodied and beaten. To add insult to serious injury, the men who inflicted the beatings lived within spitting distance of Wheeler's rented room. Wheeler never knew the impetus for the animosity but suspected it had racial origins.

Even among his staunchest supporters, Wheeler's race was an issue. Like his contemporaries, Payne could not resist speculating on Wheeler's ethnicity. "It is said here that he is a Portuguese"[24] or "a Spaniard,"[25] Payne told his readers, yet he found Peter to be "a study. Although people here fail to grasp that he is not of their phlegmatic race — but has warm southern blood coursing through his veins...he is the product of a warm clime — Cuba some say."[26]

The press were not the only ones playing the race card when it came to Wheeler. Robert Payne could not help but notice that Detective Nicholas Power seemed inordinately preoccupied with Wheeler's ancestry, sprinkling countless allusions to Wheeler's dark roots throughout his many interviews with the media. "Detective Power says Wheeler's lips took on several colors during the development of the evidence against him,"[27] noted Payne in one report, adding sardonically that "the Halifax detective is a keen observer."[28]

Whatever Wheeler's ambiguous lineage, Payne assured his readers that this was an intelligent, well-schooled man. The prisoner "reads Latin as well as English and talks French fluently,"[29] the *Saint John Daily Sun* proclaimed, adding that "in conversation he uses good language — much better than the average villager and some of his expressions indicate an acquaintance with books not read by the masses."[30] The most any Nova Scotian paper offered was the begrudging double negative: "[Wheeler] is not an uneducated man."[31]

Once in custody, Wheeler applied his formidable intellectual prowess to the case against him. In speaking with reporters, Detective Power had made much of two tiny blood spots reportedly found on Wheeler's pants and sock. Wheeler offered a reasonable explanation for the stains during his first police interrogation, saying they stemmed from his hunting expedition on the afternoon before Annie died. Although the Detective paid no heed to Wheeler's statement, Payne and the prisoner discussed the matter at length. The reporter informed Wheeler that Power had sent the clothing to Mr. McIntyre, a blood analyst with the Halifax Police Department. Wheeler asked Payne whether McIntyre "was a competent man,"[32] expressing legitimate concerns that forensic science was very much in its infancy. Wheeler's scientific acumen impressed Payne almost as much as his linguistic acuity, further endearing the prisoner to the jaded newsman's leathery heart.

Payne's admiration for Wheeler extended beyond their shared love of language. The reporter clearly respected Wheeler's character, noting: "he stood the [inquest] like a Spartan and though he must have known the thoughts of many, he never flinched. . . . if ever any man carried himself with composure, it was Wheeler. . . . he spoke in feeling terms of Annie and his heart seemed touched like all the rest."[33] It was all to no avail.

Try as Payne might to capture Wheeler in a matter that was more accurate and amenable than the image painted by his contemporaries, the reporter knew it was a losing battle: "Wheeler's appearance actually will not have the effect of eliciting sympathy on his behalf. He bears no evidence of refinement."[34] It was, however, a problem with an obvious solution, at least to Payne's way of thinking.

Refinement is in the eye of the beholder. So, too, is race, particularly if the beholding eye belongs to an agreeable newspaper artist. After more than a week of extolling Wheeler's many virtues into a vacuum, a single picture did what thousands of Mr. Payne's well-chosen words could not: make the swarthy Wheeler palatable to the masses. The *Saint John Daily Sun* put its own twist on the Goldilocks fable when it printed a picture of Peter Wheeler on the front page of its February 8 edition. If the Nova Scotian papers could portray Wheeler as "too Black," his kinder, gentler

The accused, looking every inch the English gentleman, from the *Saint John Daily Sun*.

neighbour to the north opted to render him as "too White," depicting the accused man as nothing short of a proper British dandy.

fifteen

"Don't Kick the Instrument"

It was a bold reporter indeed who cast his lot with Wheeler after the inquest. Robert Payne was one such fearless soul and his only like-minded fellow turned out to be his staunchest competitor: the crime reporter at the *Saint John Daily Record*. Like Payne, the man was never acknowledged with a byline; unlike Payne, the identity of the *Record*'s man on the scene was never publicly revealed.

Whatever his name, the *Daily Record* correspondent saw Wheeler through the same rose-tinted glasses as his colleague. "He acts like an innocent man,"[1] trumpeted the *Record*, describing Wheeler's performance during the inquest as "straightforward" and "manly."[2] The Fundy city daily marvelled at the accused man's coping skills, stating: "he maintains the greatest self-possession under the terrible strain and bears up wonderfully."[3]

The *Daily Record* had sided with Wheeler from the very beginning, noting that his sudden and unwarranted arrest caused surprise, and to "a marked degree, indignation as he is generally accepted as a hard-working, good-natured fellow."[4] The *Record* even went so far as to say that Wheeler was "not at all suspected of the crime by the people of the surrounding country."[5] Such hyperbolic rhetoric suggests that the reporter from across the bay was not speaking to the same townsfolk as his Nova Scotian contemporaries or even, for that matter, the people who were so boisterous with his colleague Payne.

The disparity in tone and coverage between the two neighbouring provinces led to some heated debates and unprecedented sales, as readers purchased every available paper to compare and contrast their accounts. The polemic and fractured approaches also generated more than a few complaints. Indeed, carping about media depictions of the tragedy began early and in earnest. The escalating war of words pitted the public against the press and editor against editor.

The first salvo was fired by the citizenry of Bear River. While testifying at Lovett's inquest, many witnesses pointed out the erroneous "facts" included in the *Digby Weekly Courier*'s first account of the crime.[6] The *Morning Chronicle* made much of the *Courier*'s embarrassing errors and gave ample coverage of the town's dismay.[7]

The *Chronicle*, sensing a winning formula in the making, took a swipe at another competitor, the *Herald*: "Considerable, it might be said universal, dissatisfaction is expressed here [in Bear River] at the report of this affair in to-day's *Herald*, as something contained therein seemed to reflect on the character of poor Annie Kempton."[8] It was an entirely manufactured controversy based on an imaginary slight. A thorough review of the *Herald*'s account reveals nothing offensive or derogatory toward the victim. If the good people of Bear River had indeed expressed animosity toward the news reports, it was likely directed to the press in general, rather than any specific account. The tendency to take offence when none was offered would become a leitmotif weaving its way through the entirety of the case.

Nowhere was this penchant for detecting unvoiced criticism more evident than in the turbulent relationship between the denizens of Bear River and the media that claimed to speak for them. A particularly salient case in point involved the notion that the community was under attack on all fronts, an idea as prevalent as it was unsubstantiated. In the hundreds of media accounts of the crime, the people of Bear River were never taken to task. There were no slights recorded, perceived or otherwise, although Payne's comments sometimes bordered on brutal honesty. Despite this absence of malice, nearly every media outlet revelled in depicting them as vigilantes under siege from all sides.

The construction of the media straw man began with the *Digby Weekly Courier* and a thinly veiled allusion to the Ku Klux Klan. On January 31, 1896, the *Courier* compared the people of Bear River and their quest for justice to "Southern negro-lynchers." As with all straw man arguments, the *Courier* never identified those making the allegations. In fact, no paper other than the *Courier* had made any such accusations. The *Courier*, contradictory to the bitter end, later qualified the remark as "perceptibly ridiculous," but the damage was done. Soon other papers began echoing the sentiment and the citizens of Bear River were alternately vilified and lionized by a media obsessed with painting them in a bad light, only then to criticize others for the poor lighting.

The *Digby Weekly Courier*, suffering a convenient lapse in memory, later reversed its stance saying: "the feeling in this community has not been of the barbarous type that it has been represented as being."[9] What the *Courier* failed to recall was its own role in casting them as "the barbarous type." Another popular leitmotif in the media's presentation of Annie's murder was ironic hypocrisy, a device employed with equal parts gusto and ignorance.

Such hypocrisy reached its zenith in an editorial appearing in the *Bridgetown Monitor*, which absolved itself of all culpability in the ongoing battle. The editor took exception to the public outcry regarding how the case (and the citizens themselves) had been depicted in the media:

> Don't blame your newspaper for what happens in the com-
> munity. [If there is something you don't like], blame yourself
> it exists, not the paper for saying something about it.... It's
> the editor's duty to make a typographical photograph of the
> town each week and if you take a homely picture, don't kick
> the instrument — try to get a better impression on your face
> next time.[10]

While Robert Payne embraced and even thrived on sharp public reaction to his contrarian stance, his colleague at the *Saint John Daily Record* did not. On February 4, the *Record*'s pro-Wheeler posturing began to buckle. The day's headline accused Wheeler of telling "queer tales." Inviolable platitudes gave way to acrimony as the paper's once unassailable belief in Peter's innocence showed its first major cracks. Within days, the *Daily Record* was wholly converted, shifting solidly into the anti-Wheeler column and leaving its city-mate Payne as the solitary white hat surrounded by black-hatted varmints and villains.

sixteen

"And a Funeral It Was"

Annie Kempton was laid to rest on Friday, January 31, 1896. In a melee more circus than funeral, Annie was venerated with a farewell befitting a fallen hero, a display of maudlin sentiment and press embellishment. Yet beneath the media distortion was a community mired in very real grief. Hundreds lined the winding streets to view Annie's remains, a sombre procession that snaked from the Kemptons' front door down the hill to the power station. Many came to pay respect to her parents, both burnt to an emotional crisp by the senseless loss of their youngest child. The horror was palpable, stunning, and — some feared — contagious. Parents held their own children a little tighter, offering silent prayers of thanks that they had been spared.

No effort was made to shield the younger generations from the stark realities of death. They had lost one of their own and were encouraged to express their grief however they saw fit. Every teenage girl and more than a few of the boys laid tissue paper flowers on her casket. Annie's classmates, along with all the children from the Oakdene Academy, marched in formation as the casket made its way through the village, crossing the bridge before climbing the hill to the Mount Hope Cemetery. The children's pageant was more than some adults could bear.

The unenviable task of eulogizing Annie's brief life belonged to Reverend John Craig. In tenebrous tones he declared Annie a martyr who had died in defence of her virtue: "in her struggle for right she lost her life at the hands of a human fiend, but her reward will follow in heaven."[1]

After a week of incessant media scrutiny, Bear River closed ranks. The town torn asunder coalesced around two unifying goals: to mourn the loss of their dear Annie and to prevent the press from feasting on their grief. For the first time since the tragedy hit their radar, reporters found themselves unwelcome and unwanted in Bear River.

The villagers' efforts were laudable but fruitless. The press were not so easily denied. Although a stalwart few tried to secure interviews with the mourners as they streamed from the cemetery, the majority of the press corps simply filled in the blanks for themselves.

In a torrent of grandiloquent prose, the *Yarmouth Herald* tried to capture the funeral for its readers, while downplaying the fact that the reporter was not present at the event: "The reverend gentleman's remarks are characterized by those who heard them as beautiful and your correspondent regrets that it is impossible to get a synopsis of it."[2] Indeed, many accounts of the funeral, most notably those of the *Morning Chronicle* and the *Bridgetown Monitor*, bore the hallmarks of second-hand reporting, foregoing specifics for trite commentary on her parents' suffering: "Words are not adequate to describe the condition of the heart-broken [*sic*] father and mother. . . No words can describe the agony of the heart-broken parents at their meeting over the body of their murdered child."[3]

The *Morning Chronicle* had been at a loss for words before the funeral began or even, for that matter, an accurate sense of time and place. One day prior, the paper announced with a patent disregard for tense that the memorial would take place "on the morrow, and a funeral it was."[4] Indeed, bizarre proclamations seemed the order of the day. Hours later, the *Yarmouth Herald* needlessly ratcheted up the pathos when it reported: "the strange thing about it is that Annie was buried on her birthday."[5] Although the declaration made for a dramatic and eerie coincidence, a quick check of Annie's baptismal record reveals the statement to be false. Her fifteenth birthday was not until February 13.[6]

The *Digby Weekly Courier* reporter was not lost for words as he described the memorial service, which was held at the Bear River Methodist Church the following day. He praised Reverend Craig's "masterly discourse," calling the sermon "one of most scholarly preparation . . . a glowing tribute."[7]

The cleric's despondency at eulogizing a murdered child was evident in the *Courier*'s summation: "With the circumstances such as they were, in all the sad commotion of the case, it was felt that all that could be said by way of comfort and admonition was included in the speaker's comments, the dead yet speaking through them."[8]

The reverend's testimonial of Annie's valiant fight to keep her virginity found a receptive audience among the parishioners as well as in the media. His healing words prompted one *Bridgetown Monitor* subscriber, a Mr. J.W. Whitman, to write with a fitting proposal: a memorial for Annie Kempton, forever fourteen, eternally pure. In a letter to the editor he asked: "are there not one hundred men — yes, and hundreds of women too — in these counties who would give a dollar each, or more if required, to place a suitable monument at the grave of Annie Kempton and thus show our appreciation of her valor and commemorate her virtue?"[9] The *Digby Courier* — having discovered a fresh vein of emotion to mine — was quick to take up the rallying cry.

> Bear River may very well call Annie Kempton a heroine, whose deeds, though they may not appear as history, are worthy of recognition because of their virtuousness. And is not a person who considers the honor of virtue before life a hero? Is a person less a hero because his or her valor is not spread before the world over a period of years? There are every-day heroes in our land, with heroism unknown. And Annie Kempton was a heroine, we think. Her example, to the death, cannot but be salutary and her name should be recorded in honor.[10]

Commemorating a murdered girl's maidenhead proved a popular charitable cause. More than four hundred dollars were donated and the commission for the monument was awarded to the Stanice Brothers of Saint John. Every nuance of its design and construction was exhaustively

The simple headstone marking Annie's final resting place within the larger Kempton family plot.

The Kempton family headstone. Note that her age gives her credit for two weeks never lived.

The commemorative memorial in the Mount Hope Cemetery
honouring Annie's valiant struggle.

chronicled by newspapers. Before the stone was delivered, both the *Acadian Recorder* and the *Digby Weekly Courier* ran lengthy treatises on the memorial's dimensions, composition, and inscription, which read: "Erected to the memory of Annie Kempton, who was murdered in her father's house, in a desperate struggle to preserve her chastity."[11]

☾

Today, no fewer than three stones mark Annie's final resting place. A small marble headstone bearing only the initials "A.K." tops her actual grave. A second memorial stands sentry nearby, a communal Kempton family headstone. One face commemorates her father Isaac and mother Mary. The adjacent face bears another salutation to Annie's noble fight. The much-lauded public memorial stands up the hill in a separate section of the cemetery. Its placement was the subject of much debate and its odd location smacks of compromise. Annual graveyard tours and commemorations to Annie Kempton continue to this day, a bit of dark tourism that has flourished in the intervening decades since her death.

seventeen

Echoes of Millman

Following the emotional crescendo that was Annie's funeral, the press once again turned their attention to the fate of Peter Wheeler. It was a fixed target, as Wheeler's case languished in legal limbo. In the week since Annie's body was discovered, there had been surprisingly little movement in the investigation. Wheeler had been arrested but not yet charged with the killing. Although there was nothing unusual about the case's pace, its glacial progress drove the press corps to distraction.

On February 3, 1896, Nicholas Power sat for an in-depth interview with the *Halifax Morning Chronicle*. Both the interviewer and subject had arrived with their own agendas, each intent on using the exchange for their own benefit. For the reporter, there was the hope of an exclusive, but he would settle for enough to fill his daily quota of ink. As for the detective, it had long been his custom to try his high-profile cases in the media. Power, never the soul of discretion, often bent the rules governing the confidentiality of evidence and leapt at every chance to present his case without the bother of opposing counsel.

Throwing caution and Wheeler's rights to the wind, Power laid out the case as it stood. He identified the key witnesses by name and summarized each of their statements. The detective also alluded to crucial pieces of physical evidence at the scene but was unencumbered by specifics.

Power forsook the criminal justice system in favour of the less exacting court of public opinion; he pointed to Peter Wheeler and proclaimed him guilty, promising that "a perfect chain of evidence will surround the prisoner"[1] by the end of the investigation. The interview was a stunning display of unfettered bravado, the dangers of unchallenged slander, and Power's considerable fortune-telling abilities. That the detective knew the outcome before he had finished the investigation spoke volumes regarding his objectivity and professionalism.

Press interviews were among the detective's fortes for a simple but compelling reason: Power's preferred mode of argument was analogy. The great man dusted every sound bite with a soupçon of metaphor, allegory, or syllogism. He had discovered in his many years that even a facile comparison or tortured simile was a powerful means of evoking emotion, particularly from an uneducated and undiscerning public. Such ploys played equally well in the courthouse and in the press, two arenas where simplicity and misdirection were encouraged.

Power closed his *Chronicle* interview with a pointed and carefully crafted aside. With a casualness intended to pass for spontaneity, Power remarked that the Wheeler investigation was similar to the case of William Millman, the subject of a highly publicized trial in neighbouring Charlottetown, Prince Edward Island. For almost a year — from July 1887 through April 1888 — the Maritimes had been riveted to the sanguinary tale of Millman, accused of killing seventeen-year-old Mary Pickering Tuplin.[2]

☾

July 4, 1887, was unseasonably hot in the otherwise beatific glen of Irishtown-Margate, sitting like a buckle on the isle's midsection, and the oppressive heat drove villagers to the banks of the Southwest River in search of relief. The bathers' dreams of a languid afternoon on the rocks were soon dashed when the bloated corpse of a teenage girl bobbed silently into view. Local men scrambled to find the grappling hooks needed to dredge the poor girl's remains from the muddy water.

Any notions that the death was an accidental drowning were quickly dispelled. A boat anchor stone had been tied to her waist to prevent her from floating to the surface. There was also no question as to the girl's identity; those gathered on the shore recognized her at once, in spite of the deplorable state of the body. She was Mary Tuplin, a pretty and popular teen who had disappeared from her home on June 28.

The anchor stone was not the lone sign of malfeasance. A coroner's inquest revealed that Mary had died from two gunshot wounds to the head. The examining physician declared that the first shot — a near contact wound that entered behind her right ear — had merely stunned her, while the second shot to the back of the head proved fatal. A far more shocking revelation was to follow: the unmarried teen was six months pregnant.

Suspicion soon fell on Willie Millman, a twenty-year-old man who lived across the river from the Tuplins. Although Willie had only met Mary three times before she died, he was widely rumoured to be the father of her child. The pair first locked eyes at a New Year's Eve party, an annual extravaganza hosted by the town's resident maven Francis Hilman. The comely young Mary flirted openly with the boisterous fiddle-playing Millman. The two danced and drank the night away and eventually gave the party's chaperones the slip. As dawn broke on New Year's Day, Willie walked Mary home.

Two months later, Mary's worst fears were realized when the doctor confirmed she was pregnant. A terrified Mary confided in her sister that William Millman was the father. Although Mary's voluminous clothes hid her growing shame, her sister was far less discreet. Village gossip ran rampant, and on June 26, an angry mob confronted Willie about the rumour during church services. He vehemently denied being the father. That evening, he called on Mary at her home, hoping to make things right, and the couple went for a walk. This time, Mary chose not to share the details of their conversation with her sister.

Mary's delicate condition was soon overshadowed by a far darker family tragedy. On June 27, one of Mary's brothers succumbed to a lingering illness. The funeral was held on Tuesday, June 28. After burying their beloved son and brother, the grief-ravaged Tuplins returned from the cemetery in the late afternoon. As the family received mourners in

MARY P. TUPLIN.

The seventeen-year-old victim, Mary Tuplin, published in the *Summerside Journal and Western Pioneer* on April 12, 1888.

The alleged murderer and father, Willie Millman, published April 12, 1888.

WILLIAM MILLMAN.

their home just after 8:00 p.m., Mary slipped from the house, never to return. By 10:00 p.m., the alarm was raised and the search for the missing girl began in earnest. Villagers pulled the girl's lifeless body from the river one week later.

Mary's murder captured headlines throughout the Maritimes. When the press learned she was pregnant, the story spread across Canada and America. In press interviews, the victim's sister painted Millman as the prime suspect when she named him as the father of the unborn child. Further aspersions were cast when it was learned that Millman was the only man in the village who refused to participate in the search for the missing girl.

Like Wheeler, the evidence against Millman was purely circumstantial. Willie lived near the Tuplins and the pair were acquainted, by all reports quite intimately. Yet despite the paucity of hard evidence, things did not look good for young William. He could not account for his whereabouts between 7:00 and 10:30 p.m. on the night of the murder. He told investigators he had stayed home alone while his parents attended a gathering at the Irishtown Anglican Church. Much was made of the fact that Willie owned a .22 calibre gun, although this was rendered moot when police confirmed that the bullets used to kill Mary were fired from a .32.

One day after the papers reported the bullet discrepancy, a man came forward to police as if cued by a stage director. Francis Power (no relation to the infamous Halifax supersleuth) told the detectives that on June 30 — two days after the murder — Willie Millman had finally returned the .32 calibre pistol Power had lent him back in May. Power's damning revelation erased any lingering doubts the public had regarding Millman's guilt.

On July 4, mere hours before Mary's body was discovered, Willie Millman made his first ever trip to the big city of Charlottetown. He was in dire need of a lawyer and Willie had learned the hard way that the local barristers were already squarely against him because of the pregnancy rumours. Millman told his new attorney that Mary's father was levelling grave accusations against him. The meeting was meant to be a simple consultation regarding slander and paternity, but by the time Willie returned home, locals had recovered Mary's body and Millman's legal troubles had grown far more serious.

A preliminary hearing was held in Clifton three days later. A grand jury was empanelled and the prosecutor presented the evidence against Millman. The media were whipped into a lather when the accused's father, John Millman, took the stand. Recanting his prior statements, Millman Senior perjured himself by claiming he was home with Willie at the time of the murder. When confronted with his overt deception, John Millman literally swooned on the witness stand. As his father fainted, Willie broke down, becoming hysterical and screaming uncontrollably. Several observers in the courtroom claimed to have heard statements that could be construed as admissions of guilt in the midst of his rant.

In spite or perhaps because of Millman's histrionics, the jury returned a true bill indicting Willie for the murder of Mary Pickering Tuplin. The case was remanded to the Prince Edward Island Supreme Court, and on July 8, Willie was delivered to the Queen's County Jail to await his fate. The trial of William Millman began in Charlottetown on January 24, 1888; the Honourable Joseph Hansley presided.

The Crown's theory was straightforward: after 8:00 p.m. on June 28, Millman took a red oyster boat belonging to John Cousins from its usual mooring on the north bank of the Southwest River. He poled across the water, bringing the boat to rest near Mud Road. The Tuplin house sat at the intersection of Mud and Princetown Roads. With the borrowed .32 calibre in his pocket, Willie met Mary at her gate and the pair walked down the road toward the boat. After a heated argument about the pregnancy, Millman shot Mary twice in the head. Several neighbours reported hearing the gunshots. Willie put Mary's body in the boat, tied the anchor stone to her waist and poled to the deepest part of the river, where he sank the body off Thompson's Point. Millman then returned the boat to its usual spot, minus the anchor stone.

All agreed Millman had a strong motive to kill Mary: fear that her pregnancy would be exposed and he would be fined or imprisoned under the Seduction Act. Still, the evidence against Millman remained circumstantial. Only one witness, a thirteen-year-old girl named Dorothy Adams, placed Millman anywhere near the scene at the time of the murder. Adams, who knew Millman well, testified that she had seen Willie tie up the boat on the night in question. Under questioning, Millman conceded he was at the river that evening. He told the court he was only there briefly to go swimming after dinner and had returned home before 9:00 p.m.

As with the Wheeler case, footprints would play a vital role in the trial of Willie Millman. Police Constable Alexander McKay took the stand and declared that he had matched some boot tracks found on the riverbank to Millman's shoes. The defence scored a major victory when they forced McKay to concede he had measured the prints by gouging marks into a stick. The courtroom erupted when a direct comparison of the stick to Millman's shoes revealed that Willie's feet were far too large to have made the sandy footprints.

Despite his lawyer's best efforts, the jury found Millman guilty of murder. Upon hearing the verdict, Millman fainted. Like his father before him, Willie's dizzy spell brought the court proceedings to a crashing halt. Willie Millman returned to court three days later for sentencing. As the judge read the verdict, the prisoner stuck his fingers in his ears and began humming to avoid hearing his fate. Although the jury recommended mercy for Willie because of his young age, the judge had grown tired of Millman's antics. Justice Hansley sentenced him to death.

Millman's childish behaviour may have enraged the judge but it initially endeared him to his jailers. Unlike most condemned prisoners, Millman was not kept in irons for the first two months of his incarceration. It was a near fatal error. In late March, Willie struck his jailer over the head with a bottle and attempted to escape but his liberty was short-lived. He was quickly recaptured when he could not find his way out of the enclosed jail yard. Both convict and jailer had learned a painful lesson and Millman spent his remaining days in shackles.

In the early morning of April 12, 1887, the executioner made his way to a makeshift gallows in the normally peaceful confines of Connaught Square, then part of the jail complex in downtown Charlottetown. A hastily assembled crowd of fifty, including the coroner's jury, were brought in to witness Willie's demise. At the prisoner's own request, Millman was blindfolded before leaving his cell so he would not see the gallows. It did not help; Millman wailed and wept openly as he was led to the scaffold. At 8:08 a.m., the signal was given and Millman was hanged.

Tradition held that a black flag be raised above the jail when the deed was done. Millman's flag was raised at 8:10 a.m. Unfortunately, Millman was not quite dead. At 8:19 a.m., the attending physician still detected a faint pulse and respiratory effort. Finally, after he had been left hanging for more than fifteen minutes, Millman was pronounced dead and cut free of the noose.

❨

While Nicholas Power no doubt left the interview feeling well pleased with himself, his tell-all proved to be one of his biggest media missteps in the Bear River case. The detective's allusion to the Millman case missed the mark and provoked an unintended negative backlash. Power had referenced Millman in the hopes of condemning Wheeler by association. Unfortunately for Power, the link Bear Riverites made was between the two victims. By raising the spectre of Mary Pickering Tuplin — an unwed pregnant teenager of demonstrably loose morals — the detective had inadvertently sullied the reputation of the beloved and virtuous Annie.

Red-faced, Power was forced to qualify his statement, insisting that, unlike her predecessor, Annie Kempton "bore a most excellent character; she was very industrious, hard-working, and was well liked by everyone in the village."[3] In trying to tar Wheeler with the Millman brush, Power had accidentally painted Annie Kempton scarlet.

eighteen

Purdy's Purview

Fortunately for Nick Power, the press forgave him everything. Once the detective had sidestepped his public relations bungle, one very real problem remained: Peter Wheeler had yet to be charged with any crime. The prisoner was left to languish in the Digby jail under a suffocating cloud of suspicion and could do nothing but await what the fates had in store for him.

The next link in the legal chain was to formally indict Peter for Annie's murder. The findings of the coroner's inquest had no judicial sway but had primed the public for a specific outcome. It was never Dr. Lovett's decision to make, but once made, there was little question that Wheeler must pass through the magisterial machinery if he had any hope of clearing his name.

The burden of proof now rested with the region's chief prosecutor, Mr. Albert J. Copp. Copp was the county's maverick; a mere thirty-six years old, he possessed a keen legal mind and formidable reputation that belied his relative youth. Wheeler represented Copp's first shot at a murder conviction, the sort of case that helped cement an ambitious man's position in the world.

Protocol dictated that Copp empanel a grand jury of Wheeler's peers: twelve local men of good standing and character. Once seated, the jurors would hear only from Copp, who would present the case without any input from the accused or defence counsel; the prisoner and his lawyer were not even permitted to attend the hearing. If the panel felt there were adequate grounds to proceed to trial, they would vote a true bill leading to a formal indictment. Given the severity of the crime, the case would then be re-manded to the provincial superior court to be heard at the next special session. Rather than send Wheeler to Halifax, however, an experienced Supreme Court justice would be dispatched to the county seat to oversee the proceedings.

There was, of course, another legal option and — this being the case of Peter Wheeler — the less-travelled path proved the preferred course. The media spotlight burned too bright and there was political hay to be made from its heat. A local county magistrate, the Honourable Wallace A. Purdy, took it upon himself to hold his own examination of the case. Purdy's inquiry was not intended to quash Copp's authority, but it was unquestionably meant to commandeer the headlines.

Judicial intent notwithstanding, Purdy's tribunal — technically known as a police magistrate's examination — featured many of the usual aspects of a trial. It was presided over by a judge — in this case, the self-appointed Wallace A. Purdy — and the accused was present and represented by defence counsel, who could cross-examine the witnesses. There were some restrictions; for example, the defence team could not call any witnesses to rebut testimony or refute evidence nor could the accused testify on his own behalf.

As the examination was procedurally at odds with a grand jury, the end result also differed. Purdy's hearing would not culminate with the indictment of Wheeler. Despite the facade of a trial, it was, in fact, little more than a rehash of Lovett's coroner inquest, right down to the exact same witness list. The only net benefit to the charade was that, if Purdy so ruled, the Crown could continue to hold Wheeler pending formal charges. There was, of course, the slimmest chance that Purdy might find the case wanting and release Peter but the likelihood of such an outcome was negligible. Still, it was opportunity for the newly appointed defence team to meet their client and hear first-hand the evidence against him.

Purdy's vanity fair found an unlikely home: the Bear River Exhibition Building, an agricultural behemoth normally reserved for livestock that retained the telltale lingering stench of manure. Unlike Lovett's inquest, which was held in the well-situated confines of the Oakdene Academy, the exhibition complex was outside the city limits and lacked all of the academy's comforts. Though reporters and spectators alike carped about the change of venue, no one seemed deterred by the inconvenience. Horse teams drove legions of the curious from across the county, and despite the venue's cavernous dimensions, many were turned away due to overcrowding. Whatever its dubious legal value, Purdy's hearing was undoubtedly the social event of the season.

The building was not up to the task. The infrastructure was strained beyond capacity as more than one thousand people crammed into every available nook and cranny. The floor had to be shored up in several locations to prevent a potential collapse. As the construction delays dragged on, the air grew blue with tobacco smoke; the open flames and carelessly discarded ash practically begged for an ill-timed disaster. As for lavatories and other crucial amenities, spectators were left to their own devices.

The humble surroundings did little to dampen Justice Purdy's mood. Knowing that the eyes of the province were upon him, Purdy assembled a stellar cast of supporting characters. Albert Copp was relegated to playing second fiddle as the Crown prosecutor, while F.R. Miller completed the roster as the clerk of the court. Such distinguished dramatis personae deserved a proper stage. In defiance of the building's distinct barnyard aroma, the judge ordered a team of workmen to craft a bench worthy of the Supreme Court, behind which the Honourable Justice Purdy took his rightful (and noticeably elevated) place.

Defending Peter Wheeler was none other than Henry Dwight Ruggles, a barrister with his own firm in Annapolis Royal (Mills & Ruggles). Ruggles, who went by both Dwight and Henry, was something of a pioneer in commercial jurisprudence. His notoriety stemmed from his revolutionary practice of advertising his services in the *Annapolis Spectator*. Dwight's advert, which prominently featured his two-digit telephone number, sat in pride of place astride the *Spectator*'s masthead.[1] He paid handsomely for such prime media real estate and his aggressive marketing strategy paid off. Ruggles, a slightly more refined precursor to the ambulance-chasers and personal injury solicitors assaulting modern society with their late-night infomercials and shock-tactic billboards, may have raised the ire and eyebrows of his staid colleagues but those in need of a lawyer knew exactly which number to call.

The star of the coming spectacle was the accused, although Purdy was no doubt loath to admit it. Negotiating a gauntlet of press and choleric citizenry, Peter Wheeler was transported to the makeshift court in chains, flanked as always by the imposing figure of Detective Power. Actually, that is not entirely true. Power made a show of accompanying Wheeler, yet history has it on good authority that it was little more than a Victorian-era photo op. When no one was looking, Wheeler was transported and guarded by the Harris brothers: C.M. Harris, who ferried Wheeler to and from the jail; Rupert Harris, responsible for supervising or "boarding" the prisoner between sessions; and brother Manning Harris, who "attended the prisoner"[2] as he sat before Judge Purdy. For their sins, the Harrises received the princely sum of $45.74, although the distribution of wages amongst them was far from equitable. C.M., covering the most miles, pocketed $23, while Rupert took home only $7.99, leaving Manning $14.75. For his well-publicized but minimal efforts, Power received nothing but his regular salary, the public's unwavering devotion, and constant media coverage.

Constant was the operative word. Reckoning that their normal publication schedule was insufficient to meet the insatiable appetite for Purdy's forum, the *Annapolis Spectator* elected to print special editions or "Extras" — single-sheet summaries of each day's events. Priced to move at one cent, the *Spectator* deferred production costs by securing a sponsor.

The Extras were brought to the masses by the good folks at "CHEROKKEE VERMIFUGE," which — if their slogan can be trusted — "kills worms every time."[3]

☾

The carnival began with a resounding bang. Judge Purdy, sporting his best judicial regalia, gavelled his examination to order on the morning of February 7, 1896. As befitted such piffle, early media speculation did not focus on the evidence or precedent. Rather, the press was atwitter with a matter of stature — specifically the colossal stature of the judge and the chief detective. Newshounds eager to paint the most vivid picture dedicated an inordinate number of column inches to ruminating on the height of the key players and debating who cut the more imposing presence in the courtroom. Judge Purdy was said to be "an unusually tall man, with a large frame."[4] The magistrate's hearty reach, however, paled in comparison to that of the well-cast Nicholas Power, who stood "six feet three inches in his stocking feet."[5] The two men, models of splendid Victorian brio, were seated side by each on the swiftly constructed dais that left them towering — figuratively and metaphorically — over the crowd below. The fuss paid to so trivial a matter seemed an apt analogy for the proceedings itself.

With such vital issues addressed, the spotlight reluctantly shifted to the matter at hand. Wheeler was escorted into the venue, bent and sub-missive, yet shackled as though he were a clear and present danger to all who beheld him. The true absurdity of the hearing was revealed in its first exchange. Although Wheeler stood indicted of no crime, Purdy asked the accused how he pleaded. Caught off guard, a bewildered Ruggles spoke on Wheeler's behalf, giving the only reasonable answer, "Not guilty."[6]

The first witness to take the stand was the coroner Dr. Lewis Lovett. Despite his inexperience, the physician was a paragon of scrupulous exactitude. He carried with him his notes from the inquest: twenty-nine foolscap pages crammed with tiny meticulous printing in Lovett's distinct hand. After summarizing the inquest's findings and admitting the notes into evidence, Copp rested the witness and Purdy signalled the defence to begin their cross.

Unlike his worthy opponent, the defence counsel was not blessed with a formidable reputation. The only way Ruggles saw his name in the papers was to pay for it. This bootless legal exercise was Ruggles's debutante ball, a coming-out party for a lawyer desperate to stake a claim among the province's affluent elite. At long last, Ruggles's moment to shine had arrived and, if his efforts helped his client, all the better.

Approaching the bench as a cat stalks a mouse, Dwight Ruggles set his sights on the novice coroner. If Purdy could play silly legal games, so could Ruggles. In a hushed yet belligerent tone, Ruggles objected to the admission of the inquest notes into evidence. He stated that the inquest related to a separate matter, namely the determination of the cause and manner of Annie Kempton's death. With a barely concealed smirk, Ruggles reminded the court that the case before them was the guilt or innocence of Peter Wheeler. As such, Ruggles argued, the inquest had no bearing on the issue at hand.

It was an audacious, almost foolhardy, opening salvo but Dwight was just getting warmed up. The defence then unleashed a litany of objections, including a motion to exclude the inquest testimony in its entirety. The move surprised Copp and Purdy, who demanded to know on what grounds. Ruggles chuckled and paused. These grounds, the advocate replied, pointing to the floor. As questioning murmurs rippled through the cowshed-cum-courthouse, Ruggles turned and played to the crowd. Purdy and his cobbled throne sat in Digby County, Ruggles reminded his rapt audience, yet the testimony had been given in another county: Annapolis. With all due respect, he gleefully told the court, the esteemed justice had no authority outside his county seat and no jurisdiction whatsoever over events in Annapolis County.

Before Purdy could rule, a bombastic Ruggles stormed ahead. He also wanted all witness statements taken in Digby County excluded, arguing such evidence was introduced absent the accused or his counsel. His client, Ruggles thundered, had been denied his right to confront his accusers; accordingly, all evidence from the inquest should be stricken from the record. The judge now had his choice of reasons to exclude the inquest materials — the county issue or the violation of Wheeler's civil rights. It was a masterfully antagonistic performance, though one doomed to fail.

Unswayed by Ruggles's theatrics, Purdy elected to overrule the objection, giving a minor victory to the prosecution. Lovett's proclamation of Wheeler's guilt would stand. The defence team could no more strike the coroner's overreaching verdict from the court record than it could erase it from every media account in the land. That genie was out of the bottle and no amount of legal showboating could put it back.

Purdy's ruling left Ruggles hobbled but re-energized. There was still some ground to be gained as the witness had not yet been excused. Lovett had sat patiently during the defence pyrotechnics, waiting to be dismissed, but Ruggles had no intention of letting the good doctor off so easily. For the first time, all would hear the uncensored version of what the coroner saw the day Annie died.

At Ruggles's urging, Lovett recounted the morning the body was discovered. The coroner arrived at the Kempton home just after nine o'clock. The corpse lay between the stove and the window, an environmental confluence that wreaked havoc on Annie's body temperature. Lovett understood that cadavers cooled after death, although he admitted having no prior experience in using body temperature to estimate the time of death. The doctor told the court he had tested the body's temperature by placing his hands on her skin, a far from exacting method. In the end, after being grilled relentlessly by Ruggles, Lovett conceded he had no way of knowing how long Annie had been dead.

Copp rose to redirect. He asked Lovett how long it would normally take for a body to cool after death. With nothing practical to draw upon, Lovett's answer was vague. It could take twelve, twenty-four, or forty-eight hours, Lovett posited, he simply could not say for certain. Although the answers were frustratingly obtuse, the exchange clarified a salient point. The question of when Annie died was quickly becoming both the linchpin and the bane of the case. It was a subject each side would return to time and again throughout the investigation.

With nothing more to be gleaned from the coroner, Dr. Lovett was dismissed. He was quickly followed by the now familiar parade of witnesses who had taken the stand during the inquest. Each of the two dozen attestants reiterated their prior testimony almost word for word, with one key exception — Hardy Benson who, as we shall soon see, revised his statement in lethal ways.

The lone piece of physical evidence introduced was the short length of firewood allegedly used to knock Annie unconscious. Although weighted with sinister connotations, the actual wood as a cudgel was rather unimpressive. As Mr. Payne succinctly stated, it was "not a formidable looking weapon."[7]

❅

Although it was an anaphora of Lovett's inquest one week prior, Purdy's folly was still the biggest game in town. And, as with all good serials, soap operas, and dime-store novellas, the secret to success lay in the cliff-hanger — that tantalizing glimpse of the next heart-pounding installment. While such prognostication often proved difficult in legal endeavours, somehow the editor of the *Annapolis Spectator* pulled it off. The tag line of each special edition announced that "perhaps the most important evidence yet will be given to-day,"[8] baiting their loyal audience to tune in next time. If such lures were not enough, the editor implored his readers to "be sure and get a copy"[9] of the next *Spectator EXTRA*, "only one cent."[10] You get what you pay for: the editor's two cents' worth, and a bargain at half the price.

nineteen

Hardy Benson Changes His Tune

Of all the cliffhangers proffered during the Purdy hearings, none garnered more attention than the appearance of fifteen-year-old Harding Thomas "Hardy" Benson. Dubbed "Annie's sweetheart"[1] by the local media, Hardy had been her gentleman caller for the past few months, an eternity in the annals of teen romance. The only son of Allut and Ruby Benson — a surname with clout in Bear River — Hardy was gawky, unerringly polite, and as docile as livestock.

Hardy may have captured Annie's heart but his public persona lacked finesse. His appearance during the coroner's inquest had been brief and entirely forgettable. The only media account of the boy came in the *Digby Weekly Courier*, which stated that "Hardy Benson was put on the stand late in the evening. His evidence was not very important."[2]

Benson's testimony was summarily dismissed because it mirrored facts presented by far more compelling witnesses. All Hardy said was that he had seen his girlfriend on the Bear River Bridge at four o'clock on the afternoon in question. In actuality, the media's apathy toward Benson could be chalked up to a single factor: his testimony in no way implicated Peter Wheeler. On the stand, Benson made no mention of the man who stood accused.

The press and public alike might have forever turned a blind eye to Hardy Benson were it not for an interview Detective Nick Power gave to the *Morning Chronicle*. Power let slip (in his practised yet casual manner) that, while transporting Wheeler from Bear River to the Digby jail, the two men had shared their impressions of the coroner's inquest. According to the detective, Wheeler claimed that one witness had perjured himself. The prisoner was outraged because said witness might have cleared his name had he told the truth. Peter reportedly told Power, "Something did not come out that may be some good to me. A respectable young fellow and I went up to Kempton's house that night. The young fellow wanted to go in but I objected and we went back."[3]

Wheeler refused to give Power the name of the respectable young fellow but inquiries in the village soon led the detective to Hardy Benson. During their initial interview, Benson stuck to his original testimony but Power leaned hard on the boy. He prided himself on his interrogation skills and scoffed at the idea that a teenager could outwit a seasoned lawman. After a few hours of artfully dodging the detective's entreaties, young Hardy began to sing an entirely new tune.

Intrigued by Power's tale of an undisclosed witness, the *Chronicle* reporter also hunted down young Benson. Hardy, his memory jarred loose by Nick Power, now claimed he had met up with Peter Wheeler at Tillie's house that night. The two went to the Kemptons' to see Annie, and Peter went inside while Hardy waited at the gate. A few minutes later, Peter came out, threw his arm over Hardy's shoulders, and the two walked back down the hill to Tillie's house.

En route, Hardy claimed Peter warned him not to tell anyone they had gone to the Kempton house. Peter then told Hardy that Annie was alone and suggested Hardy go back and stay with her. Benson said no, mindful of the scandal such action would cause, and the boy went home. Hardy told the *Chronicle* that after the body was found the next day, Peter again "cautioned"[4] him not to say anything. Wheeler told Benson he had seen two knives on the floor near her body, implying the police might think both of them were to blame.

The *Chronicle*'s report on Benson was a bombshell; every rival newspaper reprinted the account and the resulting public outcry grew deafening. Benson's revised account pounded the final nail in Wheeler's coffin. Thanks to the boy's improved recall, the detective could now place Wheeler inside the Kempton home. Of course, Hardy Benson now had a credibility problem, having changed his prior sworn testimony, but Power was confident Prosecutor Copp could overcome any and all challenges to the lad's integrity.

☾

As was often the case with Detective Power's more high-profile cases, the perfect piece of evidence had arrived at the most opportune juncture. Indeed, the timing of Wheeler's purported statement and Hardy's sudden recanting was a tad too convenient. The coroner's inquest had revealed a serious problem with the timeline of the case. Based on inquest testimony, Power could only place Wheeler near the Kempton house around 4:30 in the afternoon. Armed with Benson's surprising revelations, Power now had an eyewitness who put Wheeler through the front door at exactly the right moment.

The common denominator in all these expeditious divulgences was Nicholas Power. He was the sole witness to Wheeler's alleged declaration about a perjured witness. Power was also instrumental in convincing (some might say strong-arming) Benson to change his testimony. As Wheeler hurtled toward certain doom, it seems Detective Power was always on hand to grease the skids.

☾

When Benson's revelations became public, Peter Wheeler asked to speak to the same reporter from the *Morning Chronicle*. Peter intended to use the meeting as a fishing expedition, and the journalist later lamented that Wheeler "requested more information however than he desired to give."[5] Wheeler entertained the reporter at length in his cell, hoping to gain valuable insight into Benson's abrupt about-face. Although Peter never garnered the answers he sought, the resulting article suggests he still managed to charm the *Chronicle* correspondent: "He is very anxious to discover whether he is to be hung or not, but alleges his innocence with a clear voice and unflinching eye.... He requested and was assured that he would receive fair treatment from the CHRONICLE. If he is a guilty man, his demeanor is wonderful."[6]

Although his demeanour won over the *Chronicle*, Wheeler remained the loser in his escalating war of words with Power. The detective's statements were accepted without challenge by the media and public alike. Wheeler, an accused and all-but-convicted killer, was not to be believed regardless of the evidence he offered. Even Hardy Benson fared better — his integrity was never called into question by the press, despite having given them ample reason to do so.

☾

News of Benson's alterations sent shock waves through the community. If Wheeler had hoped Benson's tale would exculpate him, he was sadly mistaken; in fact, things only looked bleaker for the accused man. As the uproar reached its zenith, Detective Power again sat down with the *Morning Chronicle* to share his latest thoughts with the public. If Hardy Benson could rewrite history without ramifications, so could Nick Power.

After a week of investigation, Power was at last ready to reveal his theory of the crime. As he saw it, the events were straightforward. Wheeler — having lied to ensure Annie was alone — tried to rape her in the early afternoon. When she fought valiantly to preserve her honour, he picked up a piece of firewood and struck her about the head, fleeing the house as she lay moaning in a pool of her own blood. Fearing Annie might not be dead, Wheeler enlisted the unwitting Benson as cover and the two men returned to the Kempton house. Wheeler tried to convince Benson to enter, but when the boy refused, Wheeler went in and finished the job with the two knives.

It was a compelling narrative, particularly when viewed uncritically. The problem, of course, remained the timeline. Annie was seen by multiple witnesses throughout the afternoon and evening, leaving Wheeler no time to mount a single attack, much less two. Still, no one openly questioned Power's deductive skills.

When queried as to Benson's sudden change of tune, Power again put himself at the centre of the controversy, saying, "When Benson was on the stand, [I] noticed that he was not giving a full statement of what he knew of the case."[7] When Power confronted the boy, he broke down and revised his statement. What Power exalted as brilliant detective work, others might call coercion and witness tampering: potato, potahto.

Whatever else Power's one-man media campaign accomplished, it had chummed the waters for the feeding frenzy that was to follow. Purdy's exam found a new breakout star — Annie's sweetheart — and he single-handedly promised to put the knife in Wheeler's hand. As young Hardy Benson took the stand and swore his oath, he was the most exciting thing to happen in Digby County since the crime itself.

☾

With all the hype, it was inevitable that Benson's actual court appearance proved to be something of a disappointment. Hardy, the personification of a gangly awkward teen, was not a dynamic speaker. Pathologically fearful of the opposite sex and crowds, Benson's knees visibly knocked as he haltingly took the witness stand before the looming Judge Purdy. His terror was palpable and served as a delightful amuse-bouche to the hungry stable of onlookers who had travelled great distances to hear what the young man had to say.

Although Benson's oratory skills left much to be desired, his newly revised testimony still managed to pack a formidable wallop. He began his account by restating the portions of his original testimony he claimed were still true. He had seen Annie Kempton on the bridge around four in the afternoon but had not spoken to her. Then, in a painfully bumbling segue, Benson stated that his memory of the night had dramatically improved, although Power's role in the miraculous turnabout was left uncredited. Copp, who stood to gain from Benson's newest version of events, let the remark pass uncontested.

The sandy foundations of Benson's memory continued to shift. Contrary to what he had told the *Morning Chronicle*, Benson now swore he did not meet Wheeler at Tillie's house but rather had run into Peter on the road leading to the Kemptons'. The two started talking and Hardy claimed he had asked Peter, "Have you seen Annie tonight?"[8] to which Wheeler replied he had not. They decided to pay her a social call, and as the men made their way toward her house, Annie remained the sole topic of conversation. In yet another explosive revelation, Benson stunned the crowd when he stated that Wheeler had referred to Annie as "the Satan."[9]

According to Hardy's latest installment, Peter then went into the Kempton house to talk to Annie, leaving Benson alone on the road. Minutes later, Wheeler ran from the house and draped his arm around Hardy's shoulders. Shifting uncomfortably in the witness dock, Benson unleashed another new twist. He told the court that as the pair wandered back toward Wheeler's boarding house, Benson turned and saw a light suddenly appear in the sitting-room window of the Kempton house. This latest disclosure was not what the prosecution was expecting and Copp moved on quickly.

Picking up his rapidly unravelling narrative thread, Hardy soldiered on. When the men reached the road leading to Tillie's front door, Benson insisted they had the following exchange:

> **Hardy:** Was Grace Morine with her?
> **Peter:** No.
> **Hardy:** Do you suppose I had better go back and stop with her?
> **Peter:** You had better go back and stop with her.
> **Hardy:** Oh no, I have never been in the habit of stopping with her when she is alone. She might think it funny.[10]

Hardy then said that he and Wheeler met Tillie Comeau and her children on the road and the group went into the boarding house. Just before nine o'clock, Benson left the Comeau residence and swore he went straight home, arriving at about 9:15 p.m.

Benson's meandering testimony both helped and hurt the detective's case. If all the eyewitnesses were to be believed, the only window of opportunity Wheeler had to commit the crime was the time he spent in the house while Benson waited outside. Yet, by the boy's own account, Benson heard and saw nothing out of the ordinary during that time. Benson's comments during his cross-examination only added to Power's woes. When pressed for specifics by defence counsel Dwight Ruggles, Benson was adamant that Wheeler had no blood on him when he left Annie's house that night. Furthermore, Hardy's claim that a light came on in the Kempton house after Wheeler left indicated Annie was still alive as the men walked away. Benson's account also called into question the footprint evidence Bernard Parker had so painstakingly documented. If Wheeler had not gone near the pig barn or crossed any fields with Benson, how were the footprints related to the crime? The short answer was that either the footprints were irrelevant or Wheeler was not the killer. Since neither answer was acceptable to Power or the prosecution, the question was never raised.

Before releasing him from the stand, Ruggles put one last question to the trembling witness: why had he lied during the coroner's inquest? Rendered almost mute with guilt, shame, and fear, Benson finally mumbled that Wheeler had threatened him to stay quiet. When Ruggles asked how Wheeler might harm him, given that Peter was in police custody, Hardy stated that Wheeler had sent him a warning through another man, telling him to keep quiet. This proclamation elicited a burst of outrage from the crowd: was there no end to Wheeler's villainous treachery?

Although Benson would not name the messenger who conveyed Wheeler's dire threat, it did not take Power long to find him. Willie Henshaw — another fifteen-year-old boy from the village — claimed to be the envoy, and Prosecutor Copp rushed Henshaw onto the witness stand.

Once again, a timeline proved crucial to the ever-evolving saga. Power had taken Wheeler into custody on Wednesday, January 29. On Thursday, Willie Henshaw claimed Wheeler had given him a message to give to Benson just before Hardy took the stand at the coroner's inquest. According to Willie, Wheeler told him to ask Hardy to lie and tell Lovett that they had not been to Annie's house that night.

The strange house of cards did not stand for long. Under defence questioning, Willie Henshaw admitted he had not delivered the message to Hardy Benson, although the admission did little to stifle the crowd's disgust. To those assembled, Henshaw's claims were simply further proof of Wheeler's mendacious and conniving nature. Their collective certainty blinded them to the gaping hole Henshaw had just ripped in the space-time continuum.

Henshaw's testimony may have corroborated Benson's but it contained two fatal flaws — serious contradictions that are as evident today as when Henshaw took the stand. The first is the very real question of how a teenage boy gained access to a prisoner in protective custody. When cross-examined by Ruggles, Henshaw was grilled as to where his alleged meeting with Wheeler had taken place. Willie replied he had spoken to Peter "in Mr. Purdy's office in the place which is used by Mr. Harris as a harness room."[11] The conversation could not have occurred during the coroner's hearing as such an arrangement did not exist until Purdy's examination more than one week after the inquest had ended. The second far more puzzling issue is this: if Henshaw never delivered the message, how did Hardy Benson know Wheeler had threatened him from jail?

❰

Such is the nature of time — covert manipulations of it are not always apparent in the moment. The testimonies of Hardy Benson and Willie Henshaw were textbook examples of the chronological tomfoolery plaguing the Wheeler case. In all probability, the two teens were earnest in their desire to help. It is unlikely either testified purely out of spite toward Wheeler. Rather, they were influenced by adults in positions of authority who convinced them their testimony was necessary to convict an evil man accused of a heinous crime: the murder of their dear friend. With some necessary gerrymandering, the boys' statements plugged the trouble spots in Power's theory of the case. Benson put Wheeler in the house and Henshaw gave Benson a reason to lie. On the surface, the evidence seemed compelling and damning; upon reflection, both stories lacked internal logic and consistency.

Most troubling of all was Power's steadfast refusal to acknowledge the conflicting evidence in his case. The detective was so certain of Wheeler's guilt that he trusted his own hunches and suppositions at the expense of more substantial evidence to the contrary. For Power, the focus had shifted from reconstructing the crime and identifying the perpetrator to inculpating the accused at all costs. That Power's reputation for infallibility was also on the line only motivated him further. With the benefit of hindsight, it is clear that Benson's and Henshaw's respective testimony had been moulded by others and it was hard not to see Detective Power's fingerprints all over the result.

twenty

Facts Be Damned

Virtually everyone agreed Wheeler was guilty, although the ink-dappled men of the media could agree on precious little else. The story had grown too big, too popular to be contained. Sales skyrocketed as the saga of Peter Wheeler became the favoured distraction of every literate Nova Scotian.

For the papers' editors and publishers, the need for fresh content seemed to override any lingering professional ethics they may have once held. By early February, all pretense of accuracy or fact-based reporting had long since been abandoned. The region's news agencies recognized the story had legs and creative licence trumped veracity every time.

Even Homer nods occasionally and the normally truth-conscious Mr. Payne of the *Saint John Daily Sun* was caught in some overt contradictions. For instance, in the space of a single article Payne described Annie as being seventeen, only to state a few paragraphs later that she was fifteen.[1] While neither age was technically correct, the latter was at least close enough for horseshoes, hand grenades, and Maritime newshounds. Yet for all his faults, Payne was a paragon of journalistic integrity compared to many of his colleagues.

Dubious reporting became the mainstay of a media machine focused on a single criminal narrative. Competing papers still jockeyed for exclusives but seemed equally committed to including at least one Wheeler-centric story in each new edition, regardless of its merit. To fill the void and pad the word count, reporters became increasingly rococo in their descriptions. The case evoked strong emotions and editors clearly preferred overwrought copy, replete with fervent descriptions of even the most mundane details.

This new-found cynosure of the calculatingly evocative, designed to bring a tear to even the most jaundiced eye, resulted in a bewildering display of contradictory journalistic excess. In their headlong rush to wring every last drop of pathos from the event, reporters and editors chose rhetoric over logic, sacrificing substance to the gods of good story-telling. One of the most overt examples centred on some tissue paper.

As Purdy's examination dragged on, correspondents ran out of ways to make the proceedings interesting. The evidence had already been reported at length, with witness testimony repeated and dissected ad nauseam. Reporters found little need to repeat the stories, writing only that each witness account "was virtually the same as that given at the coroner's inquest, already published."[2] The once-juicy details had grown stale and readers were bored. On February 11, the stringer for the *Yarmouth Herald* needed a few potent visuals to spice up the day's tiresome account. He began the article by stating that all the tables in the courtroom had been decorated with the tissue paper flowers Annie Kempton made the night she died. It was a poignant tableau and a heart-rending reminder of the innocence of the young victim, exactly the sort of moving embellishment readers and editors were looking for.

There was only one problem: the presence of the tissue paper flowers completely contradicted the theory espoused by Detective Power. Crucial to the Crown's *res gestae* was that the murder had been committed between five and six o'clock. To bolster this claim, Detective Power pointed to three key pieces of evidence: a pan of uneaten beans on the stove, the unmilked cow in the barn, and the fact that Annie had purchased tissue paper to make flowers for Mrs. Harris's party that evening but had not lived long enough to construct the decorations. The press had reported extensively on the significance of the unfinished ornaments only days before.

The issue of the paper frippery took on biblical proportions when Mr. Payne waded into the fray. The visiting correspondent told his readers that on February 8, he had returned to his hotel room at the end of the hearing to find three vases full of pink and white tissue flowers. Payne was told the bouquet had been crafted by Annie Kempton in the hours before she was murdered. Cloistered in his jail cell, Peter Wheeler read Payne's account and took his new friend to task, joking that the few sheets of paper Annie purchased must have been "like the loaves and fishes,"[3] miraculously replicating in order to fashion all of the flowers attributed to Annie from that night.

To those possessing a keen eye and the necessary inclination, the conflicted reporting was glaringly obvious. To readers consuming the reportage without question, the contradictions passed without notice or comment. It was the unheralded dawn of a lamentable new reality: a journalistic morass more interested in entertaining than informing the public.

twenty-one

An Indictment, of Sorts

After a week of misdirecting the masses, Purdy's hippodrome was listing like a drunk on a bender. The examination lacked the explosive revelations of Lovett's inquest, offering up the same twenty-four witnesses telling the same shopworn stories. Since Wheeler was not permitted to speak in his own defence and his bombastic lawyer could not call any witnesses of his own, there was little fresh drama to be had, save of course for Hardy Benson's revisionist bluff and blunder.

As the final witness Willie Henshaw left the stand, Copp rose and proclaimed his case closed. There were no last-minute exclamations, no sudden *aha!* moments. It was a disappointingly low-key climax to a taciturn prolixity in jurisprudence. After considering the evidence for all of a minute, Purdy issued a single piece of paper dripping with all the necessary legalese, official stamps, and requisite signatures. It was a remand ordering Wheeler back to the Digby jail to await his real trial before a Supreme Court justice. Yet for all its carefully effected air of importance, Purdy's order was simply legal busywork. One local paper referred to Purdy's ruling as nothing more than a "temporary sentence."[1] Formal charges against Wheeler remained unfiled. Still, to Purdy's way of thinking, it was very much in keeping with the locals' "desire for British justice."[2] Wheeler was once again bound for jail and all was right with the world.

What once promised to be grand theatre turned out to be merely a tease. Purdy's folly was simply a way station en route to the final destination of retribution and justice, or more to the point, the appearance of justice being done. Although Wheeler was one step closer to the gallows, the pace proved excruciatingly slow for those most affected: the victim's family, the citizens of Bear River, and the media, though not necessarily in that order.

The *Digby Weekly Courier* laid the groundwork for the next phase of legal proceedings when it declared: "By English law a man is deserving of a fair trial and Wheeler should have such benefits accorded him so far as is right."[3] Having grudgingly ceded Wheeler his basic rights (within reason), the *Courier* quickly reverted to form: "The evidence points so strongly however to Wheeler's guilt that it is thought he cannot escape the conviction which would be only justice."[4] As a fair trial requires an impartial jury, the *Digby Courier* was doing everything in its power to ensure that the potential pool of jurors was as jaundiced as humanly possible.

Meanwhile, Wallace Purdy had done everything in his power to make his mark in the annals of time, but history would not be kind to him. The judge intended his examination to be a showcase for his legal prowess and a stepping stone in his career, although publicly the intent was to assess the case against Peter Wheeler. Purdy, however, had been unceremoniously upstaged by others: the accused, Hardy Benson, and the proceeding's true leading man, Detective Nicholas Power. All had garnered far greater and more effusive press coverage. For his pains, all Wallace Purdy earned was a stipend of nineteen dollars.[5]

Although codes of professional conduct prohibited both Purdy and Power from discussing the case publicly, only Purdy heeded those ethical constraints. Power, unfettered by discretion, took countless victory laps in the press, relegating Purdy to the role of spear carrier in the drama unfolding. Accessibility equalled recognition and acclaim in the quid pro quo world of the press corps; the credit went to those willing to go on the record. In what should have been Purdy's finest hour, all eyes were on the gumshoe from Halifax, prompting the *Morning Chronicle* to exclaim: "Once again, Detective Power is on top."[6] In stark contrast, the most the *Yarmouth Herald* could muster was a half-hearted nod to Purdy for the "able manner in which he conducted the examination."[7]

What undoubtedly rankled Purdy most was that Power himself never took the stand during the exam, electing instead to try the case in the media. The detective — the uncontested master of the dangling carrot — granted interview upon interview, each full of promise and portent but signifying nothing of substance. As one reporter noted: "Detective Power says he has very important evidence against Wheeler but in the interest of justice does not deem it prudent to disclose the nature of it at present."[8] How terribly convenient, particularly since prudence had certainly never stopped Power from sharing in the past.

Perhaps Power's feint toward discretion had a different motivation altogether. The detective's ceaseless quest for accolades was not vanity but rather its opposite — insecurity. Even as the press printed Power's swaggering boast that in his humble opinion "never was a case more fully proven"[9] than the one he had built against Wheeler, the weak links in the detective's self-proclaimed perfect chain of evidence were showing. They included a complete lack of physical evidence tying Wheeler to the scene and a timeline that endlessly contradicted itself. Even Power's staunchest supporters in the media acknowledged that "the evidence in the case is purely circumstantial."[10] Purdy's exam served only to remind Power of a single overwhelming reality: more than two weeks after Annie's brutal slaying, the detective still had not conclusively put the murder weapon in Wheeler's hand, and all of Power's bravado and bluster was not enough to keep that pivotal fact hidden much longer.

twenty-two

That Troublesome Timeline

Purdy's examination may have been an exercise in futility, but it provided a second and more exhaustive opportunity to consider the evidence against Wheeler. Although it was heralded by the press as a model of efficiency and exacting inquiry, Dr. Lovett's inquest lacked the structure of a court proceeding. With no defence counsel on hand, the coroner's hearing had none of the parry and thrust inherent in the adversarial exchange of opposing parties. Purdy's exam, if nothing else, had opened the witnesses to cross-examination and challenge. Even so cursory an inspection had revealed the weak foundations of the case.

The crux and the crucible of Nick Power's theory — and the prosecution's case — was the timeline of the crime. Despite the detective's concerted efforts, the window of opportunity for Wheeler to kill Annie was remarkably small and shrinking by the minute. The eyewitnesses, so crucial in establishing Wheeler's whereabouts, proved to be a double-edged sword. As each witness stepped forward to mark another milestone on the timeline, Wheeler's supposed chance to strike deliquesced until mere seconds remained.

Ever mindful of the problem, Power and the prosecutor fell back on that most trusted of legal devices: misdirection. If the evidence could not be trusted to sway the jurors, the Crown would settle for confusing them instead. The secret lay in having the witnesses present their evidence out of sequence, never allowing the jurors, spectators, or press to solidify a minute-by-minute account of the events in question.

With artful manipulation, Copp shuffled and reshuffled the witness roster, ensuring that a coherent chronology of the murder never emerged.

It is only through the deliberate compiling, parsing, and rearranging of the witness statements given during the coroner's inquest and Purdy's examination that a clear timeline develops:

Monday, January 27, 1896

8:30 a.m.
Witness: Isaac Kempton
Annie's father Isaac and brother Earnest leave the family home for work in a distant lumberyard. Annie remains at home alone, occupied by household chores.

1:00 p.m.-6:00 p.m.
Witness: Peter Wheeler
Wheeler spends the afternoon in the woods near his boarding house, checking his rabbit snares and hunting for small game.

3:30 p.m.
Witness: Grace Morine
Annie runs into her school chum Grace on the road. The girls share a brief conversation, during which there is no mention of Grace coming to stay with Annie that night. The girls exchange their goodbyes minutes later.

4:00 p.m.
Witness: Hardy Benson
Benson sees Annie near town on the Bear River Bridge but does not speak to her.

4:00 p.m.-5:00 p.m.
Witnesses: William Rice, Joseph Pictou

Annie stops in at William Rice's store to purchase tissue paper to make flowers for an upcoming party at the hotel. Pictou later sees Annie as she makes her way through town, returning home via the Bear River Bridge.

5:00 p.m.
Witness: Peter Wheeler
Wheeler meets Annie by chance near the gate to her house and they have a brief conversation. Annie asks Peter to tell Tillie Comeau there is no need for her to visit that night, as Grace Morine will be keeping her company. Peter agrees to pass on the message. Annie invites Peter in for a quick supper of beans but Peter declines the offer and the pair part company.

5:00 p.m.-6:00 p.m.
Witness: Sadie Morine
Sadie, Grace's younger sister, recalls seeing Peter Wheeler in the fields near the Kempton house, working on his animal traps.

5:17 p.m.
Source: Environment Canada Climate Data Archive
Sunset.

5:30 p.m.
Witness: Elmer Crabbe
Crabbe sees Wheeler near the Kempton home. He shouts to Wheeler but receives no reply. When the two men run into each other that evening in town, Crabbe asks Wheeler if he was near the Kemptons' that afternoon and Wheeler confirms he was there.

6:00 p.m.

Witness: Walter Comeau

As night falls, young Walter is chopping wood just off the road that runs between the Comeau and Kempton houses. Walter sees Wheeler about 140 yards from the Kemptons' gate. The two meet and Peter helps Walter carry the wood home.

7:00 p.m.

Witnesses: Peter Wheeler, Walter Comeau

Wheeler sees Annie "going up past Tillie's about 7 o'clock,"[1] as he walks home with Walter.

7:05 p.m.

Witness: Peter Wheeler

In search of his evening's entertainment, Wheeler begins walking into town.

7:30 pm

Witnesses: Hardy Benson, Peter Wheeler

Benson runs into Wheeler on the road. After a few minutes, the pair walk towards Tillie Comeau's house but do not go in, proceeding on to the Kempton house. Benson marks the time of their departure — as "the Salvation drum was beating"[2] — and estimates it took about half an hour to walk the distance.

8:00 p.m.

Witness: Hardy Benson (revised testimony, recanting prior testimony)

As Wheeler and Benson arrive at the Kemptons' gate, Benson waits by the road while Peter goes into the house via the kitchen door. Benson can see no light on in the house at that time. Minutes later, Peter comes out and wraps his arm around Benson's shoulders. There is no blood on Wheeler and he is not behaving strangely. As the two men walk away, Benson sees a light appear in the Kemptons' front window. He sees no shadows moving, "just a steady light."[3]

8:10 p.m.

Witnesses: Hardy Benson (revised testimony), Tillie Comeau, Walter Comeau, Hattie Comeau, Peter Wheeler
Benson and Wheeler go to the Comeau residence. Tillie is not home but her son Herbert is, along with his friend, Herbert Rice. Five minutes later, Tillie's younger son Walter and daughter Hattie come into the house. Peter Wheeler and Hardy Benson go out to the road where they see Tillie Comeau on her way home from work. Peter, Hardy, and Tillie then enter the Comeau house.

9:00 p.m.

Witness: Hardy Benson
Benson leaves the boarding house to return home. Peter Wheeler walks him as far as the gate. Benson says he arrived at his home at roughly 9:15 p.m. Detective Power never confirmed Benson's story nor investigated the teenager's whereabouts that evening.

9:30 p.m.

Witnesses: Tillie Comeau, Walter Comeau, Hattie Comeau, Peter Wheeler
The residents of the Comeau household turn in for the night. All are adamant that Wheeler never left the house

and all are certain they would have heard him had he tried to leave.

11:00 p.m.
Witness: John Brooks
From his house across the road, Brooks recalls seeing a lamp burning in the Kempton house. He stated that the blinds were not drawn.

Tuesday, January 28, 1896
2:30 a.m.-3:00 a.m.
Witness: Peter Wheeler
Wheeler is awakened by the sound of three men shouting, cursing, and laughing as they walk along the road that leads from Tillie's boarding house to the Kemptons'. Although Wheeler is able to describe the men, he does not recognize them.

3:00 a.m.
Witness: John Brooks
As Brooks gets up to attend to his sick son, he spies a lamp burning dimly in the window at the Kempton house.

8:00 a.m.
Witnesses: Tillie Comeau, Peter Wheeler
Tillie sends Peter to the Kemptons' to buy milk. Peter enters the home and finds Annie lying in a pool of blood in the sitting room. He kneels beside her, checks for a pulse, and then covers her with her father's coat. Wheeler searches the house, suspecting the killer might still be inside. Finding no one, he runs to the neighbours and raises the alarm.

Detective Nick Power staked his reputation on his theory that Wheeler struck Annie with the firewood between 5:00 and 6:00 p.m. on January 27. Two children (Sadie Morine and Walter Comeau) and one adult (Elmer Crabbe) reported seeing Wheeler on the road leading to the Kempton home around that time. Power also believed that Wheeler manipulated Benson into accompanying him to the Kemptons' that evening, in an effort to set up Benson to discover the body. When Hardy Benson refused to enter the home, Wheeler went in alone. Shocked to find Annie was still breathing, Wheeler grabbed some knives from the kitchen and proceeded to slash Annie's throat three times. Wheeler — drenched in his victim's blood — fumbled about the scene, leaving a trail of bloody hand- and footprints throughout the home. Power further claimed that Wheeler paused to enjoy a jar of preserves, leaving a set of bloody handprints on the spoon and jar. Wheeler, having accomplished his sanguinary mayhem in mere minutes, then left the home and rejoined Benson, somehow miraculously devoid of Annie's blood and any evidence of mental derangement.

However implausible, Power's theory of the crime found a foothold with the prosecution and the media, gaining traction through sheer repetition. Although the witnesses would tell their stories no fewer than four times in the course of the investigation, their statements were never presented publicly in chronological order. Instead, their accounts were always isolated and disjointed, disrupting any sense of temporal flow. Consequently, the holes in the timeline, as well as the direct contradictions, were never immediately obvious.

Thanks to this conscious misdirection, the problems with that troublesome timeline were not overt but they were present all the same. The very people Power heralded as unimpeachable were the self-same witnesses whose testimony proves Wheeler could not have been the killer. Although Power relied heavily on the statement of Walter Comeau to put Wheeler near the Kempton home at 6:00 p.m., the same boy later testified that he (along with Wheeler) saw Annie pass by the Comeau house around 7:00 p.m., an impossibility if Annie were bludgeoned at six o'clock. Furthermore, Power's star witness — the ever-changeable Hardy Benson — also provided strong evidence Annie was alive and well at 8:00 p.m., when he saw her light a lamp inside her home as he and Wheeler walked away.

There can be little doubt that Power was well aware of the inconsistencies of his timeline. Mapping out the witness statements was a cumbersome task, particularly given the illogical, almost haphazard way the evidence was presented, but that was entirely the point. The detective (as well as the prosecution) harped endlessly on the 5:00 p.m. to 6:00 p.m. window of opportunity, highlighting those witnesses who placed Wheeler near the Kempton home during that time span. The spotlight shone far less brightly on those statements that indicated Annie was still alive long past that point.

Even allowing considerable leeway on time estimates — a necessity in an age before wristwatches and ubiquitous household clocks — the timeline provided by the witnesses exonerates Peter Wheeler. Annie was very much alive when he and Benson left the Kempton house and Wheeler was never alone thereafter. Further, Annie's state of dress and the condition of her bed indicate that she survived much later than the 5:00 p.m. to 6:00 p.m. time of death that Power championed. The doctor's autopsy results confirmed the later time frame conclusively. It was only through the careful editing of witness statements and the adroit stage-managing of their testimony that the press, the public, and jury were unable to make neither head nor tails out of the great detective's meandering timeline.

twenty-three

The Great Divide

Thanks to Purdy's legal gambolling, the case against Peter Wheeler had become media carrion, a stripped carcass picked clean by the thieving journalistic magpies of the surrounding hills. Save for Mr. Payne, that most obstinate contrarian of the *Saint John Daily Sun*, the press had presented a united front. Speaking with one voice, the media presumed that all shared their unilateral stance. News accounts depicted the denizens of Annapolis and Digby counties in harmonious accord, allied by their singular belief in Wheeler's guilt. Yet amidst such unification there were growing pockets of resistance. Not everyone fell in lockstep behind the detective, prosecutor, and press. Payne had spawned his own small band of miscreant rebels, who steadfastly refused to accept Wheeler's inevitable conviction as a *fait accompli*.

Doubt begat doubt. Debates raged on the hardscrabble street corners and gilded parlours of the Annapolis Valley, echoing across the Fundy waves into neighbouring New Brunswick and beyond. Everyone, it seemed, had a strong opinion about Wheeler. Nick Power was no longer the only self-styled Sherlock Holmes in the Maritimes. Armchair detectives of every social stripe argued the merits of the case and more than a few bemoaned its speculative nature. Cab drivers, dorymen, and lumberjacks alike appointed themselves de facto jurors, examining the scant evidence from every conceivable angle.

Such heated dialectics needed a broader forum. The more vocal observers stepped up on the media soapbox to disseminate their views on the case and the region's news agencies were only too willing to oblige. In 1896 if you could afford a postage stamp, you too could make your voice heard. Letters to the editor flooded in, each more passionate than the last. The community polarized, battle lines were drawn, and each camp used the press to fire volleys at the opposition.

To one side sat those who feared Wheeler was being railroaded. Their rhetoric centred on the highly circumstantial nature of the case. This camp's tent poles were large enough to include those who lamented the media's culpability in the rush to judgment. A particularly heated exchange in the *Digby Weekly Courier* illustrated the crux of the debate. The opening shot was fired by an anonymous reader using the pseudonym "Observer" on February 21, 1896: "Now that the *Halifax Chronicle* has declared authoritatively that Peter Wheeler murdered Annie Kempton and the *Presbyterian Witness* has uttered a pious thanksgiving that the murderer was so soon discovered, it may be presumptuous for a humble lover and seeker after justice to say a word to check the ill-judged zeal which might hurry an innocent man to an untimely and ignominious death."[1]

As self-anointed defence counsel, Observer argued that the only evidence against Wheeler was the statement of Grace Morine, which suggested Peter had lied to get Annie alone. The letter's author was quick to point out that the absence of physical evidence — specifically blood on Wheeler's clothes and hands in the moments after the killing — was far more compelling proof of his innocence. Observer also levelled harsh criticism against Detective Power for failing to investigate properly, choosing instead to focus all his efforts on building a case against Wheeler at the expense of all other potential suspects. Observer called Wheeler "a scapegoat for the real criminal."[2] The letter closed by revisiting Payne's fears that a rush to judgment was inevitable: "It would be cruel to have a special early session to try him before the feeling dies out which the too hasty and premature assumption of his guilt on such slight ground has excited."[3]

Although the missive was strongly worded, Observer's commentary was reasoned, measured, and well argued. The author gave voice to an otherwise silent minority. The far more vitriolic majority found their voice two weeks later, when someone using the *nom du plume* "A Lover of Justice" answered Observer's fire.

"Lover" brought a cannon to a knife fight, unleashing a disproportionate response that countered cool reason with a bullying and belittling personal attack. "We think Observer's mind must be very weak if he... could not understand that this is about the weakest evidence in the case,"[4] wrote Lover, co-opting the royal "we" in direct response to the notion that Wheeler's lie was the only mark against him. Lover — who identified himself as a local and claimed to "have voiced the sentiment of the people of Bear River village"[5] — then donned the mantle of prosecutor and proceeded to try Wheeler in absentia, offering his own misguided theories as to why Wheeler had no blood on him.

Lover's ideological entrenchment left no room for differing viewpoints, dismissing anyone not of like mind as "weak and limited"[6] in their ability to see the truth and too tender-hearted to demand immediate justice.

It is also a curious quirk of the human condition that those with closed minds are best able to identify conspiracies in action and Lover saw money-minded confederates behind every door: "We have reason to believe that if Wheeler had been left alone by those who are looking after their own interests financially, he would have confessed his crime before this and thereby saved the rate payers of this county unnecessary expense.... We cannot expect justice from those who are blocking the way and warning Wheeler not to confess or say anything about it to anyone."[7]

A Lover of Justice begrudged Wheeler the right to a defence lawyer, declaring such necessities to be fiscally irresponsible. It was clear Lover wanted to simply string Wheeler up from the nearest tree in the interest of the taxpayers, a sentiment that was no doubt popular in town. Six weeks after the crime, tensions were running higher than ever as Bear River became a powder keg that threatened to explode at the slightest provocation. And there to strike the match and fan the flames were the regional tabloids, all the while decrying the entire matter as distasteful and beneath their dignity.

twenty-four

A Particularly Slow News Day

As February drew to a bitter, dreary close, the newspapers found themselves at a rare loss for words. Doldrums had set in during the weeks following Purdy's folly, and with no Wheeler courtroom dramas to fill their pages or new evidence to mull over, the press were forced to revert to their old ways: mass-distributed wire stories filled with colourful eccentrics, augmented by a few extended obituaries and some local gossip about engagements and graduations.

So it was with palpable relief that the *Yarmouth Times* announced a juicy new tidbit relating to the Kempton murder. It seemed that some folks now believed a man by the name of Joseph Pictou might be responsible for Annie's death. Joseph was a member of a Mi'kmaq band relegated to a small reserve just outside of Bear River.

According to then-unnamed sources, Pictou was seen leaving his home at 3:00 a.m. on the morning of the murder. He walked to the Bear River railway station and took the early westbound train. Although witnesses at the time assumed he was heading for his job in Hectanooga, Pictou stayed on the train until Yarmouth. There he visited with the Moffat family, whom once lived in Bear River. When news of Annie's murder reached the Moffats, Pictou — whom the *Times* referred to as "the Indian"[1] — reacted strongly and grew pale. He told the Moffats he had seen Annie on the Bear River Bridge on the afternoon before she died. Pictou then grew quiet, refusing to say another word on the matter, and soon left the Moffat home. According to one anonymous source, Pictou did not return to work or his home for almost a week, choosing instead to visit relatives and friends at various lumber camps in the region.

How such an innocuous chain of events painted Pictou as the perpetrator escapes all logic and reasoning but the story was a fresh morsel for an avaricious press pack. The *Times*, anxious to wash its hands of reporting such flimsy gossip, ran the story "for what it was worth."[2] The paper offered little comment or speculation as to the veracity of the rumour, a rare showing of editorial restraint.

Not so for the *Digby Weekly Courier*. On February 28, it scavenged the *Times* account, repackaging it as an important breaking development. Unlike its more reticent competitor, the *Courier* did not shy away from offering ample opinion regarding the unsubstantiated report, protected only by a straw man. After congratulating the *Times* for resisting the temptation to editorialize on the rumour, the *Courier* adroitly passed the buck: "We would not do so either but in talking it over with some Bear River people, we find that the idea is generally held by them as improbable.... This is as we hear it but there is enough in the rumors to make them worth investigating."[3]

The *Digby Courier*'s account then served as fodder for the *Bridgetown Monitor*, which saw things quite differently. According to the *Monitor*, the Moffats were quoted as saying: "From the first we had thought there was as good reasons to suspect the Indian as Wheeler."[4] The Moffats made a strong (if perhaps unintentional) point: there was no more evidence against Pictou than existed against Wheeler. The only strike against either man was the dark hue of their skin.

At least the Moffats were consistent in their rush to judgment. Although the *Digby Weekly Courier* had labelled Wheeler a blackguard and mongrel from the very beginning, the paper was quick to absolve Pictou of the crime on the basis of nothing but a vague character reference: "Pictou has always borne a good record, is quiet and well-inclined and the last man to be suspected of such a crime."[5] Blind to its own hypocrisy, the *Courier* argued that Pictou should not be falsely accused of a crime based solely on rumour and some odd behaviour, all the while using this exact suite of traits to condemn Peter Wheeler.

Within the succouring confines of the Annapolis Valley, no fewer than three papers had made a meal of an unsubstantiated rumour. That these three beacons of journalistic integrity derived such disparate accounts from a single anonymous source staggers the imagination. Even more bewildering, the *Saint John Daily Record* then rifled all three accounts and offered its own iteration of the tale, stating "that a strange Indian had been seen lurking in the Kempton house vicinity for some days before the murder."[6] The *Record* later amended its account, claiming the report "was traced to unreliable sources."[7] One can only hope they were referring to their competitors and not the Moffats.[8]

The Honourable Sir Charles James Townshend, Esquire, following his appointment as Chief Justice of the provincial Supreme Court.

twenty-five

A Change of Venue

Fervent pleas for sanity echoed forth from Mr. Payne, "Observer," and a motley band of pro-Wheeler forces, but the vast majority of citizens in the county and the province were unequivocally, irrevocably biased against Peter Wheeler, thanks to the concerted efforts of the region's media. The false accusations against Joseph Pictou were nothing more than a distraction, a momentary blip to tide the public over for another day. In fact, in identifying an alternative suspect with even less evidence against him, the press managed to make Wheeler look guiltier by comparison.

The story had reached its saturation point and the timing could not have been worse. As another brutal Maritime winter was sent packing and spring swept through the Annapolis Valley, it brought with it the hope that the ugly matter of Peter Wheeler would finally be resolved. To do so required a jury of his peers and that was proving to be a surprisingly tall order. Save for Mr. Payne, the media had been so effective in castigating Wheeler and so unwavering in their proclamations of his guilt, the court was hard pressed to find a single unbiased potential juror in Digby County, much less eleven others.

On May 7, 1896, Wheeler's defence team conceded defeat. Dwight Ruggles headed to the Clerk of the Supreme Court on a mission. In his fist was a motion *in limine* he had spent days crafting. The petition was battological, strident, and inarguably necessary.

The motion was brought before the newly appointed presiding justice in the case: the Honourable Charles J. Townshend. Unlike the rough-hewn Ruggles, Townshend was "a true specimen of the old-regime elite in the Maritimes."[1] Nestled snugly in the ample bosom of Old World old money, Townshend was a child of privilege. The pampered son of Reverend Canon

Townshend, rector of Amherst, Nova Scotia, Charles received a top-shelf education at the University of King's College in Windsor.

Townshend's meteoric rise through the ranks of Nova Scotian jurisprudence was based on undisputed merit tempered with unimpeachable family connections. Admitted to the bar in 1866, he partnered with his brother, J. Medley Townshend, and R.B. Dickie. Charles, arguably the more talented and ambitious of the siblings, was appointed Queen's Counsel in 1881. Just six years later, Townshend was named to the bench, becoming a Supreme Court justice in March 1887. A decade after overseeing the Wheeler case, Townshend would go on to be named the Court's Chief Justice and was eventually knighted for his illustrious service to sovereign and country.

The old school collided head-on with the new as Ruggles made his case before Townshend. The two jurists were a study in contrasts: Ruggles was bellicose and scrappy, a blustering force of nature unaccustomed to failure while Townshend was measured and sedate, a benevolent deity who demanded respect and calm in his courtroom. Shouts, threats, and theatrics did not sit well with Sir Charles. Ruggles's sharp edges cut Townshend to the quick. It was shaping up to be a long, contentious trial in more ways than one.

With great earnestness curbed by as much serenity as he could muster, Ruggles pleaded for a change of venue for the upcoming trial. Wheeler's trial was originally slated for the summer court session in the county seat of Digby, but the defence team was literally begging to have the trial held anywhere else in the province.

Ruggles, doing his damnedest to rein in his combative manner, reminded the court of the salient point he had raised during Purdy's examination. The village of Bear River was a house divided, straddling the boundary line between Digby and Annapolis Counties. The argument proved a non-starter with Townshend, and Ruggles withdrew and regrouped. He came back swinging with the crux of his plea: it was virtually impossible for Wheeler to receive a fair trial anywhere in either county due to the overwhelmingly negative media coverage.

Having vociferously aired his concerns in the judge's Halifax chambers, Ruggles filed his motion. Townshend perused the rambling typewritten petition. It included copies of newspaper articles as well as sworn affidavits from fourteen individuals, all attesting to having heard (or said) disparaging, prejudicial, offensive, and derogatory comments about the accused.

Townshend was swayed enough to grant a pretrial hearing on the matter. On May 19 at precisely 11:00 a.m., the judge convened the first of many courtroom skirmishes in the case of *Queen v. Wheeler*. Justice Townshend, an owlish man of surprisingly mordant wit, ascended the bench and laid down the ground rules for the proceedings. Despite the intense media interest in the case, Townshend made clear his courtroom would be neither a circus nor the forum for a barroom brawl.

Suitably chastised, barristers Charles Sidney Harrington and Fred T. Congdon squared off, offering sharply conflicting views on why the move was, or was not, necessary. Congdon, a local barrister hired as a temporary second chair for the defence, regaled Judge Townshend with a selection of quotes from various local newspapers, including the *Digby Weekly Courier* and the *Annapolis Spectator*. The oration left little doubt that the press had already tried and convicted Wheeler. To bolster the assertion, the defence then read a number of letters to the editor that revealed an almost pathological certainty among local residents that Wheeler was the killer.

As further evidence that the deck was stacked against the accused, Wheeler's lawyers introduced a series of sworn affidavits from prominent members of the community. Among the most damning was a statement from William Alcorn of Annapolis Royal, who overheard one of the coroner's jurors shout "of course the God damned bastard killed her."[2] Alcorn went on to say he had heard other members of the jury state they had absolutely no doubt Annie was killed by Peter Wheeler. With that, the petitioning counsel rested.

Opposing counsel Harrington rose, knowing he was on a fool's errand. The prosecution offered a half-hearted argument, including the cursory protests of added expense and the headache of moving so many witnesses to another county's courthouse. In truth, it mattered little to the Crown where the actual trial was held — the judge could move Wheeler ten feet, ten miles, or to another province. Thanks to the syndicated news agencies, there was no hope of Wheeler getting a fair trial anywhere in the Maritimes.

By this point, interest in the case extended far beyond the counties abutting Bear River. Every major paper in Halifax as well as tabloids throughout the province — great and small, daily and weekly — had printed every detail of the crime since its discovery. Even papers in the bordering states carried highlights of the case and kept their readers apprised of all the major developments. The *Saint John Daily Record* noted with some pride that the specifics of the investigation were "vividly described in both Canadian and American press and for weeks the modest town of Bear River was unenviably placed in the prominent position in the eye of the North American public."[3]

Having heard his fill from both parties, the judge brought the hearing to a close. He announced that they would have his answer by the end of the week.

With so intense a spotlight focused on the proceedings, the judge could ill-afford to overlook such overt prejudice. The provincial media had been scathing in their attacks on Wheeler, and the notion that the jury pool was tainted only in Digby County was almost laughable. Charles Townshend — a wise and experienced jurist who had already cut his teeth on a modest number of murder trials — knew all too well the outcome was a foregone conclusion. Wheeler was as good as hanged no matter where the trial took place. Still, justice must appear to be done and so, mere moments before the close of business on Friday, May 22, Charles Townshend granted the motion for a change of venue. The prisoner was to be transferred to the jail in Kentville to await trial. As Townshend headed off to begin his weekend, which included a pleasant excursion with his second wife, Lady Margaret MacFarland, he left his clerk S.H. Holmes to type the lengthy ruling and inform the respective counsels.

☾

Court documents leave little doubt as to Townshend's reason for granting the change of venue — the news media — yet the public could not have gleaned the impetus from the press coverage of the judge's decision. Most papers simply ignored the ruling, opting instead to report on more salacious aspects of the Wheeler case or other contemporaneous gruesome murder investigations. The few that did report the change failed to mention their own culpability in the ruling.

On May 22, the *Digby Weekly Courier* (which had figured so prominently in the defence's motion) ran a small article on the change of venue. Though brief, the story was a master class in denial, misdirection, and vague reporting. Stating only that "Harrington quoted from Digby County papers"[4] — as though there were countless others besides the *Courier* — the weekly tabloid managed to avoid all accountability for having tainted the jury pool. They maintained that their hands were clean, even as they continued to bloody Peter Wheeler's.

twenty-six

The Trial

After months of ceaseless chatter and miles of newsprint, the so-called "facts" of the case had been annealed into the region's collective consciousness — immutable, irrefutable, and unassailable. Memory played tricks on the unwitting and no one could remember a time when Wheeler was not guilty or when the papers had carried news of anything else.

Like the populace they so faithfully served, the local news agencies were forever changed by the Kempton murder, transformed from simple purveyors of bland rhetoric into powerful arbiters of social opinion. They had also become the self-appointed guardians of the historical record. That the media were failing miserably on both counts mattered little. The damage was done but the evidence of it was readily concealed, to be revealed only through the archaeology of time and distance.

And so it was that in the first weeks of June in the year 1896, the much-heralded yet widely perceived as unnecessary trial of Peter Wheeler hobbled toward the finish line. Wheeler was transferred to the jail in Kentville under the cover of darkness and with little accompanying hue and cry. His jail cell in Kentville became as much a watering hole for reporters as its doppelgänger in Digby.

The temporary change of scenery had little effect on the prisoner, one cell being as good as any other. The original Kentville jail and courthouse were built adjacent to the railway tracks on Cornwallis Street in 1828. A fire gutted the structure in 1849 and the centre of Kentville's legal world was hastily relocated to two wooden structures just south of the old site — one building serving as the courthouse, the other as the jail in which

Wheeler now found himself. In the decade that followed the Wheeler debacle, Kentville would build itself a towering courthouse, a beautiful brick temple of jurisprudence in the heart of the town. For now, however, the trial of the century was relegated to the drafty wooden barns by the tracks, serviceable if somewhat underwhelming.

For all the media hype, the trial of Peter Wheeler began with a whimper. Despite Wallace Purdy and his highly touted examination of February last, it still fell to Justice Townshend and the prosecutor to empanel a grand jury to do what had yet to be done: issue a formal indictment of Peter Wheeler. On June 9, the jury, duly sworn and seated, heard the same evidence from the same two dozen witnesses who had testified at both Lovett's inquest and Purdy's exam. Witness followed witness, nose to tail, as the hearing never strayed from its well-worn path. For many of the witnesses — particularly Bernard Parker, who had now testified no fewer than five times including recalls to the stand — their statements had become rote. While the case as a whole remained the biggest story in the Maritimes, the seemingly endless slog toward justice had tarnished much of its initial lustre.

As for the press, having already printed each witness's testimony on at least one prior occasion, they gave this particular exercise in jurisprudence a very wide berth. The *Bridgetown Monitor* — one of the few tabloids to report on the grand jury — allotted the proceedings a scant two column inches, buried in the back pages alongside recipes and advertisements touting cures for ladies' nervous disorders.[1] The only paper to carry news of the resulting indictment was the one it was printed on.

With Peter Wheeler finally and formally charged with the murder of Annie Kempton, the legal treading of water came to an end. His day of reckoning was scheduled for June 26, 1896. To accommodate the anticipated crowds of curious onlookers, Townshend ordered a belated start of ten a.m.

A list of potential trial jurors was prepared, and in due course, the twelve men who would decide Wheeler's fate were chosen "without much

Kentville, Nova Scotia, circa 1900. The jail and courthouse
are the white structures facing one another on the far left.

difficulty, only a few on the panel being challenged."[2] David Noth was
named as foreman, a task that normally carried a fair amount of record
keeping. Fortunately for Noth, Judge Townshend had imported from
Halifax his favoured court clerk, W.B. Wallace, to document the proceedings and Noth's duties were sharply curtailed and largely ceremonial.

As the appointed hour approached on the overcast morning of June
26, Townshend's crowd predictions proved spot-on. The gallery was filled
beyond capacity, leaving hundreds on the doorstep craning to catch a
glimpse of the accused. Teams had laboured since dawn transporting
spectators from across the province. Horse-drawn carriages strained
through the rain-soaked ruts, only to discharge their irate cargo in front
of an already filled courthouse. Even witnesses and key players had to
fight their way to the door and plead their case for admission. Bailiffs
struggled to discern the legitimate from the fraudulent as hucksters tried
every trick in the book to gain entry to the day's spectacle.

A significant portion of the courthouse gallery was reserved for the gentlemen of the press corps, a special concession that caused no end of grumbling among the unwashed masses left languishing on the roadway. That reporters could come and go at their leisure, secure in the knowledge that their premium seating awaited their eventual return, did not sit well with the hordes relegated to the great outdoors. All major news agencies were on hand, represented by stringers whose accounts found their way into every paper in their syndicate; some were even poached and plagiarized by those journals that could not afford to send a correspondent.

As the clock struck ten, the parties assembled. Barristers Harrington, Wickwire, and Copp appeared for the Crown; Wheeler's interests were represented, as always, by Mr. Henry Dwight Ruggles,[3] with an able assist from a local lawyer named T.R. Robertson. Peter Wheeler was escorted into the court by the Harris brothers who were, in turn, flanked by an excessive number of constables from the Kentville area. Despite his shackles, Wheeler appeared poised, calm, and even a little hopeful.

Following some preliminary comments from the bench, Mr. H. Wickwire rose and approached the jury. Wickwire was a master orator with a commanding courtroom presence. He could lull jurors and spectators alike with his dulcet tones, only to send them reeling as he thundered home some particularly salient point. His opening remarks for the prosecution, clocking in at just over an hour, seemed to flit by in the blink of an eye, so entranced were those in his congregation.

Wickwire opened on familiar territory. He summarized the well-ingrained testimony from the inquest, Purdy's examination, and the grand jury hearing. The prosecutor was an alchemist, deftly transforming the intangible into ineluctable facts in a conjurer's trick that mesmerized as surely as it deceived. He then claimed that he did not wish to dwell on testimony widely perceived as old hat and made a promise, swearing an oath before those assembled, that the Crown had new and compelling evidence that would, once and for all, prove beyond any shadow of a doubt that Peter Wheeler had murdered Annie Kempton. Without tipping his hand, Wickwire alluded to the bountiful physical evidence, the subject of so many of Detective Power's press interviews. The prosecutor would say only that, after months of endless baiting, the forensic clues would finally be revealed. On that tantalizing note, Wickwire took his seat and called Mr. Stanley Rice to the stand.

In spite of Wickwire's troth, those seeking this new and irrefutable evidence were in for a very long wait. The trial proceeded much along the same lines as all the prior hearings. The same witnesses rose and regurgitated the same testimony as before. The press, comfortable in their secured courtroom perch, refrained from revisiting each witness's statement, summarizing each repeat performance with the benign disclaimer: "nothing specifically new was elicited."[4]

Until the new material was released, the press pack had no interest in dancing to the classics. Instead, they dedicated their front-page columns to tiresome harangues on Wheeler's every sigh and twitch. Although body language analysis would not come into vogue for almost a century, it did not stop the assembled press corps from laying claim to proficiency in the nascent art: "the prisoner manifested a great deal of attention as Mr. Wickwire referred to the new evidence to be produced. Subsequently, as the evidence of Mr. Rice was given, he seemed quite unconcerned."[5] Like his friends in the media, it seems Wheeler was only interested in fresh meat.

As the vigil for new evidence extended into its second day, the press amused themselves with a ceaseless dissection of the defence team's approach. Few doubted that Ruggles possessed the legal acumen to mount a proactive defence, yet he opted for a strictly reactionary strategy, a ploy that outraged Canada's national voice, the *Globe*.[6] Ruggles's cautionary gambit was not well received. On cross-examination, he seemed surprisingly passive, often squandering his opportunity by simply having the witness clarify some inconsequential point. It may have been overcompensation to the presiding justice, who admonished Ruggles to rein in his normally pugnacious approach to the law. Reports from the first day of trial painted the defence as ineffectual and outmatched. Vanquished by the media, Ruggles withdrew to lick his wounds and ponder the alternatives.

It was, in the end, all for naught. The trial's opening days held no surprises and few highlights, save for those manufactured by a listless press gaggle. All eyes were fixed to the horizon, desperate for their first glimpse of the trial's apogee: the appearance of Detective Nick Power.

twenty-seven

Detective Power
Takes the Stand

As the unmistakable hefty frame of Detective Power moved through the Kentville courthouse, admiring murmurs rippled through the crowd in his wake. So great was the anticipation of his testimony that the normally apathetic press gallery was filled to capacity, keening forward at full attention. It was the watershed moment of the trial, although not for the reasons many thought. In retrospect, Power's appearance was the instant in which the prosecution of Peter Wheeler truly became the persecution of Peter Wheeler.

What gave Power's evidence such gravitas was that it carried the weight of a burgeoning new field of police work: the forensic sciences. It was a startlingly modern avenue ripe with potential, a highly technical discipline that would one day revolutionize criminal investigations. Unfortunately for Peter Wheeler, that day was still decades off. As Power took the stand, he was borne aloft solely by the promise and the hype.

This being the Victorian era, such ethereal supports proved sufficient. Jurors, judges, and lawyers alike had yet to witness the full power and emotional resonance engendered by the scientific analysis of physical evidence. Its very "newness" made forensic material so compelling. The hallmark of the age was innovation and technological advancement; science, engineering, and medicine had all grown by astronomical leaps and bounds in the past decades. Each new gadget, invention, or discovery was heralded as a cutting-edge breakthrough, a modern-day marvel that would change life as the Victorians knew it.

Embedded in this industrial revolution was the public expectation that anything driven by scientific inquiry was inherently good, unquestionably reliable, and absolutely correct. Such naïveté provided the perfect breeding ground for a wave of medical quackery, in which any device powered by the newly introduced phenomenon of electricity could boast miraculous curative properties for everything from dandruff to hysteria and find a receptive and lucrative market.

This widespread predisposition toward all things scientific spilled over into the courtroom. If medicine and engineering were experiencing such an unprecedented renaissance, why not policing? The pump was primed; all Power needed to do was throw the switch.

The public's willingness to accept scientific advancement without question was aided and abetted by the full throttle media campaign that portrayed Power as a master sleuth. Accounts of his deductive tours de force were almost daily occurrences in the Maritime press. The coupling of Canada's premier investigative mind with the latest in scientific innovation proved too intoxicating a combination to be ignored; every news outlet dispatched a representative to capture the combustible mix for their readers and in prose that enthralled even those with the most fallow imaginations. Through luck if not volition, the Kentville courthouse had become ground zero for the forensic sciences in Canada.

Time past and time present collided in the witness dock, coalescing in a veteran detective brandishing the latest weapon in the fight against crime. Dressed to impress in his finest regalia — a curious blend of gentleman's suiting accented with pseudo-military embellishments — Power looked more like the dictator of a banana republic than a police officer. As always, he spoke in the stentorian tones of someone long accustomed to being obeyed, a formidable presence who acquitted himself with equanimity in times of peril and in times of peace.

Once sworn in, the detective began with a general accounting of the case to date. He had arrived in Bear River in the late morning of Wednesday, January 29, having been personally summoned by the Solicitor General.

Immediately upon disembarking from his train, Power met with J.M. Owen, the acting prosecutor for Annapolis County. "After getting some points to work upon,"[1] Power began his investigation.

Based solely on his consultation with the prosecutor, Power was already of the mindset that Wheeler was the killer. Just the day before, the coroner's inquest had exposed Peter's supposed machinations to get the poor girl alone. The most pressing issue that remained was figuring out when the dastardly act was done. According to Power's own testimony, "it appeared to the detective, after hearing the numerous theories, that if she was killed by Wheeler, the atrocious crime must have been committed between the hours of 5 and 6 o'clock on Monday evening, as it was shown clearly that he was seen going in the direction of the house about that time."[2] By advocating such a timeline, Power had committed one of the cardinal sins of police work: bending the facts to fit the theory, rather than generating a theory based on facts.

To support this time frame, Power offered a number of observations. Dr. Ellison may have had scientific rigour on his side, but Power had his own triad of evidence. First, there was the matter of the unmilked cow. Had Annie survived until its usual milking time (6:00 p.m.), Power argued the cow would have not produced so much milk the next day. Second, there was the issue of the beans. The detective claimed he had found a dish of beans set in the oven, as though Annie were warming them for a dinner she tragically did not live to enjoy.[3] That the beans were more likely leftovers from her evening meal, rather than an untouched dinner, was a scenario never presented. Finally, there were the tissue paper flowers. In his statement to the coroner, Wheeler said that when he spoke with Annie near her house at five o'clock, she was planning on making paper flowers for a party being held in town that evening. This corroborated the testimony of a shop owner — William Rice — who had sold her the tissue paper at around four that afternoon. Power, however, noted that there were no flowers present and the package of tissue paper sat unopened in the parlour, another indication Annie was dead by sunset. In the high-stakes poker game that was Annie's time of death, Power saw the coroner's Mortis sisters and raised him a cow, some tissue paper, and a hill of beans.

A number of compelling points further contradicted the detective's theory of the crime. To begin, Annie was found in her nightclothes, wearing a red wrapper or housecoat, suggesting it was much later in the evening when the murder took place. This notion gains credence from the fact that Annie's bed was unmade and appeared to have been recently slept in, as if she were awakened in the night by her assailant. There was also the testimony of Walter Comeau (who had seen Annie alive at 7:00 p.m.) and Hardy Benson (who had seen a light come on as he and Wheeler left the Kempton house), indicating Annie was still alive until at least 8:00 p.m. Another witness — John Brooks — had seen the blinds open and a lamp burning in the Kempton house at eleven that night. Finally, there was the testimony of Dr. Ellison, whose autopsy revealed Annie's time of death to be the wee hours of Tuesday morning.

The troublesome timeline had plagued Power from the very start, but under oath he stuck to his guns, arguing adamantly that the crime had occurred between 5:00 p.m. and 6:00 p.m. Power's obstinacy balanced on a single point: he could only place Peter Wheeler alone near the Kempton home at that time and no other. To concede the crime occurred at a later hour would be to concede Wheeler was not the killer.

Unwilling to make such concessions, Power skilfully manoeuvred the line of questioning to a more agreeable topic: himself. The detective's celebrity was built on what he considered to be his trademark — his savant-like ability to unearth and interpret the physical evidence of a crime scene. In his humble opinion, Power told the court, he had a way with clues. He could see what others missed or dismissed as insignificant. If there was a scrap of evidence, no matter how trivial or concealed, Power would sniff it out and discern its true meaning. To hear him tell it, the truth lay dormant at every crime scene, waiting for someone with the proper skills (presumably Power) to seek it out. Initially, evidence might be misinterpreted but never for long and never by him. In short, the court simply needed to trust in Power and his abilities, without question or equivocation.

The detective had executed a near-perfect courtroom burlesque, simultaneously sidestepping the holes in the case while unabashedly blowing his own horn, and he nimbly set the stage for his big finish. Since his arrival in Bear River, Power had baited the press with tantalizing hints, thinly veiled allusions to all the incontrovertible proof that would seal Wheeler's fate. Eager to dispense with the treacherous quagmire that was the timeline, Power dove headfirst into a recitation of what the press had dubbed "his perfect chain of evidence."[4]

The first link in this unalloyed chain was the pesky matter of those footprints in the snow, infamously introduced at the coroner's inquest by Bernard Parker. Parker had reiterated his interpretations for Purdy and again for the grand jury, yet it fell to Power to link those snowbound tracks directly to the accused.

There were certainly obstacles to overcome. Omer Rice, a neighbour of the Kemptons and the first on the scene after Wheeler discovered the body, testified: "I think Mr. Kempton wears larrigans.... [A] great many people in that section of the country wear larrigans in the winter time and one larrigan track looks just like another."[5] Rice made some valid points—larrigans were ubiquitous and indistinguishable—and Detective Power responded the way he always did: through misdirection and showmanship.

When he took Wheeler into custody, Power seized his clothing and his winter boots—a pair of larrigans. The detective then conducted an experiment of his own design to test whether Wheeler's boots had made the tracks in the snow behind the Kemptons' pig barn. Power took the larrigans behind the barn, put them on his gloved hands and pushed them into the tracks, declaring: "they fitted the marks perfectly in length and breadth."[6] Queried by the defence, Power was forced to admit that he made the comparison several days after the murder, and in the interim, it had snowed several times. Smug as a well-fed house cat, Power explained that he overcame such difficulties by using a broom to sweep away the newer snow, exposing the older prints beneath.

It is at this point that the heads of modern-day crime scene analysts explode. Despite Power's bravado, there was nothing about his so-called experiment that was scientifically valid or methodologically sound.

Snow is an inherently unstable medium. It compacts and morphs over time and in response to oscillating temperature, gusting winds, or exposure to sunlight. In the sixty-plus hours between the crime and Power's test, the prints were irrevocably altered. Furthermore, the additional snowfalls could not simply be swept away with a broom, an approach guaranteed to result in more damage than benefit to the prints' survival. Finally, there is the feasibility of the test itself. Larrigans are soft-soled shoes, which readily conform to the appendages they contain. That Power thought his hands were comparable to Wheeler's feet showed a serious lapse of judgment. It also goes without saying that a soft-soled moccasin, worn on a hand, could easily be made to fit into a malleable substrate such as snow, which immediately conforms to any object pressed into it. Power's test proved only that snow is a highly accommodating medium and that some juries will believe anything couched in the guise of science.

Power had pushed a pliant shoe into soft snow and declared it a match, and in so doing had both condemned Wheeler and set the development of the forensic sciences back several decades in the process. Having single-handedly tarnished the as-yet-invalidated science of footprint comparison, Power then set his sights on blood spatter analysis.

When Power seized Wheeler's boots, he also took possession of the prisoner's coat, pants, and shirt. As Wheeler relinquished his clothes, he mentioned there might be blood on some of the pieces, an artifact of his recent hunting expeditions. He also mentioned that his favoured quarries were rabbit and fowl. Power scoured the clothing and found what he thought were bloodstains on one pant leg and on the heel of a sock. The eagle-eyed detective also saw evidence that Wheeler had tried to wash away the blood.

In a rare moment of humility, Power acknowledged during this testimony that differentiating human from animal blood exceeded his normally boundless abilities. Seeking an expert opinion, the detective had submitted the pants and sock to an analyst in the Halifax PD, a man by the name of MacIntyre, who confirmed Power's suspicion that blood was present on the pants but was unable to say definitively whether it was human. The analyst recommended a local doctor with training in microscopy who might be able to offer a more definitive conclusion. After obtaining an order from the Attorney General to conduct further testing, Power took the soiled items to Dr. Jacques in Halifax. The detective then told the court that he would leave it to the good doctor to explain his findings. The prosecution rested the witness, opening Power to cross-examination.

Defence attorney Henry Ruggles battled valiantly to find the chinks in the detective's armour, working Power like a prizefighter unable to land the knockout blow. Ruggles did get Power to admit that he had not made any notes at the crime scene and had failed to note the condition of the room and the location of key pieces of evidence. Actually, Power had spent very little time at the scene itself. The detective arrived in Bear River more than thirty hours after Annie's body was first discovered, by which time the scene had been highly contaminated by family, friends, and the local police. Power's primary source of information regarding the scene was Charles Dunn, the detective from the Amherst agency, who was among the first to view the body. When Power arrived, Dunn briefed him on the scene, handed over his meagre investigative notes, and took his leave of Bear River and any further involvement in the case.

Ruggles also chipped away at the detective's credibility by confronting him with inconsistencies in his testimony. When asked about the bloody handprints at the scene, specifically a bloody fingerprint on the spoon in the half-eaten jar of preserves near the body, the detective contradicted his prior statements to the press around the time of Lovett's inquest. When Ruggles pointed out Power's vacillation, the supersleuth conceded he "did not remember whether he swore at the inquest as to finger marks on the spoon."[7]

Ruggles's hawkish efforts to refute Power's testimony ultimately failed. Dwight was hampered by his own inexperience with forensic science and bested by a nemesis convinced of his own infallibility. Onlookers saw Ruggles's questions as nitpicking scurrilous attempts to discredit a highly decorated officer of the law. No one outside the defence table seemed at all troubled by Power's slipshod police work, questionable recall of key events, or poor documentation of the evidence. Even if Power had much of the science wrong, it was still science, he was still Detective Power, and all in attendance knew in their hearts that Wheeler was guilty. Ruggles's blustering struck the crowd as an exercise in futility.

The defence counsel — having been frozen out of Lovett's inquest and the grand jury hearing and marginalized during Purdy's folly — desperately wanted to have its day in court. The problem was the forensic science, a discipline about which Ruggles knew nothing. Detective Power knew even less, but his elephantine ego prevented him from admitting as much. In fairness to both men, few in Canada had any background in forensic investigations, but thanks to an American satirist by the name of Mark Twain, virtually everyone knew a little something about one cutting-edge forensic technique: fingerprints.

twenty-eight

The Myth of Fingerprints

As Nicholas Power held court in a cavernous wooden shed in Kentville, the art and science of fingerprint analysis had passed through its playful infancy and entered its awkward adolescent phase. The potential of fingerprints in criminal investigations was widely recognized but poorly understood, and the application of the technique in any particular case was still very much a matter of trial and error.

The precedents were there. In 1879 police in Argentina used fingerprint analysis to link a bloody thumbprint found on the door of a crime scene to the accused murderer, forever changing the nature of criminal investigation.[1] Eyewitness testimony — long recognized as the least reliable form of evidence — was no longer the only weapon in the prosecutor's arsenal. Thanks to fingerprints, a crime did not need to be seen in order to be solved.

One year after the Argentines opened the door to a brave new scientific world, Dr. Henry Faulds published the first scholarly work in the burgeoning field of dermatoglyphics, postulating the use of fingerprints as a means of both identifying felons and connecting the perpetrator to a crime scene.[2] Building on Faulds's ground-breaking work, academics used research and anecdotal evidence to bolster the fledgling science of fingerprinting. Advances came fast and furious, and in 1908 Sir Wilfrid Laurier signed Order-in-Council PC 1614, making fingerprints the official method of identification in Canadian criminal proceedings.

While the credit for bringing fingerprints to the courtroom goes to Argentina, Mark Twain deserves kudos for introducing fingerprints to the masses. In 1893 *The Century* magazine began serializing the adventures of Pudd'nhead Wilson, the latest creation by the venerable humorist. In one of his earliest incarnations, Wilson — a small-town lawyer dismissed by his neighbours as a simpleton — solved a troublesome crime through the use of his strange hobby: the collection and analysis of fingerprints. Although entirely a work of fiction, the serial and subsequent novel highlighted the real-world potential of fingerprints to connect criminals to their crimes. Wildly popular in its day, *Pudd'nhead Wilson* offered the general public its first tantalizing glimpse into the world of forensic science.

Whether or not he was an aficionado of Twain's colourful creation, Nicholas Power understood the probative value of fingerprints in criminal investigations — the detective had used fingerprints before. Contemporaneous with the Wheeler case, Power was embroiled in another very high-profile murder investigation, one that would take him all the way to the United States Supreme Court.

❰

On July 21, 1896, an American merchant ship, the *Herbert E. Fuller,* docked in Halifax. Its crew told a horrific tale as they staggered ashore. While bounding on the high seas, the vessel's captain Charles Nash, his wife Laura, and the second mate, August Blomberg, were viciously hacked to death with an axe. Suspicion quickly fell on a young shipmate, known to his fellows as Charlie Brown. His real name was Justus Leopold Westerberg and he became the prime suspect when he was seen changing clothes immediately after the murders. Another ensign, Thomas Bram, ordered Westerberg to be shackled and a search of the ship soon uncovered a bloody axe, presumably the murder weapon. Bram, holding the axe aloft, asked if he should throw it overboard. Another crew member — who feared the actions of a now-mutinous crew and thought the axe might once again be used as a weapon — agreed it should be tossed. In a lapse of judgment that would come back to haunt him, Bram threw the axe over the side.

As the story spread through town, the Halifax police came on board to take Westerberg into custody. Leading the investigation was none other than Nicholas Power. The detective took the accused into his office to interrogate him and, oh, what a story Westerberg had to tell. As is a sailor's want, his tale grew larger with each minute he spent ashore. By the time the interview drew to a close, Westerberg had somehow convinced Power he was innocent and that Bram was the murderer. Despite Westerberg's questionable credibility as a witness, Power believed his version of events. What ultimately convinced the detective was that Bram had disposed of the murder weapon, "which of course might have borne fingerprints."[3]

☾

The saga of the ill-fated *Herbert E. Fuller* begs an obvious question: if Power clearly understood the value of fingerprints, why did he not have the prints from the Kempton murder scene analyzed and compared with Wheeler's prints? The answer, at least according to Power, was that there were no fingerprints. When Ruggles inquired about prints on the stand, Power denied that any were present at the scene. When defence counsel reminded him of his statements describing bloody handprints and fingerprints visible to the naked eye, Power suddenly could not recall ever mentioning such prints.

Despite Power's timely memory lapse, multiple references to bloody and latent fingerprints at the Kempton house appear in the court records. Omer Rice testified to seeing bloody fingermarks all over the house, most notably on the bloody spoon, which he identified in court as it was entered into evidence.[4] The well-seasoned Mr. Payne of the *Saint John Daily Sun* also noted many bloody prints during his walk-through of the crime scene. In addition, descriptions of the fingerprints can be found in countless other media reports, which, it bears noting, inevitably cited Power as their source. Prints were visible on the two knives recovered near the body and on the spoon from the preserves — items that stood as silent witnesses in the courtroom, mere feet from Power as he denied their existence — as well as a pair of bloody handprints on the window. The evidence was plentiful, rendered in sharp relief in the victim's own blood. It does not get any easier than that for crime scene analysts, yet for reasons known only to Nick Power, he dismissed the prints as either non-existent or inconsequential.

Power's petulant stance raises two disturbing possibilities. The first is that the prints were never collected or tested, making Power grossly negligent in his examination of the crime scene. Under oath, he did admit he had not taken notes or adequately documented the room in which Annie was killed. It therefore stands to reason that he was equally negligent in preserving or documenting the fingerprints, leaving him nothing to compare against Wheeler's prints. The second and far more troubling option is that prints were tested but that no one liked the results. Power might well have collected the prints and compared them against Wheeler's, only to discover the test exonerated the accused. Had the prints confirmed Wheeler's guilt, there was no question the evidence would have been introduced at trial. Since Power had already publicly proclaimed Peter to be the killer on numerous occasions, it would have been professionally devastating for the detective to admit his mistake at so late a juncture in the investigation. In the alternative, it is conceivable he chose to bury any evidence that might have cleared Wheeler's name.

So which of these two men did Nicholas Power want to be? The incompetent investigator who failed to gather evidence or the conniving liar who destroyed exculpatory evidence? In the end, Power chose "none of the above." He took advantage of Ruggles's unfamiliarity with the still-developing science of fingerprints and simply denied their very existence. His lackadaisical approach to crime scene documentation had actually paid off. It was now simply a matter of his word against... well, his own prior words, and as always, "Detective Power is on top."[5]

twenty-nine

Power, in Hindsight

History is the view from the cheap seats. Distance from the action provides a unique perspective; one can recognize the plays and appreciate the totality of certain events.

So it is with the long and storied career of Detective Nicholas Power — chronological distance helps identify the patterns woven into his life. The phenomenon that was Nick Power only comes into focus in the cold clinical light of hindsight. In the heat of the moment, the line between charismatic leader and demagogue was readily blurred. It is with time and its travelling companion, detachment, that the distinction becomes clear. By the time Power was dispatched from New Glasgow to Bear River in 1896, his already legendary status obliterated any hope of objectivity. Perspective was warped by the sheer gravitational force of the mythology that had enveloped this seemingly humble public servant of the Halifax PD. It is only by escaping his orbit that the real measure of the man becomes evident.

Although the affliction would not be recognized for over a century, Power unquestionably suffered from "the Diana Syndrome" — those who live by the media shall surely perish by it. Power was a virtuoso at manipulating the press, much like the princess who perfected the art in the decades that followed. At the detective's behest, each of his cases was tried in the court of public opinion long before they saw the inside of a courtroom, and like Diana in her heyday, the media spotlight always seemed to catch Power's good side.

Nick Power's persona demanded superlatives: every crime he cracked was the most heinous; every criminal he caught was the most dastardly scapegrace the world had ever known. No investigation was ever simple, and at every turn, Detective Power was the lone man able to solve the unsolvable.

The very model of a modern police maverick, it was not at all surprising that Power welcomed, ánd indeed encouraged, comparisons between himself and the man he considered his professional equal: Sherlock Holmes. He openly styled himself after Sir Arthur Conan Doyle's fictional detective, eschewing humdrum investigative legwork for the cunning and cerebral solution to a crime. Pounding the pavement served little purpose in the Powerian scheme of things. The detective considered himself the intellectual superior of any criminal and he bested them all using his wits, not his mettle. Unearthing that one telltale clue was not a question of brawn but of mental acuity. And, like Holmes, there was no case Power could not solve. Ever.

The perfection of Power's arrest record should have triggered suspicion among his contemporaries. Without fail, he got his man, often well before he had the evidence to back it up. Indeed, another peculiarity of Power's record was that he tended to make arrests early, based solely on his own hunches or highly attuned read of the suspect's character. Once the supposed perpetrator was behind bars, only then would the missing pieces of the puzzle magically come to light. That such evidence always inculpated the suspect should have raised red flags for Power's colleagues or superiors, yet it appears all were entranced by the detective's uncanny acumen. Certainly the press was loath to question Nick's methods, choosing instead to call attention to his incomparable batting average. They were content marvelling over his victories and extolling the exploits of Canada's real-life Sherlock Holmes. As long as he sold newspapers, the press would let Power get away with murder.

Had any of his contemporaries taken a closer look, they would have seen a number of troubling trends in how the detective handled his investigations. The first was his marked tendency to target suspects of colour. At a time when overt racism was rampant through all aspects of society, Power was a vanguard of the trend.

One of the most egregious examples of Power's racial bias was the case of the Sydney Burglar. In the fall of 1903, Cape Breton's capital was plagued by a string of robberies targeting highly successful local businesses. Chief McEachren, head of the city's police force, called in Power to work his usual magic. With no leads to go on, Power quickly set his sights on a well-known black boxer named "Kid" Seeley, although the detective never revealed what it was about the boxer that made his nose twitch.

Power suspected Seeley may have also been responsible for a series of burglaries in Halifax, 270 miles to the southwest. Based on nothing but a hunch, Power told Chief McEachren to go to the last victim — a jeweller named White — and have the merchant file a complaint naming Seeley as the perpetrator. Power then used the complaint to arrest the boxer. It was only after the Kid was in chains that Power proceeded to search for evidence implicating him.

It was not just the colour of Seeley's skin that earned him Power's wrath, it was his lifestyle. Seeley had taken up with a white woman living on North Street. On yet another of his trademark hunches, Power searched her home, where he discovered a collection of jewellery. He also found a large axe, the type used by butchers to cleave carcasses, and immediately saw a connection. Power told reporters it was clear Seeley had taken the axe from another of his victims — a high-street butcher — for the purpose of defending himself. The detective argued that, were Seeley to be stopped and questioned by police as he made his getaway, the Kid would not have hesitated to cleave open a copper's skull. The question of why a world-class boxer needed an axe against an unarmed bobby was left unanswered. It was a flimsy argument, emblematic of Power's weak and circumstantial case, but after a fortnight of media saturation, few doubted the black boxer was guilty.

In another notorious case — the previously described triple murder aboard the US merchant ship *Herbert E. Fuller* — Power quite literally had a choice between a white suspect, Justus Westerberg, and a black suspect, Thomas Bram. Actually, he had a ship of men to choose from but Power became convinced that one of the two men had murdered their captain and two others. Before any of the facts of the case were known or any evidence was seized, Power focused on the black suspect. Worse still, his case against Bram rested solely on the testimony of the white suspect, Westerberg, who had spent much of the journey in chains, accused of the murders himself. The case, *Bram v. United States*, eventually made its way to the United States Supreme Court, where Power finally received a much-deserved comeuppance. The detective's highly questionable investigation has since become an oft-cited precedent for wrongful conviction.

Were racism Power's only shortcoming, it would be tempting to chalk it up as an artifact of the times. However, Detective Nicholas Power also had the unfortunate habit of disregarding any rule, regulation, or ethical standard that did not suit him. For instance, Power always conducted his interviews without witnesses, leaving any discord over what transpired in the legal quagmire of "he said/he said." His flagrant disdain for the rights of prisoners was evident in a significant number of cases, including the aforementioned *Bram v. United States*. The Supreme Court ruled that Power's overly aggressive style of interrogating the suspect had so flagrantly violated the prisoner's civil rights the case was overturned.

It was not the first or last time Power's conduct resulted in overturned verdicts. In 1905 Nick Power was asked to investigate the murder of a six-year-old child in Plympton, Nova Scotia. Power incessantly grilled the woman accused of the crime but failed to warn her that anything she said could be used against her. Although Power's testimony was admitted at trial, the conviction was later overturned by the provincial Supreme Court, citing Power's actions as the cause.

Power's blatant contempt for rules and regulations even led to his suspension from the Halifax Police Force in the spring of 1889. On paper, the reason for the suspension was his refusal to clarify a number of receipts he had submitted for "work-related expenses." More politic motivations for the suspension have since been floated, including jealousy among his fellow officers and superiors over the media's obsessive homage to Power. Try as they might, Power's brothers in blue could never seem to capture the ardour or even the attention of the press gaggle. Regardless of who participated in any particular investigation, it was always Power's name in the headline, relegating his colleagues to second-billing.

Latent animosity toward the grandstanding detective also scuttled his first bid to serve as police chief. Just four years after his suspension, Power was one of a handful of men who applied for the post, the first chiefdom in the force's history. Among the incentives for becoming the city's top cop was an annual salary of $1,000, with a guaranteed raise of $100 a year to a maximum of $1,300. The pay for a beat cop was $600, while detectives took home $800 a year, so the bump in salary was a tempting carrot. More importantly, the title bestowed prestige, honour, and considerable power to the man anointed. The names of the final four candidates were presented to the city council and a straw ballot was held, eliminating two men from further consideration. On the third and final ballot, Power received only two out of seventeen possible votes. The only other man left standing, John O'Sullivan, was named the first chief of police for Halifax, a job he held for the next twelve years.

Power was gutted by his defeat. He stewed over the slight, growing increasingly convinced he was the victim of jealousy and political machinations. In 1905, as O'Sullivan was set to retire, Power again applied for the top spot and this time he emerged victorious. He became the second chief of police in May 1906, only to retire one year later.

It would not be a banner year. Long accustomed to having his ears scratched by the media, Chief Power got his first taste of negative press when he failed to arrest George Stanley, a.k.a. John Ryan, for a series of thefts in Halifax. Immediately after being released from police custody, Stanley fled to Hants County, where he brutally murdered a man. Lambasted in the media, Power simply absolved himself of all responsibility, citing the classic legal argument of the "veil of ignorance": "the chief reminded his critics that he could not have known beforehand that this thug could have been capable of such a dastardly act."[1] That the point of law enforcement is to stop criminals before their deeds escalate seemed lost on the newly minted and petulant chief.

The only discernible impact Power's brief reign had on the department was as superficial as it was benign. Upon taking office, Power declared that he wanted "to make his men among the best dressed in America."[2] Gone were the days of one suit per year. Power used his considerable media savvy to ensure that the rollout of the new uniforms was front-page news. Under his tutelage, however, the clothes alone did not make the men. In what he considered his crowning achievement, Power also implemented a "service badge" system — a series of colour-coded emblems indicating the seniority of each officer. In classic Power fashion, the chief brooked no critique of the new system, arguing both sides against the middle:

> It will save the men from a lot of unjust criticism. Often an officer is criticized for not acting just up to the mark. A glance at his coat sleeve will at once show that he … is to a large extent inexperienced. Then again, remarks of a more or less derogatory nature are frequently passed about men on the force who are well advanced in years and people often ask why such men are on the force. Hereafter, when five or six badges appear on the sleeve of one of these men, it will be known that they have given the best part of their lives to the force, have grown gray in the service, are entitled to consideration and respect.[3]

It is telling that Power elected to address the problem of police apathy not through disciplinary action but with cosmetic changes. To Power's way of thinking, the bad cops were not the problem; rather, it was the public's lack of respect for them.

After a lacklustre year as chief, Nick Power retired from active duty.

In keeping with his oeuvre, he published his letter of resignation on the front page of the Halifax *Morning Herald* and the *Nova Scotian and Weekly Chronicle*.[4] The newspapers, in deference to their long-standing relationship with Power, printed his self-congratulatory treatise in its entirety.

Power's pension demands were also headline news. After only one year in office, he had the temerity to demand the same pension afforded his predecessor, O'Sullivan, who held the job for more than a decade. Power wanted four hundred dollars superannuation until his death, a small price to pay to rid the force of the increasingly troublesome Power, but it was a bill the Halifax PD ended up footing for the next thirty-two years.

Power did not go quietly into a blissful retirement. Like a high school football star endlessly reliving his glory days, Power did anything to maintain his death grip on the spotlight. Once a month, the one-time supersleuth invited his old press chums to his well-appointed home at 119 Dresden Row in Halifax. There, surrounded by his awards, commendations, and press clippings, he regaled the hapless correspondent with self-serving tales of his unequalled deductions and unparalleled crime-fighting abilities. Without exception, the story of how Power single-handedly saved the life of the future king was trotted out to remind the populace of his former éclat. The journalistic vestiges of these monthly pilgrimages appeared in the Halifax tabloids for the next three decades, rehashing the exploits of a long-decommissioned officer in perpetuity. On each occasion, Power happily sat for a formal portrait on the condition that the photo would accompany the article. Nicholas Power, always regal and nattily attired, entered his dotage still firmly ensconced in the public eye. Having risen from obscurity, Power had no intention of returning to it.

Power's insatiable need to be venerated, lauded, and immortalized reached its zenith in 1915, when the detective's ego trumped the will of a king. Edward VII, long a champion of those in uniform, wanted to find some way of honouring outstanding police officers who had distinguished themselves in the line of duty. In 1909 His Royal Highness introduced the King's Police Medal, commonly known as the KPM. Only fifty-two of the prestigious medals were ever awarded. In the historical roll call of acclaimed recipients, only one name appears with an asterisk: Nicholas Power.

The guidelines for KPM nominations were first published in the *London Gazette* on July 9, 1909. It took time for word of the award to reach Canada, but by 1912 the procedures for acclamation were in wide circulation. That year, in an unprecedented move, Power nominated himself for the medal. In a rambling six-page letter to the Secretary of State, Power outlined his illustrious career in terms that would make a narcissist blush. His application was summarily denied.

Undaunted (and with more than a hint of righteous indignation), Power wrote again to the Secretary, demanding to know why. The first response politely informed Power that he was ineligible for the award as it was created several years after he had retired from active service. Unfazed by a petty technicality, Power simply reapplied the next year, reminded the Secretary of his decades of selfless service to king and country. He was again rejected. This time, the committee told Power that his application was denied because he had self-nominated. With typical bureaucratic restraint and civility, he was reminded that the award was intended as a community's recognition of their deserving brethren and not as a vanity exercise for those who felt underappreciated.

Any nuance and subtlety on the Secretary's part were wasted on Power. He applied yet again and this time he played his ace in the hole. In his latest petition, Power reminded the selection committee how he had foiled the plot to assassinate the future king, arguing that it was "probably the most important arrest made in Canada in the past forty years"[5] and that his quick thinking had "save[d] the life of his present Majesty King George."[6]

After yet another rejection, Power sent a final letter on June 17, 1914, stating outright that if the king were queried, "His Majesty would not hesitate to grant me the King's Police Medal for my long service."[7] Sensing a losing battle, the Secretary picked the hill he wanted to die on and

Detective Nicholas Power, photographed in his
Halifax home on his ninety-first birthday.

Power's name was grudgingly added to the honorees for 1915. The lukewarm
response sent a clear message that the honour was bestowed simply to
silence Power. Forever asterisked as the lone self-nominated recipient in
the history of the KPM, Power had browbeaten a king into a final leaden
moment of glory.

Nicholas Power died in his bed in the house on Dresden Row on
Sunday, October 2, 1938. He was ninety-six years old. It would have no
doubt delighted him to know that his death was eulogized in every paper
in the province. Lauded as "the most colorful police figure Canada has
ever produced,"[8] Power commanded the headlines one last time.

With the benefit of hindsight, Nicholas Power emerges as a man driven by an unquenchable thirst for admiration, respect, and accolades. Behind the carefully crafted persona of a supersleuth lay a shallow, callow manipulator who bent the rules to serve his own purposes. In retrospect, his near-perfect arrest record seems more suspect than laudable. His unshakable belief in his own infallibility led him to make countless questionable arrests, all tinged with the misguided certainty that his hunches were somehow tangible evidence. Too autocratic to be objective and too arrogant to be credible, Power's much-touted powers of deduction were pure myth, a media-spawned fabrication that gained traction through sheer repetition.

All of Power's patent faults and foibles were manifest in the case of Peter Wheeler: the rush to judgment and arrest; the targeting of a dark-skinned suspect; the bending of rules regarding evidence and interrogation; as well as Power's long-standing practice of trying all cases in the media. Without fail, every new lead, suspicion, or scrap of evidence was leaked to the press. Those clues that refused to bend — most notably, the fingerprints — were summarily dismissed. At once corrupt and corrupting, Power may have been on top but history reveals that it was a vantage point annexed through deception and perfidy.

thirty

Bad Blood

Courtrooms attract lazy or questionable science in much the same way the hackneyed simile "like flies to honey" lures ham-fisted writers. Boffins of the lowest stripe gravitate toward the brilliant glow of the courthouse in hopes that its cleansing rays of sunlight, intended to disperse the darkness of ignorance, will somehow absolve them of their sins of scientific mediocrity and the blatant prostitution of their skills.

Detective Power's feeble efforts to link Wheeler's boots to some snowy impressions was just one such example of science gone horribly wrong, although such judgment comes through the benefit of hindsight. Power was all hat and no cattle but as the great detective made his case, those in the courthouse bought what he was selling, swayed not by the validity of the method but by the charismatic delivery of its purveyor.

The footprints were not the sole forensic evidence in the case of *Queen v. Wheeler*. There was also the matter of the blood, so copious at the scene yet somehow virtually non-existent on the defendant. When it came to the analysis of the blood evidence, Power spoke in broad yet persuasive strokes and found sanctuary in a syllogism masquerading as evidence: Annie's murder had been brutal and bloody, Wheeler had blood on his clothes, and therefore Wheeler was the killer of Annie Kempton. The argument sounded logical, particularly when delivered in Power's sonorous tones, dripping with conviction. The problem with syllogism is that the argument is only as strong as its weakest assumption, which in this instance was that the only potential source of blood was Annie Kempton.

Peter Wheeler had already provided the detective with two reasonable explanations as to why he had blood on his clothes. The first was that the blood was a by-product of a recent hunting trip. To prove this hypothesis, tests were needed to determine if the blood was human. The alternative explanation was that Peter got some of Annie's blood on him when he found her body. He admitted to having touched her when he placed her father's coat over her face and it is possible he transferred some of her blood onto his clothes at that time. Unfortunately, there was no test available in 1896 to corroborate this particular scenario. Furthermore, if the blood were human — and specifically Annie's — there was no way to tell when or how it had stained Wheeler's clothing.

Determining whether the blood came from Annie or from an animal was not exactly Power's bailiwick. His testimony served only to set the stage for the blood analyst who followed. Having whetted the audience's appetite for something new — and in particular, something scientific — Power left the more mundane technical aspects to an actual scientist, or at least someone with more claim to the title than Power: the whimsically named Dr. Hartley Spinney Jacques.

When the original blood analyst, Mr. McIntyre of the Halifax police services, was unable to adequately identify the stains on Wheeler's clothes, Power had taken them to Dr. Jacques for further testing. Reporters were quick to interpret this as a sign of Jacques's acclaim and experience; if the famous detective had such confidence in the doctor's abilities, they reasoned, surely he must be a renowned expert in his field. As was so often the case, the media's assumptions could not have been further from the mark.

On June 28, 1869, Dr. H.S. Jacques was called to the stand, giving the press, jurors, and spectators their first look at this celebrated scientist. He was, in a word, underwhelming. Nervous, unimposing, and soft-spoken, Jacques was far from the exalted silverback touted in the press. True, he was fifty-six years old — a time of life when most men had reached the height of their powers — but age had softened the line of his shoulders and chin. He came across as more caring than courageous or cutting edge.

In his early forties, Jacques had what might now be called a mid-life crisis. He headed for the City University of New York, where he took up the study of allopathic medicine, graduating in 1887.[1] The next year, he returned to his home in Nova Scotia and set up a surgical practice in Dartmouth. Technically still wet behind the ears, the good doctor had practised his particular brand of medicine for a mere eight years. Although Victorians revered physicians as a matter of course, his relative inexperience and meek persona threw the courtroom for a loop. No one knew quite what to make of the strange healer suddenly in their midst.

To his credit, Dr. Jacques displayed none of the misplaced cockiness commonly found in those overcompensating for a slim resumé. More studious than ambitious, Jacques was an awkward fit on the stand. He fumbled with his notes, needing most questions to be repeated, and he mumbled many of his answers. When asked about his qualifications, Jacques replied only that "he had taken a special course in microscopic work."[2]

Despite the doctor's rather stiff countenance, Wheeler sat transfixed and hare-eyed as Jacques unravelled his findings. According to one reporter, "the prisoner here changed his seat and leaned forward and listened very attentively"[3] as the blood analysis was presented. Wheeler's keen interest was understandable. However bumbling Jacques's testimony might be, his tests represented the only direct evidence the Crown had against Wheeler and his fate rested in the doctor's trembling hands.

Jacques grew more comfortable on the stand and he visibly relaxed as the questioning continued. Though a novice, Jacques was well trained, and before long, it became clear to those assembled that Power's faith in the scientist had solid foundations. Disquiet soon gave way to rote as Jacques described for the court the different tests he had conducted. As the allopath discussed his results, Wheeler was no longer the only one on the edge of his seat.

The first item of clothing Jacques examined was Wheeler's trousers. Contrary to Power's claims, the doctor had not found "any evidence of blood on them,"[4] nor had he identified any traces on Wheeler's vest. The bloody sock Power had described at length during press interviews appears to have been a figment of his imagination; it was never given to Jacques for testing and was never mentioned at trial.

To the delectation of the crowd, Jacques then produced Wheeler's coat. At long last there was something tangible for the spectators to sink their teeth into. Brandishing the coat high for all to see, Dr. Jacques called their attention to the locations of a number of small squares cut from the fabric. These squares, he explained, contained what he thought might be blood. Jacques had placed these samples under the microscope and examined them carefully. Most of the samples tested negative but two of the squares — cut from the area of the right shoulder — each contained one tiny drop of blood "the size of a pin head."[5]

A strange silence settled over the court. Chagrin was palpable everywhere, save for the defence table. The crowd now had it on good authority that there was blood on the coat but it amounted to two tiny specks on a shoulder, hardly the sanguinary drenching described by Power or expected from so bloody a crime scene. The prosecution, hoping to overcome this paucity of evidence through sheer repetition, asked the doctor to repeat his findings. In his loudest, clearest voice yet, Jacques "swore positively to the finding of two spots of blood."[6] On hearing it for a second time, the audience deflated like a rent balloon.

However poorly the declaration played in court, the media wanted the world to know the effect it had on the accused. According to the *Daily Echo*, "the prisoner's face now flushed and he placed his hand on his forehead, hiding his face."[7] In actuality, Peter had greeted the doctor's findings with joy, not angst. Wheeler had told Power there might be blood on his coat because he had a habit of slinging his trapped rabbits over his shoulder to carry them home. Jacques's testimony was far from a death knell for the defence; indeed, it was fast becoming a clear point in their favour.

Before releasing his witness, the Crown prosecutor asked a final seminal question: Were the blood spots human or animal? After the briefest of pauses, Jacques declared that he could not tell, unleashing another wave of disappointment through the Kentville courthouse. The prosecutor declared he had no more questions, having gained all he could from the shy scientist.

Ruggles most certainly had questions. Bounding from his seat, Wheeler's lawyer began firing at the blood analyst, a man two decades his senior. Why could the doctor not determine the source of the blood? he asked. Jacques claimed in response that "there was great similarity between human blood and that of a rabbit."[8] On this point, the doctor was entirely correct. Mammalian blood is morphologically consistent regardless of species. Had the blood been from a bird, such as the quail or partridge Wheeler sometimes hunted, the doctor should have been able to differentiate it from that of a human or rabbit. Avian blood contains nucleated red blood cells, unlike mammalian corpuscles which lack nuclei. With only standard microscopy at his disposal, Jacques had no valid method to correctly identify the source of the blood. Differentiating human from animal blood today requires either a DNA test or an antibody assay, two chemical tests that would not be developed until decades after the trial.

Despite being hamstrung by the technology of the era, Dr. Jacques's testimony was accurate, measured, and scientifically valid. Whatever he lacked in courtroom braggadocio, he more than made up for with integrity. His evidence may not have been the coup de grâce the prosecution had hoped for but the doctor acquitted himself with grace and honesty — qualities he carried throughout his relatively brief career. Dr. Jacques went on to practice medicine for another ten years, eventually becoming the revered doyen that all had expected that day in the Kentville courthouse.

❨

Reaction to the histological testimony was mixed, verging on schizophrenic. On the one hand, the very nature of the scientific evidence seemed incontrovertible. It was dispassionate, objective, and reasoned, offering exactly what the other witnesses could not, and therein lay the paradox. Dr. Jacques's even-handed tone and patient observations, as painstaking and precise as science demanded, had collided head-on with the visceral needs of the community. Following closely on the heels of the fervent tsunami that was the eyewitness testimony from those who knew Annie best, the doctor seemed detached, robotic, apathetic — empirical at the cost of emotion. Lost in the cold mantras of science were all discernible traces of Annie or, at the very least, some vitriol towards Wheeler.

The press, always choosing emotion over reason, shared none of the good doctor's integrity. Dry exposition about the limits of science held no interest for the correspondents or for the audience they served. The doctor's testimony clearly needed juicing up and the men of the press rose to the challenge. The first to give it a jolt was the *Yarmouth Herald* claiming Jacques was "prepared to swear that the blood found on [Wheeler's] clothes is human blood."[9] As if such blatant fabrication were not enough, the *Herald* tore a page straight from Detective Power's playbook and erroneously reported that the doctor had revealed "an unsuccessful effort had been made to wash some of the stains away."[10] To the contrary, Dr. Jacques was quite adamant he saw no indications Wheeler had tried to erase the traces of his crime.

Although the media reports were fallacious, the conflated accounts had two significant and lasting effects. The first was a peculiarly unexpected sociological phenomenon. Thanks to the barrage of media coverage, strange clinical terms — once so foreign — had become common currency. It was no longer strange to hear uneducated bootblacks or longshoremen bandying about terms such as "nucleated red blood cells" or "cytopathology" with an ease and familiarity heretofore unthinkable.

The second effect had far more serious repercussions. The jury in Wheeler's case were sequestered at a local hotel and kept hidden from the public "except for a short walk they had on Sunday in the company of the Sheriff."[11] Although they were cut off from society at large, there were no restrictions on their access to newspapers. Many jurors ended the day by reading about the case, no doubt hoping to catch a glimpse of themselves in the coverage. Reporters often commented on the panel, including the astute observation that no one on the jury took notes during the trial but were opting instead to rely on local press reports to refresh their memories. So great was the widely held belief in the accuracy of the press that no one stopped to question whether such a move was in their collective best interests. It was, without question, not in Peter Wheeler's best interest.

❨

The public's misplaced faith in the press went hand in hand with their unshakable belief in the power of science. Such certitudes, however, were at odds with the era's primary doctrine: religious conviction. Scientific advancement was a double-edged sword to Victorians on both sides of the pond. One well-honed face sliced through religious dogma, dispelling past beliefs that once defined even the most heinous of crimes as evidence of God's mysterious ways. Yet, having dissected away such facile platitudes, the opposing blade lacked sufficient edge to excise a superstitious world view and replace it with incontrovertible facts. Science was the new religion, and like their ecclesiastical forebears, scientists had the will if not always the way.

In the Gilded Age of enlightenment, practitioners like Dr. Jacques knew so much but comprehended so little. The Wheeler trial became an apt metaphor for the state of criminal science at that time: everyone knew the facts of the case — the news agencies had seen to that — yet it was knowledge coupled with insufficient understanding.

There was a certain circular irony to it all. The chemists and chemistry seeking the greater truths that lay in forensic evidence were still decades off, arriving far too late to be of any assistance to Wheeler, yet it was cases like Wheeler's that spawned the birth of the forensic sciences. The impetus was there although it lacked a certain moral restraint, and the needs of the justice system provided ample incentive for practitioners at both ends of the ethical spectrum. For the scurrilous and self-serving, there was the promise of personal advancement, solved cases, and high expert witness fees. For the scrupulous, there was the thrill of the hunt and the ever-present possibility of discovery. The epoch of forensic enlightenment would come, held aloft by the pseudo-science of Power and his ilk but mercifully tempered by the rational methodologies of Dr. Jacques and his peers.

thirty-one

The Minstrel Show

It is odd what some people find funny. Case in point: a strange moment of levity in the midst of a gruelling murder trial. On the second day of testimony, eleven-year-old Sadie Morine was called to the witness stand. As the child timidly made her way through the court, a skittish rabbit among the foxes, something truly unexpected happened. The wire suspending a length of stove pipe broke and a heating duct suddenly crashed down on the heads of those assembled. Amidst all the noise, shock, and commotion, thankfully no one was injured.

The correspondent from the *Daily Echo*, one from the small phalanx of bored reporters still in attendance when Power was not on the stand, knew he had seen something he could use. Ever vigilant for an opportunity to impugn the accused, the *Echo* man made hay of the unfortunate mishap: "several links came within a few inches of Wheeler's head and he laughed heartily."[1] The paper spun the prisoner's mirth as manic and wildly inappropriate to the moment, implying that Wheeler was so unbalanced as to find the potential for injury to self or others humorous. Such rhetoric played well with readers, by then conditioned to think the worst of Wheeler. The *Morning Chronicle* reprinted the incident verbatim the next day, perpetuating the myth of Wheeler's crazed indifference to his own future as well as the safety of others.

Reality is in the eye of the beholder. Mr. Robert Payne, the only remaining pro-Wheeler journalist, saw things differently. According to his report in the *Saint John Daily Sun*, Wheeler was not amused by the unscripted near-death experience; rather, his laughter was in response to a muttered comment by the bailiff, who quipped "you had a narrow escape."[2] In Payne's tale of the tape, the incident showed Wheeler to be calm and in good humour, even in the face of sudden calamity.

The prisoner had an entirely different take on the accident. It was not the danger or even the bailiff's jape that tickled Wheeler but simply a sight gag. As the heating duct fell, the pipe released a tidal wave of soot that settled on many in the court, including the prosecutors. Seeing his opponents suddenly decked out in blackface, Wheeler joked something along the lines that the courtroom had become a real minstrel show. For the dark-skinned Wheeler — long the target of racial slurs — it was a fitting allegory and he laughed heartily at the sad irony of it all.

Although the incident proved minor in the grand scheme of things, it showcased how history is skewed by the perceptions of those who claim to faithfully record it. The *Echo* turned a benign event into further proof of Wheeler's callous nature using nothing more than jaundiced editing and a practised eye for its readers' baser instincts. Mr. Payne, in sharp contrast, saw it as proof positive of Wheeler's noble bearing and remarkable strength of character. Wheeler himself couched the experience in the embittered yet resilient light of an oppressed minority.

Stripped of all bents and biases, the pipe pratfall came as journalistic manna from heaven. In a trial mired by testimony regurgitated for the fourth time, the near-miss was sorely needed comic relief for an audience all too acquainted with the intricacies of the evidence. By this stage of the game, the trial was no longer about evidence or testimony or even Power's feints at science. It had become a referendum on Wheeler's behaviour, countenance, and demeanour. One keen-eyed reporter or another managed to infuse his every gesture or utterance with sinister meaning, no matter what Peter said or did. The blackface simply exposed the spectacle for what it really was: theatre. The trial was a mere formality, the verdict a foregone conclusion. Wheeler's hearing had become, quite literally, a circus — a minstrel show to placate and entertain the masses. It is telling what some people find funny.

The courtroom lends itself well to dramatization. As Kentville's latest minstrel show revealed, the justice system is pure theatre. What greater spectacle exists than polemic adversaries debating matters of life and death? If done correctly, jurisprudence can be a poetic and stirring statement of our values as a nation. It can also be rip-roaring entertainment—lofty ideals reduced to a bar brawl between two diametrically opposed thugs, duking it out to the death.

Sadly, the law can become an exercise in stupidity — a master class in apathy, indolence, and false bravado. Lawyers often squander their opportunities, opting for flaccid rhetoric and half-baked arguments hidden beneath a barrage of bellicose thundering and wild gesticulation. Flash triumphs over substance as barristers place greater emphasis on a soliloquy's delivery than its content.

So it was with the closing arguments in the matter of *Queen v. Wheeler*. As Dr. Jacques and the last remaining witnesses stepped clear of the dock and all remnants of the stovepipe soot were wiped away, the case of Peter Wheeler — once touted as the trial of the century — faltered towards the finish line having never found its stride. The only new evidence on offer was Power, who never quite delivered on his pretrial hype, and Dr. Jacques's blood analysis, which played better in the press than it did in the actual courtroom.

Perhaps the most surprising turn of events came from Henry Dwight Ruggles. As the Crown rested its case, the defence counsel shocked the crowd when he announced he would call no witnesses. By refusing to counter the prosecution's case, the defence was ostensibly saying they were certain the Crown had not met its burden of proof. It was a time-honoured but risky gambit and one Wheeler could ill-afford. While "innocent until proven guilty" was a beloved axiom in the justice system, the credo failed to take into account those cases in which the jury was predisposed to find the defendant guilty before the trial had even begun.

Ruggles's Hail Mary ploy struck a select few as bold advocacy. The majority opinion, however, held that the team was simply outmatched, saddled with an obviously guilty client for whom no reasonable defence could be mounted.[3]

Although he abdicated his right to present evidence on Wheeler's behalf, Ruggles wanted one last kick at the can. Townshend called counsel before the bench, where Ruggles argued that the defence was entitled to address the jury last during closing arguments. The Crown took exception as Harrington also wanted the final word. More time, effort, and energy went into the protracted discussion of which side would claim the closing summation than was expended on what either team intended to say. After listening to both sides squabble for far too long, Judge Townshend had heard enough. The matter was decided by a technicality: because Harrington was simply an appointee of the court and was not a Crown prosecutor, Townshend ruled that the prosecution must deliver their summation first, thereby giving the coveted closing slot to the defence.

Neither summation would live on in judicial infamy but shame fell hardest on the prosecution. Lulled into a false sense of confidence by a trial that was always theirs to lose, the prosecution's summation barely rose to the level of trite. Harrington asked the jury a single question: If not Wheeler, then who? It was an age-old chestnut of jurisprudence, hackneyed to the point of parody, but one easily disguised as down-home common sense. It was the quintessential lazy argument, a cut-rate oracle's sleight of hand so worn at the heel it fooled only children and imbeciles.

As is always the case when such devices are invoked, it was the right question posed at the wrong time to the wrong people. It did not fall to the jurors to identify alternative suspects; that task rested squarely on the ample spotlit shoulders of Detective Nick Power. Furthermore, absence of evidence is never evidence of absence. That no other suspects were named was not proof that they did not exist; the void meant only that Power had not done an effective or thorough job. Unfortunately, this legal nuance was lost on the jury, and for reasons of strategy or perhaps incompetence, Ruggles never pointed it out for their benefit.

Prosecutor Harrington, moving with the slow deliberate stride and unflinching gaze of a caged animal, paced before the jury box as if extorting its occupants to defy him. He reminded jurors it all came down to a question of motive. "What would a stranger want to enter a house at night and kill an innocent girl for?"[4] he queried, as if the answer to that question were any different than the reasons he had ascribed to Wheeler. The motive — the ravaging of a defenceless young girl — held whether the assailant were the accused or a random psychopath. It was a poor man's shell game, seemingly based on the process of elimination but in fact predicated on the jury's insecurities and desire for vengeance. Jurors were only presented with a false choice between two arbitrary options: Wheeler or some faceless predator. The real alternative — that Wheeler was innocent — remained clumsily hidden. Eager to mete out justice for Annie and unable to pull another name out of the hat, the jurors turned to Wheeler. Shamed by their own shortcomings, the panel was propelled not by evidence but by a misplaced sense of civic duty and a lack of options.

The cheapest of tricks, it was and remains one of the most effective. It was a devastating semantic ruse. The real question for the jury should have been: did Peter Wheeler kill Annie Kempton? If the answer was yes beyond all reasonable doubt, that was a fair and reasonable verdict. If the verdict was no, the onus was never on the jury to find the real killer.

thirty-two

A Foregone Conclusion

Despite the simplicity of its fundamental argument, Harrington's guilt-inducing précis dragged on for nearly three hours. Having finally exhausted every last manipulative twist, Harrington ceded the floor to his worthy but vanquished opponent. The Crown did not get the last word but Harrington, ever the gentleman, still managed to drive his point home, trading favourable timing for profligate obloquy.

Henry Dwight Ruggles — champion of the underdog, defender of the lost cause — sat beside Wheeler and took a breath to settle his quivering nerves. Dwight was an astute observer of the hissing that was inherent in the practice of law but had never seen a case quite as venomous as this. As he rose, he carried with him Peter's last, best, and only hope for salvation. It was a crushing burden, one he seemed to bear alone. According to at least one local wag, "the prisoner looked fresh and bright, his appearance not changing any from that of the first day of trial,"[1] suggesting that either Wheeler was delusional or the reporter was. Still, the accused's calm demeanour proved infectious, a much-needed anodyne for his fretful counsel.

Ruggles's summation was, by now, a familiar refrain: the prosecution had not proven its case. There was simply no evidence to suggest — much less prove — that Peter Wheeler killed Annie Kempton. Ruggles reminded the jurors of the salient points: Annie was seen alive by numerous people until 8:00 p.m., when Wheeler and Hardy Benson left her house. Wheeler had been inside for mere minutes. By Hardy Benson's own admission, when Wheeler emerged from the house he was neither covered in blood nor was he acting strangely. From that moment on, Wheeler was never alone again and never had the opportunity to kill Annie. Several witnesses reported seeing lights within Annie's house throughout the evening, indicating she was alive well into the night. She had been found in her nightclothes, her bed clearly slept in. Despite Power's assertion that the crime occurred between 5:00 and 6:00 p.m., the autopsy results confirmed that Annie was not killed until after midnight. The only rational conclusion was that Peter Wheeler did not murder Annie Kempton.

Unlike his loquacious opponent, Ruggles addressed the jury for just over an hour, believing brevity to be not only the soul of wit but the key to holding the jury's attention. Short and sweet had proven a winning formula in the past, one Ruggles hoped might pay off again.

With the summations completed, Justice Charles Townshend checked the time and called a recess for lunch, prolonging Wheeler's agony for yet another hour. At 1:15 p.m., the court was again called into session and the judge issued his final instructions to the jury.

In spite of the petty haggling between the opposing counsels, Townshend had reserved the last word for himself. Now it was his turn to reconsider the evidence, this time accompanied by a liberal sprinkling of the judge's own thoughts and opinions. The magistrate left little doubt as to where his allegiances lay, as the *Morning Chronicle* clearly noted: "The judge's address to the jury was most eloquent and impressive but against the prisoner."[2] Townshend's biased oratory concluded: "The prisoner has been given a very fair trial and given every consideration by the crown. The defense have failed to call witnesses and the prisoner's counsel was allowed to address the jury last."[3] According to Townshend, the defence had dropped the ball, the prosecution had won, and his oversight of the case had been exemplary, even if Sir Charles was forced to say so himself.

With a final sound of his gavel, the judge sent twelve men to ponder the fate of Peter Wheeler.

☽

As the jury left to deliberate, something truly remarkable occurred. A Nova Scotian newspaper reporter experienced a moment of doubt, a brief reflexive spasm of conscience and common sense. The correspondent for the *Acadian Recorder* paused to question whether Wheeler was actually guilty. The paper had remained somewhat neutral in the previous months, opting to report the case with very little commentary, but now told its readers: "There was no direct or positive evidence [that] points to the prisoner's guilt. No person saw the crime committed."[4] Under the headline "Peter's chances good to get-off,"[5] the *Recorder* argued that the defence "succeeded in a remarkable manner in breaking down many of the strongest points of the prosecution's evidence."[6] Indeed, the *Acadian Recorder* was of the belief that "it was utterly impossible for Wheeler to have committed the crime."[7] The report concluded on an upbeat note, stating: "the feeling here at present is that from the evidence given the chances of the prisoner being cleared are good."[8]

Heaven alone knows what trial the *Acadian Recorder* correspondent was watching or from where he gleaned the notion that Wheeler's chances were good. The reporter from the *Recorder* was clearly in a boat by himself, with the possible exception of Mr. Payne from the *Saint John Daily Sun*. That Wheeler was guilty was a given as far as everyone else was concerned. That he would hang was equally certain. The only thing left to do now was sit and wait for the jury to make it official.

❧

As the minutes ticked by, Wheeler's placid facade finally cracked. His life rested in the hands of twelve strangers and the accused was wound as tight as an eight-day clock. As Judge Townshend rose to retire to his chambers, Wheeler leapt to his feet and began chattering to his defence counsel. His normally cool exterior was gone: "his eyes became glossed and his face flushed."[9] Ruggles quickly grabbed his client's arm and wrestled him to his seat. The prisoner was undeterred and, utterly frustrated by court rules prohibiting him from speaking in his own defence, he again stood tall and called out to the judge: "Your Lordship, will you allow me to speak a word?"[10]

Townshend was unaccustomed to outbursts in his court. He paused and then replied, "Yes, through your counsel."[11] Ruggles and Robertson quickly conferred, then had a sharp word with their client. Robertson, who had yet to speak in court, stood and informed the bench that they had advised their client not to make a statement at this time. The defence strategy of brevity was redacted to total silence.

☾

Countless reporters have made an informal study of the correlation between a defendant's culpability and the length of a jury's deliberations. The widely held belief is that a swift verdict means guilty. A good many covering the courthouse beat also put tremendous stock in a jury's willingness to look at the defendant as they return with their decision. If jurors fail to meet the prisoner's gaze, there can be no question as to their verdict.

In the case of *Queen v. Wheeler*, the jury deliberated for less than two hours and, as they made their way back to the courtroom, not a single member of the panel raised their eyes toward the defence table. Based on this alone, a few eager correspondents leapt from their seats before the verdict was announced and bolted for the telegraph office, hell-bent on being the first to report the jury's as-yet-undisclosed decision. With all the objectivity Ahab had for a certain white whale, the keenest of the press corps trumpeted from the rooftops that Wheeler was to swing.

Those newshounds who elected to remain seated were not on tenterhooks for long. Justice Townshend ascended the bench and called the court back into session, at which time the pronouncement of the verdict was brief, perfunctory, and ever-so-slightly anticlimactic.

Wallace — Townshend's hand-picked protonotary — stood from his desk and asked: "Gentlemen, what to your verdict?"[12] Jury foreman David Noth rose then hesitated, either from fear or the desire to give the portentous moment its proper due. A hush descended on the courtroom as all eyes turned to the jury. Noth, having milked the moment for all it was worth, uttered a single word: "Guilty."[13]

The deafening silence lingered a moment, then two. The verdict came as no surprise yet the stillness masked a broad spectrum of emotions: affirmation, acceptance, justice, vengeance, closure. After months of speculation, it was finally over. The court had validated the community's long-held belief that Peter Wheeler had murdered Annie Kempton. There was no longer any reason for doubt.

❨

As determined by the legal protocols of the day, Wheeler's one and only chance to address the court came too late. Before the judge announced his final sentence, the court clerk asked the prescribed question posed to all those condemned: "Have you anything to say why the sentence of death should not be passed against you?"[14] The query struck Wheeler dumb. The prisoner stood for what seemed an eternity, shell-shocked by reality as the earth spun beneath his feet. Finally, he answered the clerk: "I don't understand you. It's not because I am ignorant, but because I don't understand."[15] Wheeler's struggle to comprehend had nothing to do with the question posed and everything to do with the strange new world he now inhabited. Peter was trapped in a vortex in which the disparate needs of the many outweighed the rights of the one: the family's need for justice, the villagers' need for vengeance, the detective's need to protect his reputation, and the media's need to fulfill a prescribed storyline with proven sales appeal. Unable to tread water in such raging currents, Wheeler was sucked down by forces beyond his ken.

What had ultimately doomed Wheeler was a system rigged to silence him: a police force and community that would not listen to his explanations or alibi; a justice system that refused to let him speak in his own defence; a team of advocates who trusted blindly in the notion of presumed innocence; a press corps keen to talk about Wheeler but not to him. As the torrent rushing against him threatened to pull him under, Wheeler had buoyed himself on a sophistic bubble — his belief that the system would never convict an innocent man. He was sold the beguiling bill of goods that his day in court would finally set him free. Now Peter found himself without any hope of rescue from the Charybdis that would ferry him to his inexorable fate.

Dwight Ruggles tried his best to explain the circumstances to his near-catatonic client but to no avail. There was nothing left to be said, no last-minute tricks to reverse his fate. Wheeler was done and the time for impassioned pleas had passed. On behalf of his client, Ruggles waived Wheeler's right to address the court.

☾

An eerie, preternatural quiet descended over the court. The teeming crowd had finally gotten what they had come for and now sat in stony silence, savouring their victory. Judge Townshend allowed the silence to settle. Then, with a brusque clearing of his throat, he began his final soliloquy:

> The jury have convicted you of the murder of Annie Kempton and in their finding, I concur. You have had a fair trial and every effort has been made on your behalf to establish your innocence and a patient jury has given it the fullest investigation. The jury was not from the place where the crime was committed and consequently were not prejudiced and have clearly brought this awful crime against you. Probably the most hard thing to do is for one man to pass [a] sentence of death upon another. I cannot help thinking of the cruel way the poor girl was murdered. I will give you ample time to repent for the crime of which you have been found guilty. I only hope and pray that you may devote the remaining few weeks in preparation for the future world. I do not know

your religious views but I do sincerely hope you will be repentant. I hereby direct that you be taken hence to the jail in Kentville and thence to the jail in Digby and detained there till the 8th day of September, 1896, and on that day hanged by the neck till dead.[16]

Judge Townshend dropped his gavel one last time, having concluded the business of the court. Although he was not permitted to speak, Peter Wheeler suddenly found his voice. As the judge rose from his perch, Wheeler abandoned all protocols and decorum and in a clear voice said: "I hope you will find out who the guilty party is before that time."[17] The prisoner, having had the last word, was led from the courtroom for the short walk to the Kentville jail. Despite his shackles, Wheeler held his head high and met the eye of all who looked upon him with disgust or pity.

Scripture extols the faithful to "remind me Lord that my days are numbered,"[18] a cogent reflection on how fleeting life can be. Thanks to twelve sober citizens of King's County and the power invested in the robes and powdered wig of Sir Charles Townshend, Peter Wheeler's days now numbered seventy.

thirty-three

Poisoned Pens

For all the power the tabloids wielded over the fate of Peter Wheeler, there remained one last card he held against them: his steadfast refusal to act like a guilty man. The newspapers were at a standstill, having analyzed, scrutinized, and exaggerated Wheeler's every facial tic for the past five months. Even with the verdict, there remained a small but vocal minority that recognized the case against Wheeler was entirely circumstantial and the wrong man had been convicted. Robert Payne captured the absurdity of the situation best when he wrote: "it remains the fact that he was condemned, not because he went to the house at midnight and murdered the girl but because he made her a harmless visit in the evening."[1]

Pursuant to their sales strategy of reporting all Wheeler, all the time, a number of broadsheets pressed into service a duplicitous ploy, one that had proven highly successful in the past. The press would announce that Wheeler had made a very public suicide attempt. The reasoning behind the declaration was two-pronged. First, it would convince those last lingering skeptics that he was, in fact, guilty. Second, it would keep Wheeler on the front page a few days longer. The ten-week gap between his sentence and execution loomed like an unfordable abyss that hovered foremost in the mind of every editor on the eastern seaboard. Coming up with fresh copy to bridge the gap seemed a near Herculean task. A fresh scandal, particularly something as torrid and unsavoury as a suicide attempt, was just the ticket they needed to keep the story alive.

The problem, of course, was Peter Wheeler. After his momentary lapse during sentencing, Wheeler was once again the picture of bonhomie, resilience, and quiet grace under pressure. The man may have fallen into the Ninth Circle of Hell but he greeted the challenge head-on. Even the most vehemently anti-Wheeler news agencies conceded that "Wheeler was in good spirits, and indulged in jokes and frivolous talking"[2] at a time when most mortals would have cracked or run mad. The condemned man's unworldly ability to roll with the punches frustrated their every effort to portray him as a guilt-riddled menace to society.

By this point, Peter Wheeler had long since ceased to be an actual person to the scriveners in the press corps. Rather, he became the lead character in the continuing saga of "The Bear River Tragedy," a literary device subject to the whims of the creative forces crafting the script. As such, Wheeler was a puppet who could be made to say or do anything, for such are the joys of writing fiction. The question now was simply how far were the media prepared to go to create their masterpiece.

☾

On July 1, as Wheeler was led manacled and damned to his cell in the Kentville jail, the *Morning Chronicle* ran the following strategically timed, well-placed account:

> Some time ago the jailor found in a corner of Wheeler's cell a small bottle among some papers. He took it in his possession and kept it till this afternoon. The bottle contained a dark drug and is labeled outside "poison; be careful." Detective Power now has it in his possession. As soon as Wheeler was taken from the court to the jail he made for the corner of the cell where the bottle was, and he became greatly excited when he could not find it. The jailer told him where it was, and he became much alarmed. The supposition is that he intended to end his life after the sentence had been passed on him.[3]

The report was a salmagundi of every literary contrivance in a writer's bag of tricks. It had an accessible allusion: the tiny bottle so cartoonishly labelled was a clear nod to Lewis Carroll's "drink me" bottle from *Alice's Adventures in Wonderland*, although others saw a more classical reference. One pundit, perhaps spying the office copy of the complete works of Shakespeare, likened it to the apothecary scene in *Romeo and Juliet*. The story also had the requisite conflict with the protagonist's arch-nemesis, in this case ably played by the unnamed jailer, with a brief cameo appearance by everyone's favourite leading man, Detective Power. As expected, the gripping tale of the condemned man's desperate suicide attempt drove sales for the *Chronicle* and its affiliates through the roof, leaving competing papers that had missed the scoop with the option of reporting on the report.

Although Wheeler resolutely clung to his trump card, refusing to buckle to satisfy the media, the press had their own ace up their collective sleeves: human nature. Embedded in our cumulative DNA is the tendency to accept as fact anything that supports or confirms what we already believe to be true. Whether Wheeler was actually suicidal was by no means as important as the public perception that he must be, as surely the reality of Wheeler's circumstances would drive any man to thoughts of suicide. All that a savvy reporter needed to do was imply Wheeler intended to take his own life, add a few salient but unverifiable details, and readers would fill in the gaps for themselves. Where, pray tell, was the ethical dilemma in that?

❈

More than a century on, the story of Wheeler's purported suicide plot reads like a twist in a dime-store novel. The specifics of the report cannot be verified as records from the Kentville jail were destroyed in a subsequent fire. There is no mention of the incident in the court record or in any of the countless interviews Detective Power gave to the press. In all likelihood, the story is a complete fabrication, a propitious figment of an ambitious reporter's imagination.

Although far less probable, a disturbing alternative must also be considered. The stringer for the *Chronicle* was granted an interview with the prisoner as he sat in the Kentville jail during the trial, one of several reporters afforded such access. It is possible the reporter either planted the vial in the cell, knowing its discovery would be made public, or slipped it to Wheeler in the misguided hope he might actually use it when the time was right. The melodramatic label on the bottle left little question as to its content or purpose; had Wheeler somehow procured it on his own, it is absurd to think he would affix so blatant a disclaimer on the bottle.

Throughout Wheeler's ordeal, the perfect piece of the puzzle had a funny way of turning up in the press at exactly the right moment. Whether by accident or design, Wheeler's so-called suicide bid was big news and the *Morning Chronicle* profited handsomely from it. It was a heavy-handed ploy, in equal parts crass, exploitive, and unforgettable.

Somewhere, the gods of yellow journalism were smiling.

thirty-four

No Love Lost

Peter Wheeler spent a final fitful night in the Kentville jail before being remanded back to Digby. Once transferred, he was incarcerated under the watchful eye of Sheriff Benjamin Van Blarcom and his under-sheriff, William Elmer Van Blarcom, the apple at the base of the family tree. The Van Blarcoms were lawmen by choice but politicians of necessity; in 1896, policing required greater prowess in glad-handing than crime-solving. It may not have been their ideal vocation. The sheriff was a brooding, driven little man, the sort so often drawn to positions of limited authority. Young William was notoriously quick-tempered, a martinet for whom power and charm were mutually exclusive. The clan ruled the town with iron fists in dire need of some kid gloves.

Digby itself was agog with the impending execution. The gaze of the nation rarely fell on this particular dot on the map. The city's industry, then as now, rested in the oceans. Once the omphalos of the scallop-fishing world, by the late nineteenth century, Digby's most prolific export was a form of low-priced smoked herring, affectionately known as "Digby chicken."[1]

The county lock-up sat on the crest of a hill overlooking the harbour that was the city's lifeblood. The jail boasted one of the best views in the region but Wheeler never saw it. A simple wooden saltbox designed with all the mirth and creativity of a slaughterhouse, the jail was the runt of a litter that included its far more imposing brick sisters: the partially built Digby Courthouse and the newly constructed Digby Academy. The jail did double duty: the lower floor housed the prisoner's cell while the upper level served as the office and dwelling for Sheriff Van Blarcom and his family. The gratis apartment was one of the many perks that came with being sheriff. Another fringe benefit was the power to decide who gained access to his most infamous and profitable inmate.

Wheeler's cell occupied the worst of the jail's limited real estate. His keep was at the far end of the basement, accessible only through a heavy wooden door. A small hole had been cut into the top of the door, the sole means of communicating with the prisoner. A number of guards monitored the condemned man throughout the day but Van Blarcom was the lone gatekeeper of the tiny viewing portal and he single-handedly sifted through the mountain of interview requests from the media as well as from the morbidly curious social elites, who clamoured for five minutes with the lone occupant of Digby's death row. What ultimately swayed Van Blarcom to grant such requests was never formally documented but rumours lingered like an untraceable smell that if one wanted access, the right palm needed to be greased. A number of media outlets, including the *Nova Scotian*, ran editorials and scathing cartoons in retaliation, mocking Van Blarcom's alleged practice of charging admission to see Wheeler and other nefarious money-making schemes.

Despite his meagre floor plan, Wheeler reportedly wanted for nothing. According to the *Yarmouth Herald*: "he appears to have everything he desires and many articles in the cell could be used in enabling him to escape, commit suicide, or burn the building. The attention of the Attorney General ought to be called to this peculiar state of affairs."[2]

There was little cause to alert the Attorney General just yet. Wheeler was literally chained to the floor of his cell, forced to drag a heavy metal tether around his tiny dungeon.[3] Had Wheeler been foolhardy enough to "burn the building," his four-foot shackles would have prevented both escape and all hope of rescue. Even if Wheeler had all he desired, he had only an eight-foot radius in which to enjoy it. Still, no matter how restrictive his living conditions were, space was not his mortal enemy; it was time.

The *Nova Scotian* pokes fun at Van Blarcom's alleged practice of charging admission to see Wheeler.

❨

Time was also no friend to the prosecution. The longer the case dragged on, the more opportunities doubters had to voice their concerns and garner converts. Equally treacherous were the months between verdict and execution. Were the public to seriously mull over the specifics of the case, the holes in the prosecution's theory would be revealed, not to mention the complicity of the press. The "he didn't do it" chorus needed to be drowned out, if only for the sake of the Crown and the media. Any and all voices willing to step forward to berate the condemned man and shore up the shaky foundations of his conviction were promptly given a featured solo.

The first to lend his soothing baritone to the cause was the venerated gumshoe from Halifax. By the time the date was set for the execution, it was fair to say Detective Nick Power hated Peter Wheeler. The feeling was absolutely mutual.

For Power, the case had more to do with preserving his carefully crafted public persona — stalwart guardian of law and order and defender of helpless victims. The detective was adamant on that score: the murder of Annie Kempton could not go unavenged...no, not on his watch.

Power's animosity toward Wheeler in the early days of the investigation had not been personal; the detective didn't know Wheeler well enough to dislike him. Rather, the ill will Power bore Wheeler was the same contempt he bore all criminals. Power hated the sins and, frankly, the sinners as well. It was only after Purdy's examination that Power took a personal dislike to the accused. Nicholas Power was never one to favour those born in warmer climes, particularly swarthy ne'er-do-wells that took up with the pale-skinned belles of the north, and he grew to hate Wheeler on sight as well as on principle. All prejudice aside, what really irked the detective was that he deemed Wheeler to be an unworthy adversary. Power's venomous disregard was rooted in the belief that the accused was not only guilty but common and therefore a poor test of the detective's unprecedented talents. The Haligonian supersleuth craved a supervillain, an arch rival in the mould of the cunning, if somewhat demented, foes who so vexed his fictional hero and soulmate Sherlock Holmes.

If Power branded Wheeler as common, the condemned man thought the detective to be pompous and incompetent. The prisoner freely voiced his disdain for his resident nemesis to the never-ending assembly line of reporters who bought their five minutes at the tiny window to his cell. When asked by the *Nova Scotian* how he felt about Power, Wheeler admitted he "still entertained deep bitterness against him."[4] As the execution date loomed large, one reporter asked if Peter had made his peace with those involved. Wheeler replied he held no resentment toward anyone who had prosecuted him but "was very loath to forgive Detective Power before going to the scaffold."[5] Indeed, "Peter nursed his ill-feeling against Detective Power so persistently,"[6] he intended to carry "it to the grave with him."[7]

The detective was not the only one spouting vitriol against Wheeler in the press. Sheriff Van Blarcom, tasked with carrying out the execution, also grew to detest his most notable detainee. The sheriff told the *Morning Chronicle* in a fit of pique that "he can hang Wheeler with good grace,"[8] in no small part because "he styles Wheeler a cold-blooded murderer and liar."[9]

With so much animosity on display, the press boys did well not to run out of ink.

☾

Confined as he was to an eight-foot sphere, the prisoner's emotional and spiritual well-being became the subject of much speculation. Although Wheeler had paid little heed to Judge Townshend's entreaties that he repent for his sins, one man took the magistrate's pleas to heart. Police Constable Harris W. Bowles was a great side of beef of a man, well-dressed in his regulation blues, and he believed in the power of repentance. A devout and active member of the Salvation Army, Bowles thought Wheeler's only hope of redemption lay in a full and heartfelt confession.

Bowles was first assigned to guard the prisoner in the days before Wheeler was transferred to Kentville for trial, and the constable harped on his charge day and night to admit his wrongdoing and seek forgiveness from the Almighty. Peter, categorically resistant to religious dogma and even more averse to taking orders from others, thanked his warden for his thoughts but declined to confess to a crime he did not commit.

During the Kentville trial, Bowles was one of the few new faces to take the stand, regaling the court with his efforts to elicit an admission of guilt from the prisoner. At one point the officer said he had "put a mark on the prisoner's cell and said to him 'remember that date when

Constable Harris W. Bowles, Digby's resident jailer and spiritual advisor.

you are convicted.'"[10] When the prosecution urged Bowles to repeat what Wheeler said in response, the defence strongly objected, calling the testimony hearsay and the judge sustained the objection. Readers across the country were left to wonder what Wheeler had made of Bowles's prophetic proclamation.

As Bowles welcomed Wheeler back to Digby post-conviction, the constable's mark on the cell wall served as a poignant reminder of the prisoner's dwindling days. Now staring death in the face, Wheeler's hard-nosed stance toward Bowles slowly softened. As the days flew by, the burly constable chipped away at Peter's defences. According to Bowles, Wheeler initially tested the waters by asking his keeper "to get up a petition for him if he should confess the crime."[11] Spying his first glimmer of hope, Bowles heartily agreed to broker a deal between Wheeler and the press to publish his confession in exchange for cash — a common and accepted practice of the day.

Despite appearances to the contrary, it was an abrupt about-face for the burly lawman. Bowles had always advocated for Wheeler to confess purely on religious grounds, claiming a *mea culpa* would cleanse the prisoner of his sins and pave the way to the Kingdom of Heaven. Why Bowles now saw the press as a vital part of the equation was, for the moment, a mystery but there was now little question that the Digby jailkeep had empowered himself to serve as Wheeler's literary agent, as well as his redeemer.

thirty-five

The Confession(s)

The artifice of a condemned man's confession was so entrenched in the Victorian execution paradigm that the public took for granted Wheeler would make an eleventh hour admission of guilt. The only question was when and to which lucky tabloid.

There was, of course, the perennial problem of Wheeler, who "stolidly maintained his innocence and...continued to plead that he was suffering for another's fault."[1] His refusal to confess drove the press to distraction. In retribution, they wrote whatever came to mind, such as: "It is worthy of note that during his long confinement he never squarely denied having committed the murder, always evading the question by saying that he knew the man who did it."[2] That Wheeler had said no such thing was beside the point. The media had grown adroit at reading between the lines, even when Wheeler refused to give them any lines at all.

The newshawks were not alone in their dogged attempts to coax a dying declaration. After a brief but hopeful hiccup, Captain Bowles's efforts to elicit a confession also hit a brick wall. For an exclusive of this magnitude, the papers were willing to pay top dollar and impressive cash incentives were offered to both the prisoner and guard. While Peter's financial woes would end at the drop of the gallows, Bowles — a poorly paid constable and unpaid missionary — may have been sorely tempted to do more than just save Wheeler's immortal soul.

Wheeler's cavilling stance was the great equalizer. The press, normally brothers-in-arms enjoying a foxhole camaraderie born of commiseration and a shared sense of repudiation, were now at each other's throats, avowed competitors jousting for the same limp scraps. Wheeler's refusal to conform to their prescribed agenda had irked editors, cub reporters, columnists, and pundits alike and they all found themselves in the same desperate camp.

So when one paper broke ranks and rushed to market a special edition touting Wheeler's confession, it was met with legitimate shock (and more than a little resentment) by those left in the dust. A mere two days after Wheeler was found guilty and sentenced to hang, the *Annapolis Spectator* hit the streets with the headline everyone was waiting for: "Wheeler Confesses!!"[3] Richard S. McCormick — the founder of the *Digby Weekly Courier*, once the odds-on favourite for landing the exclusive — spoke for all the bested news organs when he wrote: "The general opinion, however, was that he would confess the crime, in which he seemed so irrevocably implicated, before the time of his execution; but that he would do so only a few days after his sentence was not at all surmised."[4]

The *Spectator*'s special edition, so perfectly timed and flawlessly executed, took the valley by storm, selling out every last copy as its readers and competitors scrambled to see all the ugly details. The article, ostensibly written by Wheeler in his jail cell and then conveyed to one of the paper's representatives, adhered to what was by now a well-established template for such criminal declarations. It began with a biographical sketch of the prisoner, relating intimacies of his parents and childhood intended to humanize the man convicted of "the most atrocious murder known in this province."[5] The tale then segued into his supposed activities in the hours leading up to the crime. His version of the evening, spent in the company of Hardy Benson as well as Tillie and her children, parroted the testimony of key witnesses at the trial. It was not until well into Wheeler's treatise that the story took its first stunning turn.

According to the *Spectator*'s account, Wheeler slipped out of his bedroom window just after midnight and made his way to the Kemptons' home. When he knocked, Annie called out but refused to come to the door. Wheeler needed a ruse so he told the girl that "a crowd of roughs"[6] had just attacked Tillie's house, forcing its occupants to flee in terror. Annie, believing Tillie and the kids were with Wheeler on the stoop, rushed to open the door to let him in. It was a fatal mistake.

In "that moment Satan got to work at me,"[7] the confession proclaimed. Driven by lust and immoral desires, Peter tried to embrace Annie but she resisted his advances. He was thrown by her reticence, stating: "she was rather too strong for me."[8] The pair tussled and at some point Annie fell, cutting her head.

Fearing for her life and virtue, Annie grew desperate and made a stunning suggestion. She told Peter she would not report him if he left her alone but her anguished pleas fell on deaf ears. According to the printed confession, Satan "had full possession"[9] of him, compelling him to "hit her with that stick."[10] He rendered her senseless with the firewood, then ran to the kitchen, where he grabbed a handful of knives and silenced her for good. In a nauseating aside, Wheeler tried to shift the blame back onto Annie, saying: "I wish that she had had the strength of Samson the minute I went in the room, so that she could have knocked the devil out of me."[11]

Wheeler's confession stopped people in their tracks. For almost twenty-four hours, the special edition consumed life in the Annapolis Valley as readers debated its merits and intricacies at every opportunity. Of all the so-called bombshells contained in the article, two contentious statements caused the greatest furor. The first was that Wheeler claimed Annie had "asked me to kill her."[12] The assertion packed a devastating emotional wallop by invoking a haunting image: Annie, so desperate to retain her chastity, begged to be killed rather than defiled. The notion reduced countless readers to tears — men and women alike — and secured Annie's place in the pantheon of noble victims choosing death before dishonour.

The confession's second shocking revelation was the supposed time of the attack. Despite Power's belief that Annie was killed between five and six o'clock on the twenty-seventh, Wheeler reportedly declared: "the deed was done at half past one in the morning of the 28th day of January,

1896, and no other time."[13] The confession's author could not resist a final snipe at the Halifax lawman and his sacred evidentiary cow: "So men, you can see that Detective Power was wrong as to the hour of the deed, and about the night's milk."[14]

Even after the initial eruption had laid waste to its competitors, the aftershocks of the *Spectator*'s exclusive were felt for days. Every vanquished paper was left with only two options: reprint the confession or attack it. At least one paper, the *Morning Chronicle*, managed to do both. The Halifax daily began its report by offering liberal commentary on the confession: "the description of the tragedy given by the prisoner is a ghastly and revolting one."[15]

The *Chronicle* then reprinted the entire confession, circumventing any issues of plagiarism by pulling highlights and quotes at will and paraphrasing the rest. Having repackaged Wheeler's confession, the *Morning Chronicle* promptly declared it a fraud.

In a conversation with the *Chronicle*'s representative, who was sent to the Digby jail minutes after the *Spectator* special edition first hit newsstands, Wheeler denied ever authorizing the publication of his so-called confession. Although Wheeler admitted to drafting an autobiography of sorts, one detailing his childhood and travels, he never wrote anything resembling an admission of guilt. Wheeler supposedly told the *Chronicle* that the first part — the paragraphs containing details of his life story — was correct but that "the remaining portion seems to have been to a large extent manufactured by the person who interviewed him."[16]

The idea that the *Annapolis Spectator* had fabricated the confession found purchase thanks to the concerted efforts of its competition. Virtually every paper in the Maritimes dedicated considerable space to parsing and discounting the *Spectator*'s account. The *Digby Weekly Courier* took particular offence. As the region's self-proclaimed *vox populi*, the *Courier* declared: "The people of Digby take no stock in the previous alleged confession,"[17] noting that those same people "have an idea that the one published was considerable [*sic*] of a fake."[18] Even Wheeler took up the cause, telling the *Saint John Daily Telegraph* that the *Spectator* was "way off, and I can prove it."[19]

Although Wheeler's protestations were dismissed as self-serving, all the key players in the case were given ample opportunity to comment. To a man, they seized the chance to dissect the purported confession and their sharply divided opinions followed party lines. Crown Prosecutor C.S. Harrington was not at all surprised by Wheeler's admission of guilt, telling the *Morning Chronicle*: "all expected that he would confess."[20] Wheeler's defence lawyer Dwight Ruggles found the confession a little too scripted. Ruggles reminded everyone that Power's supposed perfect chain of evidence was "only completed by Wheeler's confession."[21] He was also quick to add that the confession made better sense of the evidence than did the prosecution.

Such sniping between opposing counsel was standard operating procedure for the adversarial justice system. The papers printed the comments as a matter of course and courtesy but saved their front pages for discussions relating to the burning question of when the crime occurred. C.S. Harrington remained adamant that the murder was committed on Monday in the late afternoon and not the early morning of Tuesday. Cherry-picking the sections that suited him best, Harrington claimed that he did "not believe in that part of his confession,"[22] but he readily accepted the remaining sections that supported his theory of the crime, adding that the Crown "had no misgivings as to his guilt."[23]

As for the convicted man himself, Wheeler voiced his disgust early and often then fell silent, frustrated by constantly being misquoted. A second reporter from the *Morning Chronicle* later hammered away at a mute Wheeler in his cell, trying to elicit any reaction. When it came to that most contentious issue of time, apparently Wheeler spoke volumes with his eyes: "When questioned as to whether he had committed the crime between the hours of twelve and one o'clock that night, he refused to answer, and *the impression conveyed* is that he now regrets that such a statement has been published. He evidently thought that by reflection on the character of his victim in making the statement that she admitted him to her bedroom at 12 o'clock at night that it would palliate his offense in the eyes of the public, but he did not anticipate the wave of indignation which the statement aroused."[24]

It was quite a lot to read into a simple "no comment." Freed from the shackles of relying solely on the spoken word, the *Chronicle* went on to say that Wheeler's real confession was yet to come. Since the correspondent had grown quite adept at intuiting Wheeler's every thought, it went without saying that the *Morning Chronicle* already possessed the highlights of that upcoming confession, gleaned entirely from the look on Peter's face.

With the lawyers having had their say and the press speaking on behalf of the accused, the lone voice left to be heard belonged to Nick Power. Immediately following the release of the confession, Power talked exclusively to the *Morning Chronicle*, a pro-Power vehicle if ever one existed. The scoop was a gift, payback for being the only paper to hold tight to the detective's timeline of the case. Flying in the face of convention, the *Chronicle* sided with Power and declared: "your correspondent is in a position to state that Wheeler's correct and true confession will reveal the fact that the theory of the crown was correct in almost every detail; that Annie Kempton was murdered by Wheeler between the hours of five and eight o'clock, and that the murderer did not visit the house after that hour."[25]

When asked about the contentious claim, Power dismissed the notion that Wheeler had crept out his back window after midnight to commit the crime. The detective emphatically stated that "in company with others I examined the fresh snow there and it was impossible for footprints to be there without being detected."[26]

As for the confession as a whole, Power offered a perfectly circular argument. He claimed that Wheeler's admission "proves him a liar,"[27] then argued, "Why should he want to lie if he did not commit the crime?"[28] When pressed for specifics Power knew to be lies, he pointed again to the unmilked cow: "a thing that was certain to happen if the girl were alive."[29] Whatever his other faults or human frailties, Power was nothing if not consistent, tenacious, and intractable.

❨

If one confession was good, two were better. Say what you like about its veracity, the *Annapolis Spectator*'s special edition had struck gold and at least one other paper gambled there was still money to be made. On July 7, the *Yarmouth Herald* ran its own version of Wheeler's guilt-induced revelations. Best of all, the *Herald* acted as though it had the exclusive, making no reference to any prior confession in a competitor's paper. It, too, appeared to be woven out of whole cloth; for example, beyond reporting that Wheeler was born in Mauritius, his so-called biography bore no resemblance to the one given in the *Spectator* confession.

The tone, syntax, and language were also entirely new; modern methods of forensic linguistic analysis[30] indicate that both so-called confessions were unquestionably written by two different people. Further, the *Herald*'s rendition contained no talk of Satan. If the Devil had indeed made him do it, Peter was no longer sharing the credit.

Also at odds were the two versions of the crime itself. In the *Herald* report, Wheeler supposedly sat on Annie's bed with her and "made some improper proposals"[31] that were soundly rejected. The two then "wrestled in the bed room and from there to the sitting room."[32] Unlike the earlier *Spectator* account, the Wheeler portrayed in the *Herald* seemed hazy on the specifics of his crime: "I can't tell whether I struck her first in front or on the back of the head."[33]

On one crucial point, both articles agreed: Annie had begged Peter to kill her. The *Yarmouth Herald* offered a far more embellished account, complete with dialogue: "Before she fell on her hands and knees she said 'Peter, kill me, and put me out of the way.' I said, 'Annie, do you want to die' and she said 'yes, kill me right now.'"[34] The two purported confessions also ran parallel on the much-debated question of when the crime was committed. Like its predecessor, the *Herald* placed the time of death well after midnight on Tuesday, January 28.

As for the act itself, apparently Wheeler felt little remorse: "Annie made no noise after her throat was cut. When I went home I went to sleep and slept soundly until morning."[35] Such gross indifference sickened the interviewer. Having heard more than his fill, "the reporter could stand the brutal confession no longer and he condemned the murderer in strong terms."[36] Unlike his *Spectator* colleague, the *Herald* correspondent supposedly then cut Wheeler off mid-confession.

Disgusted by Peter's callousness, the *Herald* representative tried to turn the conversation toward a more agreeable topic: the accused. Always happy to talk about himself, "the wicked creature laughed but grow more sober"[37] as talk turned to his pending execution. Wheeler "was anxious about the matter of the drop,"[38] fearing the mechanics of the hanging more than its eternal repercussions.

☾

The flurry of ersatz Wheeler confessions continued for weeks. Each paper, in turn, claimed to have finally secured the one "correct and true confession."[39] Crafted by whatever reporter drew the short straw, each account supposedly stemmed from a jailhouse interview with the condemned man who was at long last ready to unburden his troubled soul. All offered only minor variations on the theme: an increasingly brief and inaccurate biography followed by a disturbingly apathetic account of the crime. The sheer volume and repetition of it all became numbing. Sales plummeted as readers grew jaded and distrustful, by now certain that each new report was a hoax.

On July 18, more than two weeks after the first confession appeared, the *Saint John Daily Telegraph* decided to try a different tack. It dispatched a correspondent to visit Wheeler in his cell. There he found the prisoner in good spirits, even though his body bore traces of his prolonged incarceration: "Wheeler is somewhat fat but is very pale."[40] Wheeler blamed his rapid physical decline on a prison-issue diet of nothing but stale bread. To prove his point, Peter showed his guest his weekly rations: twenty slices of an inedible loaf, already showing signs of mould.

Whatever toll the prison food had taken on him, Wheeler's mind remained sharp and he insisted he was putting it to good use. Peter claimed to be hard at work drafting his life story, which he hoped to sell to the highest bidder. It was not a confession, per se. Rather, it was Wheeler's take on how he came to be facing death for a crime he still vehemently denied committing. Peter reportedly showed the *Telegraph* reporter an impressive thirty sheets of handwritten foolscap, filled from margin to margin in his tiny precise script.[41] Wheeler explained that there were actually two versions of his story: one he intended to sell shortly and one that he planned to give Constable Bowles, with instructions that it be sold after Wheeler's death to help cover his burial expenses.[42]

When queried about the onslaught of so-called confessions he had reportedly penned, Wheeler scoffed and dismissed every last one as a fabrication. To prove it, he pointed to a single fact: each one had ended with his signature (typically translated into type for publication). Wheeler was unequivocal — he never affixed his name to anything in his life.[43] He made it a habit not to sign any of his personal letters or to put his name in his books. He jokingly told the journalist that in the past few weeks, countless people had asked for his autograph but he had always refused to give it on the advice of counsel.[44] If there was one message he wanted the public to hear, it was this: any confession that bore his signature was a forgery.

Wheeler also expressed distrust and more than a little contempt for the lengths the media were prepared to go to try and elicit a confession from him. To illustrate his point, Peter directed the newsman's attention to the inmate occupying the adjacent cell. The prisoner, a recent addition to the cellblock, was a "colored youth"[45] who was "very annoying to Wheeler,"[46] constantly peppering him with questions from the minute he arrived. Wheeler told the *Telegraph* that the inmate was clearly a plant working in cahoots with the press to sink him even further. Peter intended to ride out his time in silence, tuning out the man's incessant droning.

With that one simple report, the *Saint John Daily Telegraph* did what none of its competitors had managed to do: revive interest in Wheeler's confession, at least among the press. According to its correspondent, Wheeler had written about the crime, even if his treatise could not be construed as confessional. The real thing was there for the taking, waiting to be sold to the paper with the deepest pockets. Even if the *Telegraph*'s interview did little to excite the public, it most certainly caught the attention of those in the news game.

☾

Intrigued though the competition may have been, most had already run what they claimed was Wheeler's true confession. The *Digby Weekly Courier* — one of the few yet to offer its own version — was quietly interested in Wheeler's self-penned biography but needed to proceed with caution. The paper had been vocal in its coverage of all prior confessions, as well as Wheeler's role in them, writing that "Peter has been surprised at the indignant way in which his statement has been received, he has a new confession to make. In fact he has a different one for nearly every visitor."[47] It was not Wheeler's story that changed, however; each reporter took liberties and modified it to suit his own agenda. Even in the scrum of false confessions, revelations, and admissions of wrongdoing — none of which were traceable to Wheeler himself — the *Courier* still saw incontrovertible evidence of guilt: "However much Wheeler's multi-confessions may vary from this out, the fact is now known as much, that he is the person guilty of the murder."[48] How the paper made the immeasurable leap from fabricated confessions by anonymous sources to irrefutable proof of guilt was not expanded upon. The *Digby Weekly Courier*, ever the bastion of hypocrisy where Peter Wheeler was concerned, denounced the man as a liar and "even more of a villain than was thought."[49] It again declared his confessions to be fabrications, not to be trusted, which was true, although not for the reasons the *Courier* implied.

The Digby weekly was desperate to remain above the fray but that tantalizing morsel of bait offered up by the *Saint John Daily Telegraph* proved too great a lure, even for the *Courier*. On August 4, the *Digby Weekly Courier* announced it had secured the exclusive rights to print "the only truthful confession of Peter Wheeler."[50] What separated this particular version from all prior missives was simply that the *Courier* had paid handsomely for it. Whether this version would indeed be the much-lauded thirty pages seen by the *Telegraph* man or just another in the endless series of imposters was fodder for much speculation among the *Courier*'s competitors.

Speculation was exactly what the *Courier* wanted. The paper had learned two valuable journalistic lessons: the first was that murder sells; the second was that it pays to advertise. Any paper could simply print the news as it happened; it took a special kind of moxie to promote what had already become old news.

❨

The deal was done and the *Digby Weekly Courier* abandoned its usual caterwauls of protest and dismay at being forced to print base and reviled commentary regarding Peter Wheeler. There was more money to be made from jumping in and wallowing in the mire than mocking those who did. Having thrown in its lot with the lowest common denominator, the tabloid unleashed a marketing campaign that guaranteed every last citizen of Nova Scotia knew the confession was coming. The *Courier* announced it would print the confession as part of a special edition, "numbering several thousand copies and containing engravings descriptive of the leading features of the tragedy, together with a complete history of the terrible affair, Wheeler's confession and an account of the execution."[51] Timing was key, and the *Courier* planned to release its exclusive on the

The press room of the *Digby Weekly Courier*, circa 1900,
centrally located in the heart of the city's bustling harbour front.

same day Wheeler was executed, leaving him no opportunity to refute
any disputable claims it might contain. It would be the most comprehensive
compendium available on the tragedy, or so their advertisements promised.

To ensure maximum market saturation, the *Courier* expanded its
normal distribution network, urging merchants and even rivals to carry
their exclusive: "newsdealers and others interested should write for
particulars."[52] What was truly shocking was the number of direct competitors
who accepted the *Courier*'s brazen offer, using their own pages to promote
their adversary's exclusive. The *Bridgetown Monitor* heralded the upcoming

commemorative, and informed its subscribers that "the special edition of the *Courier* will be on sale at all important points along the line of railway from Yarmouth to Windsor."[53] The *Saint John Daily Record* also tweaked its readership with news of the *Courier*'s coup, touting that "indeed the country roundabout, across the bay and all Canada was deeply stunned"[54] by Annie's death and that no man of woman born was immune to the illicit charms of the upcoming spectacular.

To whet the public's appetite, the *Digby Weekly Courier* began running a series of provocative teases, hinting at the startling revelations its special edition would feature. In breathless text that begged for a decent copy editor, the weekly proclaimed: "the interest in this matter will, we believe, be sustained when it is known that Wheeler's confession completely disproves the theory of the crown but in such a way that a number of points that have hitherto stood in the way of a popular recognition of the facts as being otherwise than thought by the crown are fully explained and brought into a story more reasonable than any yet produced."[55] In other far less convoluted words, the *Courier* promised a version of the crime that finally fit the evidence, a novel concept at this late stage.

And, there would be pictures.

thirty-six

"But It Had to End"

In the wake of the *Digby Weekly Courier's* big announcement, its competitors divided into two camps: those who awaited the special edition with bated breath and those possessed of a decidedly more cynical view of the upcoming extravaganza. Whether it was the green-eyed monster alone that prompted the backlash is difficult to discern; jealousy is easily hidden in critique. The *Annapolis Spectator* may have trounced its competition by being first on the "Wheeler confessional" bandwagon, but the *Digby Weekly Courier* made it perfectly clear that its goal was to commandeer the vehicle and ride it, solo and triumphant, across the finish line.

The folks at the *Morning Chronicle* saw it as their mission to ensure that did not happen. If other papers planned to simply roll over and accept the *Courier* as alpha, the *Chronicle* had no intention of joining them. The paper was also prepared to play rough.

By this point in the twisted tale of Peter Wheeler, it was virtually impossible to know how much of any particular news account was true and what could be believed. To this day, there is no means of verifying many of their assertions. Journalists seemed free to take considerable liberties and, at times, offer up outright deceptions. While some exercises in poetic licence remain glaringly obvious, other amended vignettes buried in the wreckage are harder to categorize.

When it comes to the honesty, integrity, and reliability of the press, one of the greatest innovations of all time was the introduction of the byline. Forcing correspondents to put their name (and often face) to their words caused a good many to rethink their approach to reporting. In the age before credited stories — which unfortunately included the Wheeler era —the reporter's anonymity provided the perfect shield against accountability. Stories could rarely be traced to their source, much less their sources. As was often the case, particularly with the smaller weekly tabloids, it was possible there were no actual reporters at all. The "news" such papers belched forth was nothing more than a reprint of wire service issue and openly plagiarized rehashing of the larger dailies compiled by a lone editor or publisher.

In such a tenuous environment, all accounts of reporters holding private interviews with Peter Wheeler — which were legion in the lull between the court and the gallows — must be viewed with a skeptical eye. No jail records survive and there is no independent means of confirming whether the visits even occurred, much less what was said. Since no correspondent's name was directly linked to a story, the checks and balances that hold fabrication at bay were minimal and the temptation to embellish was more than some reporters could bear.

☾

By the end of August a strange normalcy had descended on the Digby jailhouse. Wheeler, having called his barren cell home for the past few months, settled into a daily routine. He met each morning with a few prayers and a crust or two of his mouldy prison fare then Peter would prepare to receive his guests, the day's allotment of journalists and other notables who had secured an audience through the largesse of his guardian, Sheriff Benjamin Van Blarcom.

As September dawned and Wheeler's time on earth dwindled to a handful of days, one particular morning brought two red-letter visitors. The first was an unnamed correspondent from the *Morning Chronicle*. The second, at least according to the first, was Matilda Comeau.

The ever-shifting sentiments and loyalties of Bear River had become quicksand beneath Wheeler's feet. Tarred, feathered, and pilloried by his cronies and detractors alike, Peter found himself without a friend in the world. Only Tillie Comeau had stood by him, whether out of a mother's love or something more carnal. Whatever had passed between them, whatever understanding they once enjoyed, the relationship had endured long after Wheeler's more fair-weather companions had abandoned his sinking ship, as rats notoriously do.

Tillie's visit was much welcomed by Wheeler, who despaired of ever seeing her again. As the *Chronicle* noted: "She had promised to come from Bear River last Tuesday to see him, but when that day and the remaining days passed without her putting in an appearance, he began to lament over his disappointment and feared that he would never meet her again on earth."[1] When Tillie finally cropped up at the cellblock door, Wheeler's joy was evident to all. She reportedly made her apologies and excuses, saying she was employed every day and "could not afford to lose a day's labor."[2]

Always on the lookout for drama (be it real or manufactured), the *Chronicle* rep let slip that Tillie's absence had nothing to do with her work schedule: "it required a number of urgent messages to induce her to pay Wheeler another visit, as she had no particular wish to see him again."[3] One key element of drama, however, is unpredictability. Having just informed his readers of her supposed reticence, the reporter suddenly shifted emotional gears, noting that "tears were shed copiously on both sides, Tillie Comeau seeming to feel the situation fully as deeply as did the man whose crime has brought him to the gallows."[4] It seems the reporter was having difficulty taking the emotional temperature of the room.

Although the *Chronicle* correspondent was willing to go with the fervent ebb and flow of the moment, he had arrived with his own agenda. His task for the day was to expose the sordid details of the *Digby Weekly Courier*'s purchase of Wheeler's final words and the love story quickly gave way to more pressing financial matters. "There was a little business to transact,"[5] said the *Chronicle*, regarding the "proceeds from the sale of Wheeler's confession to be published this week, of which one-half is to be given to whoever Peter designates."[6] The report fails to note exactly how the *Morning Chronicle* became privy to such information. At no point does the reporter suggest Wheeler was his source and it was unlikely anyone at the Digby tabloid had been so loose with the specifics of their contract. What was clear was that the *Chronicle* hoped to unmask the *Courier*'s hypocrisy. In spite of the *Digby Courier*'s wall-to-wall promotion of its special edition, it was careful not to appear too venal. The paper never once revealed that it had paid for the publication rights; indeed, it maintained its normal haughty tone, implying such mercenary ploys were beneath the organization's dignity.

If one accepts the *Chronicle*'s contract claims at face value, one must also accept the paper's report as to the identity of Wheeler's designate — his long-time landlady love: "Peter wants Tillie Comeau to receive this money to do with as she pleases."[7] According to the *Morning Chronicle*, what pleased Tillie was to give the money to her youngest son, Walter, as "she does not want it herself and would not use it for her own benefit."[8] How much Wheeler was paid for his confession was never stated — a frustrating omission.

At this juncture, the once-emotional meeting takes a discernibly legal turn. "An agreement was drawn up this afternoon"[9] giving Tillie all of Wheeler's meagre worldly possessions, including his share of the proceeds. Who drew up this agreement was not stipulated, another glaring omission. As the documents were being signed and duly executed, the *Chronicle* added one last brush stroke to complete its tableau. The reporter offered up a strident variation on the "Tillie-as-wanton-harlot" theme by stating that Wheeler paused during the transaction and "besought her with all the Christian eloquence at his command to turn from the error of her ways…and join the Christian throng."[10] Tillie made no such promises.

Having failed to save her immortal soul or even line her earthly pockets, Wheeler was forced to bid Tillie "a heartbreaking farewell."[11] In prose both purple and prosaic, the *Chronicle* brought the couple's love story to an abrupt halt: "But it had to end at last and Tillie bore herself from the embrace of the condemned man and mounted the stairway from the jail basement, crying bitterly. Ten minutes later she was on her way back to Bear River."[12]

Readers could not help but think a precious opportunity had been squandered. Still, the reporter's gambit paid off, no matter how clumsy its execution. The headline story struck a chord with romantics, cynics, and sinners alike. His scenario encompassed all the necessary narrative elements: a classic tale of unrequited love, the perils of crass commercialism, and last-minute redemption, all neatly tied together in a bow that strangled its chief rival, the *Digby Weekly Courier*.

Once the *Morning Chronicle* had let the *Courier*'s well-kept secret out of the bag, the lesser papers piled on. The *Digby Weekly Courier*'s special edition suddenly seemed less of a media coup and more of a triumph of chequebook journalism. The *Digby Weekly Courier* — which had so callously led the chorus taunting Tillie Comeau for her wanton ways — now found itself exposed as the media whore it truly was.

❬

If the *Courier* took home the gold medal in media slatternliness, the silver went to a relative unknown — a local barber by the name of Charles Trask. The deluge of press coverage afforded every one of Wheeler's visitors invariably caught the attention of the wily Mr. Trask, who saw an opportunity for a little free advertising. It all began innocently enough, a refrain familiar to every john ever busted in a solicitation sweep. Barber Trask, who owned a shop in the town of Digby, offered to give the accused a final shave and a haircut, sending him to the hereafter looking his very best. Van Blarcom approved the request with no concern as to Wheeler's wishes.

As expected, Trask's pilgrimage to death row garnered plenty of media interest, if for no other reason than the introduction of a straight razor into the cell of a condemned man under suicide watch. The visit left many wondering what Van Blarcom could possibly have been thinking. So great were public fears that Wheeler might have grabbed the razor and hurt himself or others that Trask later amended his account by saying he had demanded the prisoner's arms be bound behind his back. The barber's belated histrionics were good copy but there had been little need for such precautions. Peter made no effort to seize the blade or run his visitor through. Rather, Wheeler spent their time together offering words of advice and comfort to the barber, counselling him to "turn his back on temptation and become a Christian."[13] Trask later told reporters he was so moved by his encounter that he assured Wheeler he would lead a better life from that day forward. However self-serving Trask's initial intentions might have been, he had gained not only his sought-after publicity but a whole new spiritual outlook on life. For days following the visit Trask made the rounds, sharing his redemption song with every news organ in the Maritimes. In addition to printing Wheeler's healing prescription, most articles provided directions to Trask's barbershop.

Other local merchants could not help but notice the upswing in business such notoriety brought Trask and his razor and they were soon clamouring to get in on the act. Charles Mason — a shoe and boot dealer in Digby — provided Wheeler with a new pair of black patent-leather shoes for his final walk to the gallows. Although Mason claimed he made the gift out of the goodness of his heart, he later expressed disappointment that, while every paper had noted the prisoner's shiny new footwear, only the *Morning Chronicle* had identified him as the donor.[14]

Corporate sponsorship of Wheeler's impending execution quickly took on a life of its own. The Salvation Army received front-page coverage for their gift to the condemned: a pair of black trousers and a crisp white shirt.[15] The ensemble was meant to serve double duty, to be worn at both the execution and as Wheeler's burial suit. Having read the accounts of Wheeler's shameful death-house diet, a number of bakeries and local restaurants delivered meals to the prisoner, although the honour of making his last meal went to the sheriff's own wife.[16] Local outfitters offered much-needed rope for the noose, while a well-known carpentry firm made quick work of a coffin.

These feints of altruism began to rub the reading public the wrong way. A few of the more vocal throng questioned why there were no such signs of generosity at the funeral of Annie Kempton. To stem the tide of publicity seekers, the papers stopped printing the names of donors and the flood of donations instantly dried up.

thirty-seven

"The Hole in the Floor of the Gallows"

It takes a special sort of man to serve as an executioner. The job is not for the faint of heart or those ruled by heated passions such as vengeance or hatred. Hanging requires a cool head, a steady hand, and more than a passing knowledge of physics and human anatomy. Sending a man (or on rare occasion a woman) to meet the Almighty was no small feat, as dozens of botched executions in the 1800s can attest. And so when the powers that be learned of a particularly gifted hangman, his services were prized and in high demand, particularly in the era of the Bloody Code, the golden age of British law in which virtually every offence was punishable by death.

When Canadian courts imported the Code across the Atlantic, British traditions of execution followed close behind. Chief among them was the practice of naming an official executioner, a professional in the art and science of state-sanctioned death. Like the nation itself, Canada's legal system was growing by leaps and bounds in the 1890s but the country's anointed executioner was a man of proven mettle and long experience, unfazed by the awkward growth spurt. His name was John Radcleve.

Although the official tally puts the number of men hanged by Radcleve at 69, the actual number was likely closer to 150. Hanging was, after all, his entire life's work. British-born, Radcleve's formative years were spent in the Royal Navy, where he learned his dark art by hanging pirates in the South China Sea. Later he apprenticed under England's official executioner, William Marwood. After immigrating to Toronto, Radcleve quickly made a name for himself by conducting several successful executions in Ontario at a time when "successful" was not a word often associated with the process. Word of the hangman's unique talents reached then-Ontario premier Oliver Mowat, who enlisted Radcleve to serve as provincial executioner. His promotion to the nation's first commissioned hangman came in 1892, when he was appointed to the newly created post by Canada's fourth prime minister, Sir John Thompson.

Despite his macabre title, Radcleve was little more than a federal employee. As Wheeler lay cooling his heels in the dock, Radcleve's salary was just seven hundred dollars per year. To supplement his meagre wage, he had a grisly stipulation written into his governmental contract that entitled him to literally keep the clothes off the dead men's backs. Radcleve sold those items that neither fit nor struck his fancy. Another lucrative sideline was the pedalling of souvenirs to the morbid collector. He once famously clipped the ponytail of a recently dispatched Chinese national, which he divvied up and sold to the bolder members of the assembled throng. Radcleve also sold lengths of rope supposedly used to hang infamous prisoners, although with few exceptions, the ropes were fakes. Legal constraints prohibited him from selling the actual nooses used, but Radcleve still profited handsomely from the public's ignorance of the intricacies of government bureaucracy. One west coast sheriff reported seeing Canada's hangman in a hardware store just before a particularly contentious execution, purchasing a spool of rope to shill to eager memento seekers. It all smacked of a premonition Robert Payne of the *Saint John Daily Sun* had in the weeks after Wheeler was arrested: "if the murderer of Annie Kempton is executed, bits of the hangman's rope will be worth their weight in gold."[1]

Given the nature of his calling, it comes as no surprise that Radcleve was not what anyone would describe as a sensitive or compassionate man. He was, for want of a better word, an absolute bastard. Forgettable in his calmer moments, it took only the slightest provocation for Radcleve to become a cauldron of seething emotion, liable to scald any who ventured near. Prone to vocal tirades from the gallows, Radcleve was far from the sombre and silent executioner depicted in popular culture. There seemed to be nothing he enjoyed more than raising the hackles of the populace who revelled in his violent trade. In 1892 he was sent to dispatch a murderer in Hull. Walking into a crowded local tavern, Radcleve announced with his usual barroom gusto that he "had come to hang a Frenchman and hoped it would not be the last."[2] During the ensuing brawl, Radcleve gave as good as he got but was vastly outnumbered. He was badly beaten, saved only through the timely arrival of a police paddy wagon.

Radcleve's tendencies toward bellicosity, mendacity, and belligerence may have escaped the notice of his superiors, who chalked up his cantankerous nature to the price of doing business, but his choleric ways soon had press pundits up in arms. In 1900 a correspondent for the *Toronto Star* wrote: "if he were a man of delicate sensibilities, he would not be the hangman. He is a necessity in our system but he should be treated as if he is the hole in the floor of the gallows."[3] Those were decidedly harsh words for a man tasked with a job few others wanted or knew how to do.

As the population soared and crime rates kept pace, gallows began springing up across the nation, which — in a country the size of Canada — meant constant travel for the so-called necessity to the system. Although he was once married with kids, blissful domesticity offered no succour to John Radcleve. Sickened by his increasingly volatile nature and frequent absences, Mrs. Radcleve took the children and returned to her native England, leaving the nation's hangman to a life of bitter solitude. Like many of his ilk and chosen vocation, Radcleve turned to the bottle to soothe his embattled soul. He often appeared intoxicated or hung over on the gallows, and in his later years, he failed to show up at all for a few executions. Drink would prove the death of him. He was found dead in his home (or a Toronto hotel room, depending on which account you believe) on February 26, 1911. Cirrhosis of the liver had claimed him at the age of fifty-five.[4]

Radcleve's unique job title, colourful life story, and ignominious death have since secured him a place in the nation's history books, but in the summer of 1896, such infamy was still a mere blip on the horizon. John Radcleve was very much alive, though universally despised, and had just received word there was a man in Nova Scotia that needed killing. Radcleve put down the bottle, picked up his ropes, and headed for the Toronto train station.

❦

By this time, Wheeler had achieved a measure of celebrity large enough to generate its own weather system. His infamy preceded him all the way to Toronto, where it reportedly struck a responsive chord with the country's leading hangman. On July 22, 1896, the *Bridgetown Monitor* gleefully reported that Radcleve actually "wants to hang Wheeler." In point of fact the paper called him Radcliffe, a common occurrence. His name was often butchered by the imperfect machinations of Victorian journalism and telegraphy. The article went on to say that the renowned executioner was begging to do the dark deed, going so far as to make an application to Sheriff Van Blarcom to carry out the Queen's verdict. Van Blarcom, whose role as sheriff made him responsible for the execution, reportedly welcomed Radcleve's interest and wrote back asking how much his services might cost. It was, by all accounts, a rather genteel exchange, more akin to a garden party invitation than the methodical killing of a human being.

The *Monitor*'s exclusive interview with Van Blarcom gave them a meaty scoop. Other papers were forced to play catch-up, reprinting the *Monitor*'s account second-hand. The Bridgetown editor's delight at besting his competition was almost visible from space.

His joy was to be short-lived. One month later, the *Bridgetown Monitor* ran a small correction, buried deep between some local town gossip and its regular feature, the much-loved "Joke Corner." The tiny headline proclaimed "Radcliffe will not hang Wheeler"[5] and declared that any prior claims he would to be "altogether unfounded."[6] As usual, the *Monitor* deftly sidestepped the fact that such prior claims emanated from its own pages. Van Blarcom, who now claimed to have never spoken with the *Monitor*'s reporter, also denied having corresponded with Radcleve and confirmed that he alone would be responsible for carrying out Wheeler's sentence. Like all good tight-fisted bureaucrats, Van Blarcom was loath to spend money on luxuries, and for the first time in his professional career, Radcleve's services were deemed a hedonistic indulgence.

The word echoed forth from that day — John Radcleve, the "hole in the floor of the gallows," was not welcome in Digby County. Annie Kempton had been one of their own (as was Wheeler, for that matter) and Bear River would take care of its own. If the "negro-lynchers"[7] of the South could hang a man, Sheriff Van Blarcom reasoned, so could he. John Radcleve put down his ropes, took up his bottle, and sat back, content to watch Van Blarcom make a shambles of it all.

Annie's father, Isaac, from the *Digby Weekly Courier*, September 8, 1896.

thirty-eight

Meeting the Kemptons

During the last week of his life, Peter Wheeler entertained the usual fraternity of reporters in his cell. Depending on Van Blarcom's mood, the prisoner also played host to the curious, the publicity seeking, and the cream of the county's polite society. Rubbing elbows with the condemned became a strangely fashionable craze during the Victorian era and Wheeler was the only game in town.

If nothing else, visiting a dead man walking was a good way to garner a little media attention. For example, the *Yarmouth Herald* dedicated considerable coverage to the story of Mr. James McMillan, a former police officer of the paper's namesake city. On a weekend jaunt to Digby to visit relatives, Mr. McMillan paid the price of admission and was granted a few minutes with the county's most notorious prisoner. Interviewed later at his home, McMillan expressed surprise at how easy it was to gain access to Wheeler, whom he found to be "in good spirits"[1] as the two "indulged in jokes and frivolous talking."[2] Despite the two having no prior acquaintance, McMillan told the *Herald* that Wheeler was quick to share intimacies, including the details of his recent visit with Tillie Comeau as well as his ongoing efforts to craft his life story. Wheeler told his new best friend that the recent spate of so-called confessions had riled him and he longed to set the record straight. Finally, in passing and apropos of nothing, Wheeler let slip that "he had never denied that he had killed Annie Kempton,"[3] a startling admission from a man who had steadfastly proclaimed his innocence.

Such reports must be taken with a grain of salt. The papers were littered with these supposed first-person accounts, each brimming with odious rumours and spurious claims. For the press, it was a convenient device to keep the Wheeler saga on the front page. For the sources themselves, it was a fast track to their fifteen minutes of fame, the Victorian precursor to today's reality television pseudo-celebrity.

Wheeler's chockablock social calendar served its various purposes: the prisoner was distracted and amused, the sheriff's pockets grew heavy, and the press had something to write. Traffic through the revolving door to Wheeler's cell only increased as the execution date drew near. The press, having finally crossed Tillie off the list of highly anticipated emotionally wrought visitors, found that only one set of names remained. All the media mavericks could do now was take a collective last gulp of air and wait for the denouement of this particular picaresque: the predicted death-row visit from the victim's parents, Isaac and Mary Kempton.

Although they were of markedly humble social status, the Kemptons were well liked and highly regarded members of the community. The *Acadian Recorder* had once described Isaac Kempton as owning "a productive and comfortable farm,"[4] but it was clear its reporter had never set eyes on it. The Kempton home was located on a steep hill adjacent to the river and had little land under cultivation. Isaac was, in fact, a lumberman who struggled to eke out a steady living. His misfortunes were sordid grist for the tabloid rumour mill: "formerly well to do. . . the prevailing hard times have made a change for the worse and Mr. Kempton, together with the members of his family, are compelled to save their rather comfortable home by the sweat of their brows."[5] While some papers discreetly excused Mrs. Kempton's absence from the home under the guise of "visiting relatives in the United States," the *Morning Chronicle* laid bare the Kemptons' reduced circumstances when it reported that mother Mary was forced to work as a maid in her son-in-law's tony Somerville, Massachusetts, home to help keep the family afloat.[6]

Despite his failing finances, Isaac Kempton remained a proud man.

Born in the eponymous village of Kempton, Nova Scotia, Isaac came to Bear River in the early 1860s. There he met and married a local girl, Mary Parker. Although Mary was never considered one of the region's great beauties, it was by all accounts a loving and happy union. The couple had one son and four daughters, Annie being the youngest and the only one still living at home full-time. Her sisters had married well and relocated to the northeastern United States. Isaac was fifty-nine years old at the time of Annie's death. When he was not consumed with grief and financial strife, Isaac was normally considered avuncular and gregarious. The *Acadian Recorder* commented that, despite his present hardships, he looked young for his age and was "a medium sized man with dark face and brown side whiskers"[7] who was "a pleasant talker."[8]

According to the *Recorder*, Kempton was understandably bitter towards Wheeler, whom Isaac once considered a close friend. Kempton took a chance on the then-fourteen-year-old Wheeler, giving the boy his first job when he arrived in Bear River. Isaac now called Wheeler "a bad lying scoundrel"[9] and dismissed his alleged confessions as pure fabrications. Kempton — who had testified at the inquest, examination, and trial — possessed an almost encyclopedic knowledge of the case. The bereaved father told one reporter that the bloodstains and condition of the room proved that the murder was committed in the afternoon, although he offered no specifics to support his claim.

Mary Kempton, whose taciturn manner belied a steely core, never took the stand to testify. As she was out of the country at the time of the murder, she had little to offer the court but her grief and guilt. Since Mary had no open avenue to express herself, the media elected to speak for her. Some news services (including the *Bridgetown Monitor*) painted her with broad dark strokes, suggesting she was an ineffectual guardian. To the vast majority of news organs, however, she was the silent, long-suffering mother, a stock character needing little back story or embellishment.

Although Mary preferred to harbour her grief out of the media spotlight, she was occasionally thrust into its searing glare. Shortly after his arrest, Peter Wheeler wrote a letter to the Kemptons. In it, he denied having anything to do with the crime and begged them "to not be too down on him."[10] Mary chose to share the letter with the *Acadian Recorder* correspondent during the only interview she ever granted the press.

According to Mary, Wheeler had sent word to the Kemptons as his execution drew closer, saying he hoped he could meet with them before he died. With time running out, Isaac and Mary reluctantly made their way to the Digby jail. Although she was distraught almost to the point of hysteria, Mary Kempton stepped into the jail with her own agenda. Mary, in equal measure racked with guilt and paralyzed by the unknown, needed to know her daughter's final words.

The meeting did not go as any had hoped, although what actually took place depended on which paper one read. According to the *Acadian Recorder*, the Kemptons questioned Wheeler ruthlessly for hours on end. Wheeler begged their forgiveness but they refused to absolve him, claiming he was "lying in the face of death."[11] As the heated exchange wore on, Mary broke down and Isaac drew back his arm, intending to strike Wheeler through the tiny window in the door of his cell. Stepping in at the last minute, Sheriff Van Blarcom caught Kempton's fist and restored order.

Both the *Morning Chronicle* and the *Nova Scotian* heard different. According to their reports, there was neither the threat of physical confrontation between the victim's father and her accused killer nor did Wheeler beg for forgiveness. Rather, Peter was "deeply agitated and was glad the meeting did not last long."[12] As no punches were thrown, Van Blarcom was conspicuously absent from their accounts.

The *Digby Weekly Courier* had an entirely different spin on the meeting, which reportedly had left Mrs. Kempton's "very heart bleeding."[13] Although Mary was always in excellent health, the encounter made her "dangerously ill."[14] Unlike its competitors, the *Courier* made no mention of fisticuffs, forgiveness, or Wheeler's feelings.

Although none of the rival media factions could agree on the specifics of the meeting, they all found their way clear to end their accounts with the same question: would Isaac Kempton attend Wheeler's execution, and more importantly, would he — if asked — throw the lever that would send Peter Wheeler to his death?

thirty-nine
Wheeler Gets Religion

Despite appearances to the contrary, Digby considered itself a progressive town where all manner of odd behaviour was excused, as long as it didn't frighten the fish. Peculiarities were tolerated, infelicities were comforted, and the world's heavy burdens were eased by an enduring spirit of community. It was a fellowship born of a life lived on (or at least near) the sea, with all its inherent perils and pleasures. So precarious an existence was made possible and even tolerable through faith: faith in each other, faith in the bounty of the waves, and faith in a higher power. Digbians were hardly united in their faith — Methodists lived peaceably alongside Baptists and Catholics alike. How or where a man chose to worship was not important; what mattered was that he did worship. The concept of freedom of religion extended just far enough to embrace the Almighty in all His guises but snapped when stretched to include agnostics or atheists.

As if being a highly pigmented convicted murderer were not enough, Wheeler's other unforgivable sins included what his neighbours perceived as a chronic, pathological disinterest in religion or, more to the point, his failure to practice religious piety as others deemed acceptable. Actually, Wheeler was a highly spiritual man, well-versed in the Bible and well-acquainted with the code of Christian conduct. The problem was not that Wheeler did not believe in God; the problem was that Wheeler wanted to worship his deity on his own terms.

Alternately stymied and outraged by the prisoner's steadfast refusal to bow to social pressure and repent before he took leave of this world (or was forcibly ejected from it), a veritable "who's who" of local clergy beat a liturgical path to the Digby jail with one goal in mind: to convert the heathen sinner and make him atone his wicked ways. They could have saved themselves the trip. Without exception, Wheeler dismissed "clergymen of different denominations from Digby, Annapolis, Bear River and other places,"[1] proclaiming to all who came calling that: "I belong to the church of Christ and I am satisfied I have found the Lord, who is now my only comforter."[2]

Whatever their collective sins, the media were one thing above all: consistent. When it came to the matter of religion, as with every other aspect of Wheeler's behaviour or speech, Peter was damned if he did and damned if he didn't. His proclamation that he had found the Lord did meet with the heartfelt approval of his self-appointed spiritual advisor, Captain Harris Bowles. Bowles, a pious foot soldier in the Salvation Army, told the *Morning Chronicle* that: "Peter's conversion occurred some six weeks ago and that ever since then the murderer has been most Christian-like in his conduct and manner of living."[3] The *Nova Scotian* was not so easily swayed: "Wheeler's talk was always so filled with lying contradictions that it is safe to concede his professed conversion was a sham."[4] The *Saint John Daily Record* wholeheartedly agreed, stating Wheeler was "too blatant"[5] in his newly minted piety to be sincere.

As for Peter, his was no hackneyed foxhole conversion. Wheeler was a man mired in godless despair, who esteemed a saviour that, by all appearances, had forsaken him. Receiving little solace from above, Wheeler thought of his salvation less as a passage into heaven than as a reprieve from the fiery pits of hell. With his tongue firmly planted in his cheek, Peter told reporters that his deliverance from Satan had made him "the happiest boy in Digby."[6]

Public skepticism aside, Wheeler's private spiritual journey continued apace. In one of his final acts on earth, Peter sat in his tiny cell and wrote three letters, each begging its recipient to forsake all earthly temptations and hold tight to the ways of the Lord. The letters, all unsigned, were eloquent and stirring departures from the prisoner's usual heavy-handed secular rhetoric. Having written his fill, Wheeler slipped the letters one by one into envelopes, addressed each in turn, and then handed them to Captain Bowles, with strict instructions that the letters be mailed immediately. As Bowles mounted the stairs from the basement dungeon, he made note of the intended recipients. The first envelope bore a familiar name: Tillie Comeau. The second was addressed to her eighteen-year-old daughter Hattie, a girl Peter had often called sister. The last letter was marked for Charles Trask, the mercenary barber whose ablutions had prepared Peter to meet his maker.[7] As Wheeler stood "on the threshold of Eternity,"[8] poised on the brink of the abyss, it is disheartening to think how tenuous his tethers to the outside world had become.

forty

Ottawa Weighs In

Although the press, public, and Digby power brokers lamented the lengthy pause between Wheeler's conviction and his execution, those months served a real purpose. It had nothing to do with the appellate process — not an option for Peter at that time, at least as we understand appeals today — but it provided the necessary buffer for one of the legislative hiccups lingering in the country's nascent system of jurisprudence. While many perceived the jury's verdict and the judge's sentencing as the final word on Wheeler's fate, nothing could be further from the truth. Capital crimes were still affronts to sovereignty — the case was, after all, *Queen v. Wheeler* — and so Peter's future was wrested from provincial hands. Whether the prisoner lived or died was now a matter for the Crown, and in the decades since Confederation, the "Crown" in Canada was, for all intents and purposes, the Governor General.

As a matter of legal course, sole discretion for clemency fell to the current resident of Rideau Hall, who, in 1896, was the Right Honorable John Campbell Hamilton-Gordon, Earl of Aberdeen, the once and future Lord Lieutenant of Ireland and Canada's seventh Governor General. In his prime, Sir John possessed an impeccable sartorial sense, the perfect foil to his sometimes unruly beard, and a haunted piercing gaze that sometimes bordered on cruel.[1] His fearsome countenance was well earned, as he had the misfortune of overseeing Canada during a period of considerable political turmoil. Although Campbell only held the post for five years (1893-1898), his term coincided with a revolving door of Prime Ministers: John Thompson, Mackenzie Bowell, Charles Tupper, and Wilfrid

Laurier. Sir John used this period of uncertainty to reform his office's rather ambiguous political mandate. He is credited with transforming "the role of Governor General from that of the aristocrat representing the King or Queen in Canada to a symbol representing the interests of all citizens."[2] Such progressive views may have heralded great change in Ottawa but it did not bode well for Peter Wheeler. If the media were to be believed, the interests of the citizenry were to have Wheeler hung from the highest yardarm at the Crown's earliest possible convenience.

While the buck unquestionably stopped at Rideau Hall, it first had to make its way through the mille feuille that was the bureaucracy of Ottawa. Judge Charles Townshend initiated the process minutes after he sentenced Wheeler to hang, when he sent a letter to Sir Charles Tupper Bart, then Secretary of State. In it, Townshend makes his position perfectly clear: "Although the evidence on which he was convicted was almost entirely circumstantial, yet that in my opinion the verdict was fully justifiable by the evidence adduced on behalf of the Crown."[3] Townshend also made the rather bold decision to not send any documentation or evidence for the Crown's perusal, saying only that such materials were available, should they be deemed necessary. The letter's brevity and terse tone raise some question as to whether Townshend — a puisne provincial Supreme Court justice — resented such judicial review or merely thought it unnecessary.

Ottawa clearly felt it was necessary, as the immediate response from Undersecretary of State Joseph Pope indicated.[4] Pope instructed Townshend to send the case file immediately, a request the judge grudgingly granted,[5] although the documents forwarded were parsed to the point of bias.

The judicial cherry-picking continued as the file marked "Capital case of Peter Wheeler"[6] wended its way through the hallowed halls of the nation's capital. Its first stop was the Privy Council Office, where the standard petition for the release of Peter Wheeler was denied.[7] The file's next port of call was the desk of a junior unnamed lackey in the office of the Ministry of Justice, who had the thankless task of preparing a brief for the justice minister to review.[8] The resulting memorandum, dated August 8, 1896, laid out a revisionist timeline of the case to rival that of Detective Nicholas Power's. The brief, drawn from the court documents, argued that the crime was unambiguously committed by Wheeler at 6:00 p.m. Unfortunately, the file did not contain a full court transcript but rather selected witness statements and heavily redacted testimony. As a consequence, the brief was a highly skewed and prejudicial take on the trial, riddled with calculatedly edited quotes designed to shore up the circumstantial case.

In early August, the memo reached its target audience: Sir Oliver Mowat, minister of justice. Despite his lofty post, Mowat looked more like a vaudeville performer than the country's top legal mind. Regardless of circumstance, Mowat wore a look of distracted bemusement, as if recalling a favoured joke.[9]

There was little cause for levity at the moment. Mowat reviewed his underling's case summary and recommendations. On August 13, Mowat fulfilled his statutory obligations by redrafting the memorandum, signing his own name, and forwarding it to the Governor General for his consideration. The case had travelled to the top of the legal food chain, if salary and rank were any indication. What began at the feet of a six-hundred-dollar-a-year Halifax detective then passed before the bench of Judge Townshend who cost the taxpayers of Nova Scotia some four thousand dollars that year. From there, it transferred to the well-manicured hands of the Minister of Justice, whose annual salary topped seven thousand dollars before ascending to the rarefied air of the royal retinue, who took home ten thousand dollars per annum for his troubles,[10] all in service to Wheeler, a journeyman who never made more than a dollar a day in his life.

The justice minister had no qualms in stating his recommendation: carry out the execution as sentenced. Despite its incessant tone, Mowat's letter would sit on Sir John Campbell Hamilton-Gordon's elegant yet cluttered desk until the eleventh hour.

Mowat's recommendation was hardly the only paper being generated on the question of Peter Wheeler. Missives ricocheted across Ottawa and between the capital and the little Maritime province where the problem first began. Without question, the singularly most damning dispatch was a seemingly innocuous letter sent by Digby Sheriff Benjamin Van Blarcom to the Attorney General on August 17. The note, typed on the sheriff's engraved stationery, was sent in response to a query from Ottawa, asking if Wheeler had confessed to the crime. With unwavering certainty but only a passing concern for the truth, Van Blarcom declared: "Wheeler confesses to the fact that he committed the crime, and has done so ever since he was convicted, that he committed it after twelve o'clock and not between five and eight, as in the evidence given at trial shows. I have never seen the written confession but am sure there is one."[11] Van Blarcom's assurances stemmed from the *Digby Weekly Courier*'s promotional campaign, trumpeting its soon-to-be-published confessional coup.

The evidentiary rules regarding confessions were clear. If such an admission was offered by the convicted man, then a signed copy of the confession needed to be forwarded to the Ministry of Justice for final review. Failing that, signed affidavits were required from anyone claiming to have heard an oral confession from a prisoner. Van Blarcom's letter circumvented all such mandates, providing nothing but his word as a gentleman that Wheeler had confessed.

Van Blarcom's declaration unleashed a second flurry of letters, as everyone weighed in on this fortuitous development, and in so doing, created a paper trail perfectly crafted to cover behinds and absolve all parties of any culpability. Deputy Minister of Justice E.L. Newcombe wrote to the Attorney General of Nova Scotia, seeking assurances that the confession was legitimate. One has to wonder if Newcombe knew whom he was dealing with. Nova Scotia's Attorney General was James Wilberforce Longley, a born and bred Bluenose who was as tightly wound a creature as has ever walked. Blessed with a rapier wit, Longley was a man long accustomed to taking up more than his fair share of oxygen. Longley's response to Newcombe was a breathtaking exercise in plausible deniability. With one deft stroke of his pen, Longley managed to speak his piece without committing to anything: "I gather from your letter that you invite any observations from myself in relation to [the confession]. I can only say that any observations from me seem superfluous. It was one of the most cold blooded and brutal murders on record and not the shadow of doubt exists as to the guilt of the accused."[12] Deputy Newcombe, amply placated, then communicated Longley's affirmations to his boss, Oliver Mowat.

The ripples caused by Van Blarcom's letter did not stop there and were quickly building into a lethal tsunami. Weeks had passed with no official decision from the Earl of Aberdeen and Mowat was growing impatient. On September 1, the justice minister issued an addendum to his "*Regina vs. Peter Wheeler*" Memorandum to the Governor General. To bolster the prosecution's case, Mowat emphasized two salient points. The first was to highlight that "it is noticeable that there does not appear to be any circumstance of suspicion against anyone else, and no one else appears to be suspected of having committed the murder,"[13] a fainéant revisiting of the lazy argument foisted on the jury during the Crown's trial summation. The second more troubling issue was a pointed reference to Van Blarcom's letter: "Since considering the case, letters have been received stating that Wheeler has confessed his guilt."[14]

With that, Sir John Campbell Hamilton-Gordon had heard enough. He issued Executive Order-in-Council PC-2631, ordering the execution of Peter Wheeler for the crime of murder. After months of inquest, examinations, trials, and tribulations, it was the final word on the subject and the last gasp of hope for the very lowest of the Queen's subjects.

forty-one

Trouble Brewing

As Wheeler's now certain day of reckoning drew near, the crowds swelled and overwhelmed Digby, a town never before witness to so wretched a gaggle of men. A catena of railcars and horse teams disgorged their cargo, unleashing a tide of humanity bent on seeing evil in the flesh and justice done before their very eyes. The mercenary mixed freely with the merely curious. Street urchins hawked the latest editions of local rags and jostled cheek by jowl with working girls and buskers, all in a desperate quest to part the assembled gawkers from their coin. The end result was a bizarre saturnalia heightened by the strange menace of the occasion. The final fatal ingredient was the liberal flow of alcohol, as if inebriation might somehow temper the Lucullan scale of the debauchery. Robert Payne of the *Saint John Daily Sun* contended that "the hotels, livery stables and rum shops all did a big business, especially the later. [*sic*] Several arrests were made, all for drunkenness."[1]

Yet it was not the demon drink alone that caused such mischief. Reports circulated that the residents of Bear River intended to take matters into their own hands. No less a source than the *Toronto Evening Star* declared: "it is feared that an attack will be made in the jail by neighbors of the Kempton family who desire to witness the hanging."[2] The *Saint John Daily Telegraph* ratcheted up the threat and added props, with the report: "it is said that they have had 25 or 30 large iron hooks made with which they will pull down the jail if Wheeler is not publicly hanged."[3] Exactly who was doing all this saying and fearing was never stated, for such were the benefits of blind sources.

The *Daily Telegraph* took a dim view of its neighbours across the bay, openly chastising the residents of Digby County and their duly appointed sheriff: "the execution will either be bungled or Wheeler will be lynched."[4] Rival Saint John tabloid, the *Daily Record*, kept a firm grasp on the obvious when it printed that if the hanging were "done by another than the sheriff or deputy, it would have been murder."[5] Having blithely forsaken the services of the nation's hangman, it seemed the sheriff had his work cut out for him.

Indeed, the run-up to the execution was a gauntlet designed to test the fortitude of Sheriff Benjamin Van Blarcom. As the clock on Wheeler's remaining hours ran down, the sheriff was consumed with details large and small. Van Blarcom never saw a bed in the forty-eight hours leading up to "Wheeler's necktie party," as a sardonic few had taken to calling it. Van Blarcom oversaw every facet of the preparations, steadfast in his desire that "the law of the country, if not God's will"[6] be carried out to the letter. On September 7, an intoxicated crowd gathered to jeer as several sheriff's deputies began to dig Wheeler's grave at the rear of the jail.[7] The commotion caught the eye of the *Saint John Daily Record* correspondent, who mistakenly reported the work detail was erecting the scaffolding and gallows in the garden behind the jail.[8]

The subject of Wheeler's final resting place quickly became a hot button issue among the assembled rabble. Vested clergy were accosted on the streets by drunken louts seeking assurances that Wheeler's bones would never rest in consecrated soil. No churchyard or sanctioned cemetery had agreed to take his body, or that of any other executed convict. If Harris Bowles had succeeded in using the proceeds from Wheeler's confession to secure a burial plot, the captain was keeping the grave's location a closely guarded secret. For the drunken masses, where Wheeler ended up was of little interest; they had come to see a guilty man swing. J.W. Whitman, in a passionate letter to the editor of the *Bridgetown Monitor*, aptly summed up the feelings of many when he wrote: "Let him die the death of a vile cur and be buried with the burial of an ass."[9]

☾

In hopes of securing a front-row seat to the death of the vile cur, newsmen from across Canada and the United States descended on an already overtaxed Digby.[10] On Water Street, the town's main thoroughfare, the number of newshounds scrambling for "man-on-the-street" interviews sometimes exceeded the number of actual men on the street. Swamped with press requests to interview the prisoner, Van Blarcom settled on an expeditious but controversial plan. The sheriff announced that the condemned man would no longer be seeing journalists, much to the disappointment of the throng who sat waiting their turn on the jailhouse steps. Instead, the sheriff declared that Peter Wheeler would hold a press conference in his cell at precisely 6:00 that evening. Shouting to be heard above the resulting outcry, Van Blarcom extended a formal invitation to the gentlemen of the press to attend, then turned and beat a hasty retreat.

At the appointed hour, Van Blarcom and his deputies packed the press corps into the tiny holding cell. The fourth estate found themselves in a basement with no windows or air and the room quickly grew fetid and dank. Peter seemed genuinely bemused by all the fuss. As Van Blarcom opened the floor to questions, the prisoner deftly returned each volley from the gallery, answering every query with honesty, high spirits, and more than a little humour. He maintained his innocence but admitted he had accepted his fate. Having lived a life built on happenstance, Peter conceded he had little control over what was about to unfold. When asked if he had made his peace with those who prosecuted him, Wheeler laughed. After a brief pause, Peter stated for the record that he had forgiven everyone but reserved the right to "have a very poor opinion of Detective Power"[11] till the bitter end.

For the intoxicated and idle masses in the streets, word of the press conference seemed an ideal opportunity for a little mayhem. In the era before press credentials, a few puckish civilians simply pretended to be newsmen, forcing their way in with bluster, bravado, or overt deception.

During the press conference, a half-drunk man from the distant town of Canning overheard Wheeler's swipe at the Halifax detective. The man pushed his way to the fore and announced to the crowd that he was Detective Power. Spinning wildly and unsteady on his feet, the inebriated fraud caught Wheeler in his sights, shouting: "I have nothing against you."[12] One novice correspondent mistook the drunkard for the real deal, to the absolute delight of his more seasoned fellows. The rookie fired a string of questions at the would-be detective before finally being let in on the joke. A correspondent from the *Saint John Daily Telegraph* recognized the drunken impostor; earlier that day, the same man was seen in town trying to pilfer free drinks by pretending to be Radcleve, the nation's hangman.[13]

With the media's curiosity quenched, Van Blarcom drew the press conference to a close. In response to a final shouted inquiry, the sheriff confirmed that the execution was scheduled for seven the following morning.[14] Van Blarcom refused all further entreaties and the press filed out into the waning daylight in search of drink and distraction. Van Blarcom was glad to see the back of them, as he knew something they did not — the execution was subject to change without notice, a platitude very much in keeping with the commercial overtones of the event to date. The execution's timing, mechanics, and particulars were entirely at Van Blarcom's discretion. The sheriff, sensing trouble on the horizon, had already decided that things would not go according to plan.

Van Blarcom's spasm of conscience at having deceived the media was admirable but misguided. The illustrious men of the press corps suffered from no such moral censure. They lied often and without remorse. Case in point: the *Saint John Daily Record* and its timely coverage of the execution. In a narrative polished to a shine that bordered on slick, the *Daily Record* correspondent described Wheeler's final moments: "when the dull thud of the fatal death trap was heard and the groan for mercy, that the black cap smothered and cut short, half uttered."[15]

The astonishing thing was the *Daily Record* reporter had somehow managed to witness this poignant display a full twenty-four hours before it actually occurred. A deadline can be such a heartless mistress. Indeed, saddled with the burden of knowing the news before it happened, the *Daily Record* hedged all bets by seating itself on both sides of the fence, with little regard for consistency. For instance, when it came to Wheeler's demeanour, he was "morose and sullen at times — childlike and apparently simple at others."[16] It is hard to be wrong when you cover all bases.

The reporter's clairvoyance was as impressive as it was vague. Overflowing with colourful prose (much of it purple), the *Daily Record*'s prescient account was merely a morass of clichés, a recycled tableau of every public hanging ever committed to print. When it came to misleading the press, Van Blarcom need not have worried, for one cannot shame the shameless. Despite their lapse in journalistic integrity, the men behind the *Daily Record* considered themselves guilty of nothing more than giving the public exactly what they expected and precisely what the paper thought they wanted.

forty-two
"Lord, I Am Coming"

Seconds before the clock in Van Blarcom's parlour struck one on Tuesday, September 8, 1896, an anxious band of thirteen men[1] began a convoluted and silent journey. They were shepherded in teams of two and three through the rear entrance of the Digby jail, down an ill-lit flight of stairs, and along a narrow corridor. Having arrived at their final destination, the men — coroner John Daley and the twelve panelists selected for his jury — stood huddled in a cramped room deep in the bowels of the cellblock. It was a rushed and inauspicious start to a hastily conceived clandestine event.

The coroner and his men were sequestered from another group, who at that very moment were having a similarly strange evening. The second assemblage sat in awkward silence, enjoying "a basket of delicacies and a cup of warm tea, the kind remembrance of Mrs. Bowles and Mrs. Allen."[2] The composition of the second gathering fluctuated throughout the night, but had, at various times, included Sheriff Van Blarcom; his son and under-sheriff, William; Captain Bowles and his colleague from the Salvation Army, Captain Ellias Allen; and three members of the medical profession, including the prison's staff surgeon, Dr. J. Edgar Jones. The physicians were on hand to pronounce Wheeler dead when the time came, although why such a straightforward task required three doctors defies explanation. The only constant in the second group was Peter Wheeler, whose attendance at the odd soirée was anything but voluntary.

When William Van Blarcom arrived in Wheeler's cell bearing the tea and pastries, the prisoner partook of his final meal "in a sparing manner,"[3] eating just enough to avoid offending the cooks or their spouses. Despite

Wheeler's marked lack of appetite, "he was in the best of spirits, and he kept continually assuring his spiritual advisors that he was confident of pardon and salvation."[4]

Peter's faith in a last-minute reprieve was to be sorely tested. Although his execution was originally scheduled for seven that morning, Van Blarcom elected to alter the schedule. The iron-hook-wielding rioters had yet to materialize in Digby proper but Van Blarcom chose to err on the side of caution. The two disparate groups — Daley and his jury to the one side, Wheeler and his attendants on the other — had been hurriedly assembled six hours early, under the cover of darkness as the streets lay quiet and bare. Many others had announced their intention to attend the hanging but only those deemed absolutely essential to the process were summoned, a hedge against a press leak or retaliatory violence by the as yet non-existent mob.

Most notable in his absence was Isaac Kempton or any representative of the victim's family. Fevered speculation in the press held that Kempton would attend the hanging, with a few rogue newshawks going so far as to suggest Kempton be allowed to "man the drop," sending Wheeler to his fate. Given Van Blarcom's methodical preparations, Kempton's absence in the exclusive enclave was hardly an oversight. Indeed, Isaac Kempton abstained from watching his daughter's convicted killer pay the ultimate price. Having met with Wheeler in the days before, Kempton had made his peace with what was to come.

❲

Public executions had been outlawed several decades prior to 1896. Though Peter Wheeler would be denied a conspicuous final exit, the condemned man made the best of his sorry lot. Peter was a surprisingly vain man, always neat and tidy in his appearance, who prided himself on maintaining an air of cultured civility in the most feral of environs. Surviving as he did on meagre rations, Wheeler's weight had fluctuated throughout his incarceration. Idleness stripped him of his once work-hardened muscles, leaving him bloated and corpulent.

Harris Bowles, having witnessed ample evidence of Wheeler's sartorial vainglory in the preceding months, had procured — on behalf of the Salvation Army — a fresh set of clothes in which Peter could spend eternity. The raiments proved to be a godsend in more ways than one. Sometime after midnight, Wheeler and Bowles were informed that the prisoner's time on earth was to be shorter than originally planned. To soften the blow, Bowles quickly presented his gift to a stunned but grateful Wheeler.

Peter donned his new clothes and asked for a mirror. It was the first and only time he had seen himself during his long incarceration. Striking a series of poses, Wheeler "surveyed his figure, [and] pronounced himself satisfied"[5] with his new appurtenances. Suitably coiffed, Wheeler then knelt to pray. With his head bowed and arms bent in supplication, Peter offered up a final prayer then rose and faced his jailers. With one final check that every hair was in place, Wheeler announced that he was as ready as he would ever be.

☾

Angry mobs bent on lynching were not the only trouble Van Blarcom fought to circumvent. An equally unruly horde — the press —were also being kept at bay. The slight did not go unnoticed: "Newspaper correspondents have been treated like all others today and have not been allowed near Wheeler's cell,"[6] one irate reporter carped. The sheriff broke with his long-standing policy of accommodating the press. Since he could not afford access to all, Van Blarcom reasoned, his only option was to prohibit them all. Accordingly, no journalist, editor, or media representative was present as Wheeler took his last steps towards the gallows. All first-hand accounts of his final moments came from those select few in attendance. To fill the void, the press did what it had always done: they invented the narrative.

With its stark and potent visuals, the execution seemed to bring out a touch of the poet in every journalist. Each moment was deemed worthy of exalted and soaring rhetoric: "As the shadows of the Unknown loomed before him...the war of waters of the Great Divide sounding in his ears,"[7] "Annie Kempton's murderer met death without a tremor."[8] With pens dipped in garish ink, the press strained to give the condemned man an ending worthy of this sublime tale.

To their bitter disappointment, Peter Wheeler once again failed to co-operate. He remained maddeningly stoic to the last. "The expected 'break down' did not occur,"[9] the *Saint John Daily Record* informed its crestfallen readers. Whatever tawdry emotive displays the press craved, Wheeler refused to provide. Left to their own devices and furtive imaginations, journalists painted a vivid, if inaccurate, portrait of a man experiencing a very literal memento mori: "No sound escaped him during this time. His countenance would change to a brown pallor, then flush visibly and forcibly, as if the forces within him were greater than the manifestations otherwise without."[10]

The *Morning Chronicle*, hamstrung by Wheeler's lack of histrionics, simply crafted its own melodramatic version of his final minutes. If its readers wanted emotional fireworks, then by Job the *Chronicle* would give them some visceral pyrotechnics. According to its correspondent, who openly cited Sheriff Van Blarcom as his confidential source, Wheeler broke down "under the weight of woe which for some weeks he had succeeded in smothering from public view."[11] Peter's weakness softened Van Blarcom's heart, a man who had always been vocal in his contempt for the prisoner. Moved by the prisoner's tears, the sheriff "placed his hand on the condemned man's shoulder and said softly, 'Don't take on so, Wheeler; I feel as bad about it as you do.'"[12] Wringing every last ounce of maudlin sentiment from the proceedings, the *Chronicle* claimed: "Wheeler turned to the sheriff and answered, 'well, sheriff, if you can stand it, I can.'"[13] No self-respecting novelist could have written it any better.

Having shared a last tender moment together, the sheriff and the condemned then slipped back into their prescribed roles. Wheeler's arms were pinioned to his sides using a new leather strap created for just such a purpose. Flanked by Bowles and Van Blarcom Junior, "Wheeler stepped strongly and boldly into the death chamber."[14]

It was a death chamber in name only. Prohibited by law from erecting an open-air gallows, Van Blarcom was forced to improvise but his solution bordered on the bizarre. Wheeler's "threshold of Eternity"[15] was in fact the empty space beneath the porch of the sheriff's living quarters. Normally used for storage, the erstwhile charnel house was "of limited dimensions, being little more than four feet square."[16] At just under nine feet in height, the space could not accommodate a long-drop gallows. In its stead, Van Blarcom had constructed a Rube Goldbergesque hanging contraption, designed to kill by "a sudden and violent hoist towards the ceiling."[17]

Only two portions of the apparatus were visible within the chamber. The first was the noose itself, its lead disappearing into a hole cut in the porch floor. Through a second hole came the anchor of the noose attached to a five-hundred-pound metal weight. A guide rope held the weight aloft. At a predetermined signal, the executioner would cut the guide rope, releasing the weight. The downward thrust was enough, in theory, to pull Wheeler upward. It was understood that the force was insufficient to break his neck and that Peter would be left to strangle, his feet mere inches from the dirt floor. It would not be a clean or quick death but it was the best Van Blarcom could do. Prior to Wheeler's last press conference, the sheriff had given the correspondents a tour of the chamber. Each reporter examined the makeshift gallows in queasy silence. Escaping from the miserable little room, every last correspondent no doubt held the same thought: Van Blarcom should have hired Radcleve. Even Wheeler's staunchest critics agreed — no one deserved to die like that, assuming of course that the contraption worked at all.

At a few minutes past 2:00 a.m., Harris Bowles led his charge into the little room, lighted only by a single oil lamp. Peter was positioned under his noose and Bowles secured a second leather strap to his legs then

The Digby jail and the porch that was
to be the epicentre of the coming drama.

stepped back. Satisfied that all was as it should be, Van Blarcom made his way onto the porch, axe in hand, to await the signal. The witnesses were called into the chamber and packed tight within its minuscule confines; those who could not fit remained in the hall, craning their necks to take in the macabre scene.

Tradition held that the prisoner be afforded one last chance to speak. "In a firm voice,"[18] Harris asked Peter if he had anything to say. What came next reveals the true depths of the press corps' malignant machinations in this case.

No official record was made of Peter Wheeler's last words. Although he was known to wax eloquent, no one felt compelled to commit his final utterances to paper. Unbridled by the truth, the media simply ran wild and each paper offered up a version of Wheeler's last words in keeping with their own political bent. The *Toronto Evening Star* opted for biblical allusions and contrition: "I killed Annie Kempton and will pay the penalty. I suppose it's all right. I have taken one life for the devil and will now give my own life for Jesus' sake."[19] The *Acadian Recorder* thought Wheeler needed one last confession: "I committed the deed at 12 o'clock. Tillie Comeau was wrong when she said the cow was not milked."[20] According to the *Morning Chronicle*, Wheeler had the region's taxpayers on his mind: "I am sorry to have been so much trouble and expense to the county and ask you men here to forgive me."[21] But the award for the most egregiously self-serving work of revisionist history went to the *Digby Weekly Courier*, which claimed Peter had used his last breath to promote their upcoming special edition. According to the *Courier*, Wheeler's final words were: "the confession I gave to the DIGBY COURIER is the only true confession I ever made. If I am lying it is not before men, it is before God."[22]

On one lone point, all papers agreed. Wheeler's last utterance was: "Lord [or Jesus, depending on the publication], I am coming."[23] In all probability, that final sound bite represented Wheeler's actual last (and likely only) words. The ubiquitous reporting of the quote suggests it came from a number of informants, since each of the selected witnesses gave "exclusives" to different news agencies. The rest was nothing but journalistic licence — nothing more than a polite term for calumny.

Whatever the content of Wheeler's final proclamation, it was punctuated by the draping of a black hood. Bowles then positioned the three-quarter-inch noose around his neck, drawing the simple slip knot down to encircle the hood. After a moment of silence, Bowles knocked twice — the signal for Van Blarcom waiting above. It was 2:21 a.m. In an instant, the percussive thwack of the axe resonated through the small room. The weight plummeted to the floor, wrenching Wheeler toward the ceiling "some two feet and eight inches, followed by a slight rebound and the unmistakable snapping of the cord."[24]

Wheeler did not die quickly, even though the *Acadian Recorder* tried to persuade its more sensitive readers that "the breaking of his neck was distinctly heard."[25] Indeed, Peter dangled for several minutes, slowly suffocating as he twitched and laboured against his leather restraints. "On the advice of the attending physicians,"[26] the body was left hanging for a full twenty minutes, although the *Courier* reported it was closer to twenty-five.[27] When the doctors were at last certain he was dead, Bowles and the younger Van Blarcom cut Peter down and carried him back to his cell.

To placate the bureaucrats, skeptics, and naysayers, coroner Daley and his jury filed past Wheeler's body, examining it just closely enough to satisfy themselves he was dead. The men stood silent sentry as Daley wrote his autopsy report and each juror in turn affixed his signature, attesting to the cause and manner of Wheeler's state-sanctioned demise. It was the last meaningless yet necessary step as Peter Wheeler finally crossed the threshold to eternity.

forty-three

Mob Mentality

So what became of the advertised angry hordes with their hooks and diabolical plans to overrun the execution? It appears they were just another media fabrication. The *Toronto Evening Star* summed it up best when it reported: "the mobs failed to arrive before night and it is not likely they ever started."[1] At the moment Wheeler rocketed skyward, the grounds surrounding the jail were barren. Van Blarcom's scheme had worked and, despite Radcleve's predictions of failure and the nebulous threat of rioting, the execution had gone off without a hitch.

Eventually the press realized they had been duped and the media spin machine cranked into full gear. Having once trumpeted the threat of the maddening crowds, the news agencies now scrambled to explain their absence. The *Acadian Recorder* blamed the dearth of crowds on Wheeler's inherent lack of sex appeal: "The idea appears to impress itself on the popular mind everywhere that Peter Wheeler was a very low order of criminal indeed — there was nothing mysterious or romantic about him."[2] Sheriff Van Blarcom took offence at the notion, arguing it was his quick-witted rescheduling of the hanging that averted certain disaster. A strange competition ensued over who or what deserved the credit for thwarting a non-existent threat, a pointless bout with no true victor.

Although the crowds were thin on the ground at 2:21 a.m. — even as Wheeler's feet dangled inches above it — the throng grew quickly just before daybreak. In the bluing dawn, thousands roused themselves from their drunken somnolence and began the slow march up the hill toward the jail.

When met with the news that they had been robbed of the much-anticipated main attraction, all the crowd could do was wonder, horror-struck, at the sheer effrontery on offer. They had come to see a hanging and, suffice to say, they did not respond well.

Word soon spread throughout town: Wheeler was dead. The execution was done. Digby's waterfront had its charms but none could compete with a man being put to death. The crowd, at first dumbfounded and visibly disappointed, quickly grew petulant and punishing. Flower beds were trampled, gates were pulled down, and a growing number of revellers took up residence in the church graveyard adjacent to the jail, hell-bent on retaliation.

The more inebriated in attendance began hurling taunts and barbs aimed squarely at the sheriff's head. Although the drunken jeers of a mob rarely leave room for misinterpretation, one publication managed to find a silver lining in the thunderheads growing over the Van Blarcom residence. Nimbly sidestepping the pickled taunts and slurred threats, the *Yarmouth Herald* put its finger squarely on the pulse of the throng and declared: "the work of the sheriff was much admired by the multitude."[3]

The crowd's fictitious admiration aside, Benjamin Van Blarcom now found himself in a rather tight spot. In his efforts to circumvent civil unrest, Van Blarcom had inadvertently kicked a hornet's nest of pent-up anger and liquor-fuelled rage. The disgruntled crowd were not wielding hooks or pitchforks but their propensity for violence was clear. As the teeming masses surrounded the jail, Van Blarcom became a prisoner in his own home and it would take nothing short of a miracle to placate the crowd at this late juncture.

Van Blarcom prided himself on two things: being a man of action and thinking on his feet. As the abuse and hectoring echoed throughout his home, an idea began to hatch in the sheriff's quicksilver brain. It was unconventional and more than a little distasteful, to be sure, but it was the only notion he could summon on such short notice.

To satisfy a mob cheated of a brutal death, Sheriff Van Blarcom would give them the next best thing: what remained of Wheeler himself. He ran to the basement and ordered his deputy son to put Peter's body on display for all to see. The lid was pried off of the cheap pine coffin and the box was mounted on a bier in front of the jailhouse. At the sight of the corpse, the legions went wild. Thunderous applause erupted in waves, peppered with cheers and hoots of joy as the herd surged forward en masse to catch a glimpse of the recently departed.

The coffin proved the perfect focal point for their rage and a sort of ordered bedlam ensued. Staggered lines formed as the curious filed past the open box, poking and prodding at Wheeler, as if hoping he might sit up and take offence. In keeping with Victorian notions of modesty and decorum, the *Daily Sun* reported that "women were conspicuous by their absence,"[4] although no other source noted any such segregation of the sexes. By all other accounts, both genders embarrassed themselves in equal measure.

Peter Wheeler, now well past caring, endured the indignity with his usual stoic grace. According to the *Morning Chronicle*, Peter's face "wore a peaceful, contented look with an entire absence of anything to indicate that any suffering had been felt at death."[5] So placid a countenance no doubt disappointed the gawkers, who wanted the dead man's face to be locked in a mortal grimace befitting so terrible an end.

Van Blarcom left Wheeler "laying in state"[6] for more than two hours as the throng converged on the coffin. When all seemed satisfied with their glimpse of mortality, the sheriff ordered the coffin lid to be affixed and the remains were carried to the waiting grave in the jail's rear courtyard. Captains Bowles and Evans of that army of salvation attempted to hold a simple graveside service, but by this point, the angry mob numbered several thousand "and many of them joined in raising a frightful howl, using all sorts of shouts, jeers and other noises"[7] to interrupt the eulogy. Having been denied a public execution, "their ill-feeling had to work off in some way."[8]

As Harris and Evans made ready to lower the coffin, the crowd erupted in a chorus of chants: "throw him in,"[9] "tear him open,"[10] and "pitch the bastard in head first."[11] The taunts served only to rile an already hostile and unruly crowd into full-blown mayhem. As the people relegated to the rear began to push forward, those lining the grave were thrust onto the coffin and a few were forced into the open grave itself. Hoping to avoid complete pandemonium, Harris ordered the coffin lowered and the grave swiftly sealed. The crowd, drunk and disorderly almost to a man, continued their jeering to the very last. As the final clump of dirt was tamped down, there was nothing left to shout about and the hordes decamped in search of livelier entertainment.

❨

Diversions were not hard to come by, as the day seemed to make even the sanest man run mad. In the hours before Wheeler was hanged, Walter W. Payson seemed as normal as any of his good Christian neighbours. He was fifty-three years of age, a relatively successful farmer and "a resident and rate-payer of the town of Digby."[12] He and his wife Anne were active members of the local Methodist church and together they had raised nine fine children. It was said, on good authority, that Walter was as solid as they come. He was not given to wild flights of fancy or obvious bouts of paranoia; he never had any trouble with the law and never showed much interest in local politics. Those who knew him thought he was the salt of the earth.

Like everyone else in the county, Walter had some loose association with the Wheeler-Kempton debacle. In early May, Payson was among the witnesses who provided affidavits to Judge Townshend in support of the motion for a change of venue.[13] His testimony recalled numerous caustic comments about Wheeler that Payson had overheard in town. Aside from that, Payson had never met Wheeler prior to the unfortunate events of January 28, 1896, or had any direct dealings with him in the months since.

But as Wheeler shuffled off his mortal coil, something in Walter W. Payson came unglued. Never one to espouse conspiracy theories — at least not in polite company — Walter became convinced there was something hinky about Wheeler's execution and he intended to do something about it.

In the cold, clear light of dawn, as the crestfallen hordes formed outside the courthouse complex, Walter Payson muscled his way into the Digby jail. Tumbling down the stairs, Payson thrust a handwritten note into the hand of Sheriff Van Blarcom. The message was penned in a shaky cursive but contained surprisingly coherent text, demanding an immediate public autopsy of Wheeler "on the grounds that when hanged, Wheeler was under the influence of an opiate."[14] The note offered no explanation as to how its author reached this conclusion. Walter W. Payson, who held no public office or civic powers, ended with a final bold declaration: he forbade Sheriff Van Blarcom from burying Wheeler's body until an autopsy could be performed.

The note left Van Blarcom scratching his head and mildly amused. The sheriff had conducted the execution and was with Wheeler in the hours before his death. The autopsy, cursory though it was, had been completed hours before and the coroner and his jury had already signed off on the report. Even if Payson was granted his request, comprehensive toxicology testing and drug screens — now a standard part of every medico-legal death investigation — were still decades in the future. At that moment in history, there was no way of knowing if the allegations were true. What the sheriff knew for certain was that the farmer had no jurisdictional authority to stop the proceedings. Van Blarcom shook his head. He had predicted the execution would bring out the loonies; he just never thought Walter Payson would be among them.

With as much patience as he could muster, the sheriff informed Payson that an autopsy had been conducted. Van Blarcom gave Payson his personal assurances that drugs were not involved in the death. Deeming the matter closed, Van Blarcom excused himself, having far more pressing issues to attend.

The sheriff was satisfied but Payson clearly was not. Walter would not be denied and if the sheriff refused to listen to reason, Payson knew a far more powerful ally who would mark his words. He had read every inch of the media coverage for the past eight months and Payson knew journalists were hungry for any fresh scandal on the case. Spying a huddled mass of newsmen, the gentleman farmer held an impromptu press conference on the steps of the Digby Courthouse. He once again identified himself as a town resident and taxpayer, then Payson laid out his conspiracy theory for the assembled media throng.

The response was not quite what Payson had hoped. As a unit, the press corps turned their backs in the middle of his tirade and moved on, looking for more palatable fare. Only two papers — the *Morning Chronicle* and the *Saint John Daily Telegraph* — bothered to report on Payson's accusations. Both publications treated the story as just another footnote in their vast compendium of the day's tragic events. Undaunted, Payson fired off letters to the editors of the local papers but his conspiracy theory never found traction. Eager as they were for scuttlebutt, no editor wanted to dive into Payson's troubled waters.

Weeks later, rumours began to circulate that Payson had taken matters into his own hands. Local gossips whispered that the farmer was so convinced he had discovered a major governmental conspiracy, he went to the small graveyard behind the courthouse and dug up Wheeler's body. The strange rumour took hold because of an auspiciously timed coincidence. The insinuations began making the rounds right about the time Wheeler's remains were disinterred from the temporary gravesite and moved to his permanent burial plot. Nothing in the historical record suggests Payson actually exhumed Wheeler's coffin, but oddly enough, the suggestion that he did received far more attention than his initial cries of conspiracy.

forty-four

Wheeler's Last Laugh

Before the body was even cold, the *Digby Weekly Courier* made good on its threat and rolled out its special edition, welcoming all in the Annapolis Valley to share in the cruel intimacy of the moment. The coverage was penned by a number of reporters prone to taking themselves a little too seriously, yet they somehow failed to give the event the sober reflection it deserved. Furthermore, it was clear from its content that the vast majority of the three-page spectacular was written well in advance of the day.

The special edition sold for the unprecedented sum of five cents a copy, highway robbery compared to the cost of the paper's first "Bear River Tragedy" handbill just eight months prior, the exposé that had started it all. In lieu of the cogent analysis promised in the advertising, the special edition was nothing more than a regurgitation of the *Courier*'s coverage to date, replete with all the errors of facts and haste-driven typos of the earlier editions. The reportage was also a gallimaufry of tone and sentiment. For example, the extra opened with the kindest comment the *Courier* had ever afforded Peter Wheeler: "If he were not a murderer, it would be said he died bravely."[1]

The *Digby Courier* also held to its promise to include illustrations. Its pages were festooned with line-art representations of the principal sites — including a rendering of the Kempton home, "the scene of the tragedy"[2] — as well as portraits of the key players. All of this was, of course, window dressing to the main attraction. The majority of the front page was dedicated to the "only true confession,"[3] the subject of such manufactured debate, speculation, and envy.

Aside from its ponderous and inflated length, this confession still bore an eerie resemblance to all past confessions attributed to Wheeler. To pad the word count, this rendition contained a substantial sprinkling of direct quotes, including every utterance that had passed between the killer and his victim. As for the most contentious issue — the slippery question of when the crime was committed — the *Courier*'s pricey confession mirrored all prior accounts. Detective Power be damned — the crime had occurred just after midnight.

Anticipating considerable public outcry, the *Courier* ran an accompanying sidebar entitled "Some points explained."[4] The foundation of the aside was an interview reportedly conducted with Wheeler "a few days before his death."[5] The correspondent was mindful of the criticism generated by prior attempts to force Wheeler's actions into Power's timeline. Accordingly, the *Courier* expected strong resistance to its version of events, "in which it is shown that the idea of a midnight visit is not so unreasonable as it is thought."[6] In a pre-emptive strike, the tabloid had sent its reporter to question Wheeler on "the doubtful portions of the confession."[7]

The *Courier*'s precautions were wasted effort. The final confession was no more credible than its predecessors. The tone, language, and syntax in it ranged wildly, suggesting a minimum of three authors, each with a hand in crafting a particular section.

The *Courier* did include something no prior confession had presented. The tabloid spared no expense and went to great lengths to affix one last illustration to the end of the confession. If it were possible to speak from beyond the grave, Wheeler was having the last word and the last laugh. The confession was signed:

forty-five

Reclaiming the
Moral High Ground

The *Courier*'s special edition was ethically questionable but there was no arguing its commercial success. The Digby tabloid bested its competitors by a very healthy margin, sticking like a bone in its rivals' collective craw. Itching for a fight, the *Windsor Tribune* went on the offensive. Its editor's bitterness was evident, as was its source:

> The *Digby Courier* has obtained the only true confession ever written by the condemned man and will issue a special edition with details of the execution etc. It would seem as if this miserable murderer, liar and fool had had about enough advertising as it is, but the public demand this sort of thing and the *Courier* has the scoop, and it would not be business if it did not use it. The special edition of the *Courier* with the ghastly details of the wretch's taking off and his miserable lying confession will be greedily bought and read by all classes, while a special edition containing a full and complete description of our Heavenly Home and the way to get there would not sell enough copies to pay for the ink. We hope the *Courier* as well as the daily press will omit no details. The public want to know just how the condemned man drew up his legs when the drop fell, just how long the body twitched and whether the knot remained in the proper

place under his ear or slipped around to the back of his neck, as sometimes happens.[1]

In a fit of pique, the *Tribune* editor had broken two cardinal rules of journalism. First, he provided free advertising to a competitor, naming it no fewer than four times. Second, he offended his readers by disparaging their interest in the case as purulent and morbid. His righteous indignation at the disappointing sales of his "Heavenly Home" issue revealed an editor in the throes of a childish tantrum, sickened by printing salacious details only to be trounced by others doing it better.

❨

On that fateful day in September, the *Yarmouth Herald* dedicated two pages to the execution of Peter Wheeler. Page one recounted Wheeler's hanging in full and graphic detail. The *Herald* devoted its second page to an editorial screed against its competitors. The editor saw no hypocrisy in chastising his fellows for the very sin he had committed just one page prior: "For months the provincial press has been teeming with details of this most horrible murder, until it has become nauseous in the minds of the public.... Whilst admitting the fact that the details of such murders should not be passed over lightly, we must regret that no good result can follow the re-publication of such ghastly details.... We hope by the execution of this condemned criminal that this murder will be allowed to drop out of sight, as far as the newspapers are concerned. "[2] Lest the paper's duplicity be lost on any of its readers, the tirade ran adjacent to an account of another gruesome crime.

Three days later the *Digby Weekly Courier* fired back. In an editorial entitled "The Last of a Disagreeable Affair," the paper managed to offend its readers and competitors alike:

With the events of last Tuesday [Wheeler's execution], we gladly note the last of a case to which it has been our disagreeable duty to give considerable attention from the first. For the benefit of the entire community let the Bear River tragedy now drop.

As a local paper and the recognized news organ of the community in which the murder took place it has been our duty to report all the essential features of the case. This we have done in as clean a manner as possible. Our aim is to publish a family paper and we consider that one of the characteristics of such a paper is the absence of criminal or sensational matter. We have followed this rule in the past and intend to in the future. We have broken it in this instance because it was necessary and our publication of all the details, revolting though they may have been, was entirely within our province. The public, also, demands this. Our issue of Tuesday sold almost faster than our press could supply and was rapidly gathered up by the crowd. Had it been filled with a description of a great moral revolution we would have lost rather than have made money.

But now it is a thing of the past. The case has been a terrible one but justice has been done according to British law. We are glad to be free of it and we trust that we can again settle down to our duties with cleaner association.[3]

Like its shameless predecessors, the *Digby Courier* placed the blame squarely on the shoulders of its readers, a gambit that persists among tabloid editors to this day: if no one bought it, the sleaze peddlers argue, we wouldn't be forced to print it. That the *Courier*'s editor managed a tone of righteous indignation whilst simultaneously trumpeting his record-breaking sales figures was an impressive feat of journalistic funambulism.

For all their protestations and hand-wringing, the Maritime tabloids would settle down to their duties with cleaner association, although not always by choice. In the century since the Wheeler trial commanded the headlines, the Canadian news media have undergone tectonic shifts. A slew of libel and defamation lawsuits have put a much-needed damper on irresponsible crime reporting. Gone are the days of openly declaring the accused guilty immediately following a crime. The symbiotic relationship between the press and law enforcement is another victim of the media's prior excesses. Police now feverishly guard the facts of a case, spoon-feeding the press only the barest details of a case while holding in reserve evidence crucial to securing a conviction or identifying a false confessor. Today, a peace officer trying a case in the media is seen by the public as the blatant act of desperation it has always been.

Yet for all these changes, society's hunger for the gruesome details in high-profile murder cases persists unabated. Many of the newspapers featured in this tale remain in business to this day, steadfast in spirit if not always consistent in name. The *Digby Courier*, the *Halifax Chronicle* and *Herald* (now merged), and the *Annapolis Spectator* survived just as surely as Peter Wheeler did not. Furthermore, no editor or reporter was fired or even reprimanded for the liberties taken in the Wheeler debacle. They had done nothing wrong according to the journalistic ethos of the time. Those who played so freely with the truth held their thrones, presiding with an enduring smugness over the ruin they had so carelessly wrought.

The advent of the Internet has welcomed a new age in crime reporting, reducing the wait time between action and information to mere seconds. The immediacy of the World Wide Web, coupled with an almost animalistic need to scoop the competition, means that unvetted and unreliable reports continue to flood the market, just as they did in Wheeler's day. In cyberspace, accuracy is inevitably sacrificed on the altar of expediency and nothing gets in the way of a good story, least of all the truth. The evolution of crime reporting has come full circle, leaving us exactly where we started.

forty-six
None the Wiser

David Milgaard, William Mullins-Johnson, Anthony Hanemaayer, Steven Truscott, Kyle Unger, Romeo Philion, Guy Paul Morin — a tragic litany of wrongful convictions plague the Canadian justice system, men falsely accused of murder and caged for decades for crimes they did not commit. Their faces form a dire and haunting portrait of a legal system fraught with injustice, bias, and all-too-human error. We sit equally transfixed and paralyzed by their nightmarish tales of agony and salvation. The nation's news cameras focus on these exonerated men but only by widening the lens to include Peter Wheeler does a clearer picture emerge. More than a century on, it appears we are none the wiser when it comes to understanding how wrongful convictions occur.

Public perception holds that such mistakes occur during trial. As the calamitous case of Peter Wheeler shows, the die was cast and the erroneous accusations were made long before the falsely accused set foot in a courthouse. Such tunnel vision is costly. Attempts to right the wrong that focus solely on legal errors inevitably fail to capture the exogenous elements that implicated the innocent man in the first place. Although virtually all wrongful convictions are now overturned through the introduction of cutting-edge scientific evidence, technology cannot address the external factors that wield such portent. Even the most sophisticated DNA testing could not have identified the moment when the press declared Wheeler to be guilty or measured the impact that decades of casual racism had on the jury of his peers. Microscopes could not have detected Nicholas Power's deep-seated insecurities or his pathological need to be right.

And erroneous verdicts cut both ways. Judge Ito's jury mistakenly acquitted football legend O.J. Simpson of murder, but the deciding factors in the case began long before the gavel dropped. The courthouse antics were merely the endgame of a judicial miscarriage that started when the first newschoppers locked onto the white Bronco creeping along a California highway. More to the point, the mitigating circumstances really began when the first merchant ships arrived in Africa in search of free labour and continued through the dawn of the mass media and the building of a temple to celebrity, in which all were free to worship the god of their choosing. To believe otherwise is to miss the actual catalysts of wrongful verdicts.

The true problem remains one of focus. Because the legal system demands it, appellate lawyers stare myopically at trial transcripts, hoping to find an impeachable error but they are missing the bigger picture. Those metered pages do not reveal the real reasons their client was wrongfully accused, for such social factors dwell outside the courthouse: racism, media manipulations, the force field that is celebrity, a community's need for justice, and police officers with personal agendas.

❰

In the pantheon of the wrongfully convicted, Peter Wheeler may be a newer and lesser light but his is the perfect cautionary tale. By modern standards, errors proliferated during the legal proceedings but the damage was done long before Wheeler stood in the dock. As summer gave way to fall in that most terrible year, Peter Wheeler was repeatedly passed through the *machina carnis* of the Maritime journalistic cabal. Yet the tabloids alone do not bear the full weight of Wheeler's untimely demise. Some of the burden must fall on Dr. Lovett, whose well-intentioned naïveté led to that first intractable proclamation of guilt. Even greater iniquity rests on Detective Nicholas Power, who cared more for preserving his aura of infallibility than the pursuit of true justice. Some measure of blame must also be shared among those witnesses who manipulated the truth to seal Wheeler's fate with their malleable testimony, including Bernard Parker and his magical footprints; his brother Herbert, who turned Wheeler's locker-room banter into a motive for murder; and Hardy Benson, whose ever-changing tale shoved Peter headfirst into the crime scene.

In the end, there was ample blame and shame to go around. The system failed Peter Wheeler, delivering a verdict that was not justice but simply mindless vengeance. And, if the system failed Wheeler, the media failed the system and society. The fourth estate proclaimed itself the ultimate seeker of truth, the last bastion of fidelity and candour. Self-appointed as society's watchdogs, journalists were supposed to keep the lawmakers honest by exposing corruption and wrongdoing wherever it may reside. Modern-day balladeers, the media professed to chronicle the exploits of the great and small, kings and everyman, sinners and saints. But, as they will be the first to tell you, the market wants the sinners, not the saints — the adventures of the virtuous do not move much ink.

At the very least, the media should have reported the facts accurately and objectively. In this regard, the tabloids failed miserably. By favouring verisimilitude, the editors and reporters lost sight of their higher calling, opting to wallow in the mire for the sake of the bottom line, peddling half-truths and outright fictions for a few measly shekels.

As we toss yet another unwanted local circular into the recycling bin, it borders on the ridiculous to think that the *Digby Weekly Courier* ever wielded such power or influence. It is hard to believe that a local paper, with its part-time reporters and limited circulation, could have ever held a man's life in their feeble grasp. But in the decades before broadcast radio or television, and more than a century before the birth of the Internet, newspapers reigned supreme. They scripted rather than recorded history and all the news that was fit to print was disseminated according to their agendas and political bents. The local tabloids not only informed the citizenry, they controlled it. Newspapers had a stronger hand in shaping public opinion than any other social institution, save for the church.

Born of such a tainted journalistic womb, the myth that Peter Wheeler killed Annie Kempton has survived longer than most other old wives' tales. After his execution, the doubters and heretics who refused to toe the party line of Wheeler's guilt eventually fell silent and were all but forgotten. A sparse and dusty court docket book records only that he was tried, convicted, and hanged in accordance with the law. A century on, the only public record of Peter Wheeler remains the one limned by the media. It is a portrait reminiscent of the works of the great master Pablo Picasso, which feature a vaguely recognizable subject that is beautifully disturbing yet an unambiguous distortion of reality, a once tangible solid taken on an entirely artistic flight of fancy. It is well past time to set the record straight.

It is, in hindsight, almost too easy to see how it happened. Despite his discernible innocence, things never looked good for Wheeler. There was no escaping it: Wheeler was an African-born man in the snowy white confines of the "Switzerland of Nova Scotia." Worse still, he had never learned his place. He had the temerity to live in proximity to an innocent white girl and the gall to be friendly to her. Wheeler, who was among the last to see her alive and the first to find her dead, had signalled his guilt to all those predisposed to see it. Anyone that needed further proof of his reprehensible nature need look no further than his unholy relationship with Tillie Comeau, a white woman reputed to have questionable morals. And what of Wheeler's morals? In a land where a well-thumbed Bible was the hallmark of piety and righteousness, Wheeler preferred to spend his days lost in the heathen words of Shakespeare and Tennyson, blasphemously forsaking all organized religion in favour of a self-guided spiritual journey. What was the town to make of such a man? How could anyone have ignored all these signs pointing to his guilt?

There is no denying that Peter Wheeler was far from perfect. His was not a guileless life and he was not deserving of accolades or reverence. He sometimes enjoyed a casual relationship with the truth and was rootless and untethered, an outsider in a land anchored by family and community.

But a second glance reveals another set of truths. Wheeler had no say in his ancestry or how his physical appearance was judged or interpreted by others. He could not help the circumstances of his birth or control the era in which he found himself, replete with its mythology of demonic criminals and the supersleuths who waged war against them. He held no sway over the media and their portrayal of him. Peter never cast himself as a victim or begged for the nation's sympathy. He possessed no great wisdom and offered no profound insights into the mysteries of life, save this: he did not kill Annie Kempton and he did not deserve to hang for her murder.

❨

Should you ever lament that the system favours the accused at the expense of the victim, recall well the saga of Peter Wheeler, a man stripped of all rights or any hope of a fair trial. Not only was the system at odds with Wheeler, it was clearly aided and abetted by a media wholly unbridled by the constraints of journalistic integrity or the forced protections of libel laws.

Among the so-called favours lavished on the defendant was the right to a speedy trial. Swift justice was originally intended to protect the wrongfully accused from languishing in perpetuity without due process. It is a noble and vital tenet of our practice of jurisprudence, yet — if Peter Wheeler teaches us nothing else — there is a razor-fine line between swift justice and a rush to judgment. Time is the enemy of those incarcerated but it is the saving grace of those unjustly accused. In the wake of a heinous and inhumane crime, the emotions of the afflicted community run high. Passion obliterates reason and the thirst for vengeance drives otherwise sane men to desperate and sometimes unconscionable acts. The difference between David Milgaard and Peter Wheeler is that the former lived long enough to see justice done and Wheeler swung before cooler heads prevailed.

Like laws and sausages, the mechanics of crime and punishment are best left to the public's fertile imagination. In the case of *Queen v. Wheeler*, the law's viscera have been flayed open for all to see. Such forthright disclosure reveals an empty vessel: there was no evidence, no smoking gun, no irrefutable proof. There was merely fear and supposition tinged with xenophobia and a healthy dose of racism overheated by a news media hungry for a homegrown story to rival the Ripper.

And what a story it was. Reporters tripped over themselves in their mad search for superlatives to describe the horrific act. Wheeler was dubbed "a wretch of the deepest dye,"[1] quaint Victoriana now but harsh words at the time. Florid excess was the fashion during the reign of Alexandrina Victoria, and gonzo journalists of the day heeded the trend with narratives dripping with glorious surfeit and nugatory extremes.

The sad tale of Annie Kempton and Peter Wheeler runs the gamut of negative and painful emotions: fear, prejudice, lust, deceit, cowardice, indifference, insecurity, and unfathomable rage. And through it all, the one common thread was the media's reptilian embrace, a fetid clutch that chilled even as it feigned concern. Duplicitous, exploitative, and mercenary, the Maritimes' earliest tabloids eagerly fed on the all-too-raw emotions of victims and villains alike. There was no subtlety; like vaudeville, it was designed to entertain by appealing to the lowest common denominator. The editors contended they were merely giving the people what they wanted, in spite of their own oft-voiced disdain for such reprehensible subject matter. Then, as now, we get the media we deserve.

Flash-forward to modern day. Digby bears no trace of the short life and brutal death of Peter Wheeler; no gravestone denotes his final resting place, no historical plaque was affixed to the jail or courthouse. All of the relevant institutions have been demolished or rebuilt in the intervening decades. Little from Wheeler's time survives and nothing of Wheeler himself: no descendants, no siblings, no recognized heirs. In contrast, the village of Bear River pays ample homage to its fallen daughter Annie, as many no doubt feel befits their respective roles of perpetrator and victim. The case lingers, familiar as the scar of a wound long-healed.

Yet for all that has been written about Peter Wheeler and his part in the crime of that century — after all the trials, inquests, and tribunals and in the wake of an execution made all the more public for its feigned secrecy — one question still haunts Bear River more than 110 years later: who really killed Annie Kempton?

Acknowledgements

I am eternally grateful to Philip Hartling and the curators of the Nova Scotia Archives. I also cannot say enough about Mary Munk at the Library and Archives Canada Genealogy Room in Ottawa, who went above and beyond the call in hunting down the right doctor named Jacques — you set me on the straight and narrow. Thanks also to Susan Beard, Sheryl Stanton, and the staff of the Admiral Digby Museum, located in the heart of the Digby Town in Digby County — the centre of all things Digby. I am indebted to curator Bria Stokesbury at the Kings County Museum in Kentville and the good folks at the O'Dell House Museum in Annapolis Royal and the James House Museum in Bridgetown. I could not have done it without John Boylan of the Public Archives and Records Office of Prince Edward Island, who was so helpful with the case of Willie Millman. The same can be said for Susan McClure and Dave Cogswell of the Halifax Regional Municipality Archives, who never gave up the search until they found the Holy Grail. A nod of thanks is also due the supportive staff of the Archives of Ontario.

My heartfelt thanks to the helpful souls at the reference desk at the Saint John Free Public Library and to Kelli Janson of the *Digby Courier*. I would also like to acknowledge the lovely folks in the *Toronto Star* Newspaper Reading Room at the Toronto Reference Library for their help in tracking down early editions of the *Star* and the *Globe*. Thanks are also due to Louis V. Comeau and Lynne Milbury of the New Horizons' Centre for their assistance with photographs. I want to acknowledge Constable Holly Smith, Public Relations Officer for the Halifax Regional

Police, for her efforts, along with Bev at the *Annapolis Spectator* for pointing me in the right direction. Thanks also to Suzanne McLean of the Bata Shoe Museum in Toronto for hunting down some larrigans. A shout-out is due to Lois Jenkins, who shared her encyclopedic knowledge of the region and a long-lost copy of the *Annapolis Spectator*. And, as always, I am beholden to the wonderful staff of the Annapolis Royal branch of the Annapolis Valley Regional Library — many thanks Dorothy, Sandy, and Ken.

If I had a first-born, I would owe it to Jenny Milligan at the Bear River Heritage Museum and Historical Society, who was helpful to a fault and marshalled the powers of Facebook to answer any question she could not. If I had a second-born, I would happily hand it to my agent, Carolyn Swayze, for all her guidance, wisdom, and hard work. I am out of imaginary children but would still like to thank the usual suspects at Goose Lane Editions. I am eternally indebted to Susanne Alexander, James Duplacey, and Colleen Kitts-Goguen for taking a chance on an unknown author and giving me a safe, supportive place to grow. Paula Sarson has now guided me through two books, saddled with the unenviable task of tempering my sharp tongue and breaking my myriad bad habits. Thank you, Paula, for always knowing what I mean, even when I don't. Thanks also to Julie Scriver, Chris Tompkins, Martin Ainsley, Angela Williams, Cheryl Norrad, and Corey Redekop for all their hard work and support. I send thanks to those who have worked on manuscripts past and present, including Barry Norris and Dr. Megan Woodworth.

Finally, to my friends and family, who have patiently put up with all this nonsense for years now — your support means more to me than I can say — words just aren't my thing.

Notes

The primary evidentiary files for this case (Crown v. Wheeler, also known as Regina v. Wheeler or Queen v. Wheeler) are retained in the Library and Archives Canada (LAC) (RG 13, vol. 1430, file 278A, 1896) and in the Nova Scotia Archives (NSA) (RG 39, series C, vol. 17 #761).

One — And So It Begins
1. "Bear River Murder," *Saint John Daily Sun*, February 3, 1896.
2. "Curse of a Fiend," *Saint John Daily Record*, January 28, 1896.

Additional sources: Details were drawn from testimony and physical evidence presented in court, now retained in the case file at the NSA, RG 39, series C, vol. 17 #761. The description of the crime scene comes from the trial testimony of Omer Rice, the first person to see the body (after Peter Wheeler); see Queen v. Wheeler, Trial transcript, [1896] LAC. Annie's surgery and prior victimization were reported in "Seeking the Slayer," *Saint John Daily Record*, January 29, 1896. Additional information was taken from "Murder at Bear River," *Digby Weekly Courier*, January 28, 1896; "14-year-old Girl Murdered," *Morning Chronicle*, January 29, 1896.

Two — "Nearer Brute Than Human"
1. "Murder at Bear River," *Digby Weekly Courier*, January 28, 1896.
2. Ibid., original emphasis.
3. Ibid.
4. "A Diabolical Murder," *Saint John Daily Telegraph*, January 29, 1896.
5. "A Horrible Murder," *Saint John Daily Sun*, January 29, 1896.
6. "Murder at Bear River," *Digby Weekly Courier*, January 28, 1896.
7. "Murder at Bear River," *Digby Weekly Courier*, January 31, 1896.
8. "Murder at Bear River," *Digby Weekly Courier*, January 28, 1896.
9. Ibid.
10. Ibid.
11. "Seeking the Slayer," *Saint John Daily Record*, January 29, 1896.
12. The *Toronto Evening Star* ("Told by the Wires") reported that "she had been outraged" on January 29, 1896.

13. "Foul and Shocking Murder," *Bridgetown Monitor*, January 29, 1896.

14. "14-year-old Girl Murdered," *Morning Chronicle*, January 29, 1896.

15. Parker, *Historic Annapolis Valley*, 48.

16. "Wheeler Confesses," *Annapolis Spectator*, July 3, 1896.

Additional source: "The Bear River Murder," *Saint John Daily Sun*, February 8, 1896.

Three — Blame It on Saucy Jack

1. Newton, *Encyclopedia of Serial Killers*, 131; see also Sugden, *Jack the Ripper*.

2. Curtis, *Jack the Ripper and the London Press*, 65.

3. Newton, *Encyclopedia of Serial Killers*, 132.

4. Ibid.

5. Sugden, *Jack the Ripper*, 48.

6. Curtis, *Jack the Ripper and the London Press*, 65.

7. Ibid., 38.

8. Newton, *Encyclopedia of Serial Killers*, 132.

9. "Wheeler's Confessions," *Digby Weekly Courier*, July 10, 1896.

10. "Murder at Bear River," *Digby Weekly Courier*, January 28, 1896.

Four — The Ineffable Detective Power

1. "Letter to the Editor," *Halifax Herald*, February 13, 1919.

2. "Drunkenness the City's Worst Problem," *Halifax Herald*, May 4, 1906; see also McGahan, "Detective Nick Power."

3. "Detective Nick Power," *Halifax Herald*, November 21, 1903.

4. "Nicholas Power Obituary," October 3, 1938, MG 100, vol. 209 #31, NSA; "Planned Death for Prince at Halifax," *Halifax Mail*, n.d.

Additional sources: McGahan, "Crime and Policing"; McGahan, "Police Commission"; McGahan, "Halifax Police Department"; Halifax Police Staff Register, 1892-1914, RG 35, 120 series, 16H vol. 6, NSA; "Nicholas Power, Colorful Haligonian, Passes to his Reward," *Halifax Chronicle*, October 3, 1938; "Eventful Life of Ex-Chief Power," *Morning Chronicle*, March 30, 1918; "Chief of Police Power Resigns after Forty-Three Years Faithful Service," *Morning Herald*, November 4, 1907; "Chief Nicholas Power Resigned from Head of Police Force," *Nova Scotian and Weekly Chronicle*, November 8, 1907.

Five — The Inquest

1. Lovett's biography was taken primarily from Hall, *Heritage Remembered*, as well as from all additional sources listed below.

2. Canada, "Service Record and Biography of Lewis Johnstone Lovett."

3. Finn's biography is from Nova Scotia, "Nova Scotia Medical Examiner Service — History."

4. Knight, "Crowner."

5. Ibid.

6. "The Bear River Tragedy," *Annapolis Spectator*, February 8, 1896.

7. Trial transcript, Queen v. Wheeler, LAC. His mother, Tillie Comeau, also testified that Annie had told her "someone had been inside her house" in the days before her death.

Additional sources: Canada, 1891 Census; Dinn, "Old Saint Edward Cemetery"; Woodman, "Lovett Family"; Johnson, *Canadian Directory of Parliament*; Bear River Tides, "Tour of Historic Houses"; "Tribute to the Late Dr. Lewis Johnstone Lovett," *Digby Courier*, May 7, 1942; "Dr. Lovett Passes Away in Carolina," *Digby Courier*, April 30, 1942; "14-year-old Girl Murdered," *Morning Chronicle*, January 29, 1896.

Six — The "Lie"

1. "Dies in a Few Hours," *Saint John Daily Record*, September 7, 1896.

2. "Is Wheeler the Murderer," *Morning Chronicle*, January 30, 1896.

3. "Murder at Bear River," *Digby Weekly Courier*, January 31, 1896.

4. Ibid.

5. Ibid.

6. Ibid.

Additional sources: Lewis Johnstone Lovett, Report of the Coroner's Inquest, including List of Witnesses and Fees, July 14, 1896, no. 4 (hereafter "Lovett report"), Queen v. Wheeler, NSA.

Seven — The Parker Brothers

1. Bernard Parker, Map of Kempton Property in Bear River, 1896, map 1, Queen v. Wheeler, NSA.

2. Bernard Parker, Revised Map, with Witness Locations Denoted, 1896, map 2, Queen v. Wheeler, NSA.

3. Larrigan prices quoted are from F.B. Miller's Bear River store, as noted in Hall, *Heritage Remembered*, 93.

4. "Murder at Bear River," *Digby Weekly Courier*, January 31, 1896.

Additional sources: Environment Canada, Meteorological data from Digby and Yarmouth weather stations for January 1896; Canada, 1881 Census, LAC, FHL film 1375809; Canada, 1891 Census; Parker, Last Will and Testament; Edmund Rice (1638) Association, *Genealogical Register*; "Murder at Bear River," *Digby Weekly Courier*, January 31, 1896; "Is Wheeler the Murderer," *Morning Chronicle*, January 30, 1896.

Eight — The Mortis Sisters

1. Camps, "Time of Death," 78.

2. Spitz, *Medicolegal Investigation*, 95-96.

3. A description of Annie's fatal injuries and Ellison's post-mortem interval estimate were reported in "Murder at Bear River," *Digby Weekly Courier*, January 31, 1896, and were included in his autopsy report—Ellison, Coroner's Inquest.
4. "Murder at Bear River," *Digby Weekly Courier*, January 31, 1896.

Additional sources: Spitz, *Medicolegal Investigation*; Van Den Oever, "Review of the Literature."

Nine — The Verdict

1. "Peter Wheeler to go on Trial," *Morning Chronicle*, January 31, 1896.
2. The issue of the cow was addressed repeatedly during the trial. Under oath, Isaac Kempton admitted to milking the cow Monday morning before he left for work (approximately eight o'clock) and Omer Rice milked the cow Tuesday morning after discovering Annie's body (approximately nine o'clock). On the stand, Rice stated he had no idea how much milk the cow normally gave.
3. "Murder at Bear River," *Digby Weekly Courier*, January 31, 1896.
4. Ibid.

Additional sources: Lovett report, Queen v. Wheeler, NSA; Ellison, Coroner's Inquest (Autopsy Report); "14-year-old Girl Murdered," *Morning Chronicle*, January 29, 1896; "Peter Wheeler to go on Trial," *Morning Chronicle*, January 31, 1896; "Murder at Bear River," *Digby Weekly Courier*, January 31, 1896; "Bear River Murder," *Saint John Daily Sun*, February 3, 1896; "Seeking the Slayer," *Saint John Daily Record*, January 29, 1896.

Ten — Out of Bounds

1. "Peter Wheeler to go on Trial," *Morning Chronicle*, January 31, 1896. A similar unequivocal expression of guilt was published in "Very Strong Evidence Against Wheeler," *Saint John Daily Telegraph*, February 3, 1896.
2. Lovett report, Queen v. Wheeler, NSA.
3. "Murder at Bear River," *Digby Weekly Courier*, January 31, 1896.
4. "A Horrible Murder," *Saint John Daily Sun*, January 29, 1896.

Eleven — With Friends Like These

1. "Is Wheeler the Murderer?" *Morning Chronicle*, January 30, 1896.
2. Trial transcript, Queen v. Wheeler, LAC.
3. Ibid.
4. Ibid.
5. Rice was confronted about his outstanding warrant for arrest during Ruggles's cross-examination of him at trial—ibid.
6. "Is Wheeler the Murderer," *Morning Chronicle*, January 30, 1896.
7. "Peter Wheeler's Execution," *Digby Weekly Courier*, September 8, 1896.

8. Ibid.
9. "Another Record of the Crime," *Acadian Recorder*, September 8, 1896.
10. "The Bear River Tragedy," *Digby Weekly Courier*, February 28, 1896.
11. Ibid.
12. "Murder at Bear River," *Digby Weekly Courier*, January 31, 1896.

Additional sources: Richard Godfrey, letter to W.B. Stewart requesting witness fee, April 24, 1897, no. 1, Queen v. Wheeler, NSA; Death certificate — Richard Godfrey, 1918, Death Registry, book 33, p. 484, #1261, NSA.

Twelve — The Harlot of Bear River

1. "The Bear River Murder," *Saint John Daily Sun*, February 7, 1896.
2. "The Bear River Murder," *Saint John Daily Sun*, February 8, 1896.
3. "The Bear River Murder," *Saint John Daily Sun*, February 7, 1896.
4. "The Bear River Murder," *Saint John Daily Sun*, February 10, 1896.
5. "The Bear River Tragedy," *Bridgetown Monitor*, February 5, 1896.
6. "Wheeler Suspected," *Saint John Daily Sun*, January 31, 1896.
7. "Only a Circumstantial Case Made Out Against Wheeler," *Saint John Daily Sun*, February 1, 1896.
8. Tillie's inquest testimony, paraphrased by Detective Power and published in "Not a Midnight Murder," *Morning Chronicle*, July 6, 1896.
9. Ibid.
10. Ibid.
11. Mrs. Rice's account of Mary Kempton's itinerary was published in "Bear River Murder," *Saint John Daily Sun*, February 3, 1896.
12. "The Bear River Tragedy," *Bridgetown Monitor*, February 5, 1896.
13. Ibid.
14. Ibid.

Additional source: Canada, 1891 Census.

Thirteen — In Black and White

1. "Straightening their Eyes," *Bridgetown Monitor*, February 19, 1896.
2. Ibid.
3. Ibid.
4. "The Negro's Curly Hair," *Bridgetown Monitor*, February 19, 1896.
5. Ibid.
6. Ibid.
7. Ibid.
8. "Three Popular Blacks: They Belong to the Diamond Family," *Digby Weekly Courier*, February 21, 1896.
9. "Is Wheeler the Murderer," *Morning Chronicle*, January 30, 1896.
10. "Murder at Bear River," *Digby Weekly Courier*, January 31, 1896.

11. "The Bear River Tragedy," *Bridgetown Monitor*, February 5, 1896.
12. "The Bear River Murder," *The Globe*, January 30, 1896.
13. "Seeking the Slayer," *Saint John Daily Record*, January 29, 1896.
Additional source: The *Time* magazine O.J. Simpson mug shot cover (in which the image was manipulated to make him appear "blacker") was published on June 27, 1994.

Fourteen — Mr. Payne Takes Exception
1. Competitors reporting on Payne's arrival included the *Annapolis Spectator EXTRA*, "The Bear River Tragedy," February 8, 1896, as well as "The Bear River Tragedy," *Bridgetown Monitor*, February 12, 1896.
2. "Only a Circumstantial Case Made Out Against Wheeler," *Saint John Daily Sun*, February 1, 1896.
3. "A Horrible Murder," *Saint John Daily Sun*, January 29, 1896.
4. Ibid.
5. "The Bear River Murder," *Saint John Daily Sun*, January 30, 1896.
6. "A Horrible Murder," *Saint John Daily Sun*, January 29, 1896.
7. "The Bear River Murder," *Saint John Daily Sun*, January 30, 1896.
8. "The Bear River Murder," *Saint John Daily Sun*, February 7, 1896.
9. "The Bear River Murder," *Saint John Daily Sun*, January 30, 1896.
10. Wheeler's full statement to the coroner's inquest ran in "Only a Circumstantial Case Made Out Against Wheeler," *Saint John Daily Sun*, February 1, 1896.
11. "The Bear River Murder," *Saint John Daily Sun*, January 30, 1896.
12. "The Bear River Murder," *Saint John Daily Sun*, February 7, 1896.
13. "Bear River Murder," *Saint John Daily Sun*, February 3, 1896.
14. Ibid.
15. "The Bear River Murder," *Saint John Daily Sun*, February 10, 1896.
16. "Wheeler Suspected," *Saint John Daily Sun*, January 31, 1896.
17. "Only a Circumstantial Case Made Out Against Wheeler," *Saint John Daily Sun*, February 1, 1896.
18. "The Bear River Murder," *Saint John Daily Sun*, February 8, 1896.
19. "Only a Circumstantial Case Made Out Against Wheeler," *Saint John Daily Sun*, February 1, 1896.
20. Ibid.
21. Ibid.
22. "Bear River Murder," *Saint John Daily Sun*, February 3, 1896.
23. Quoted in "The Bear River Murder," *Saint John Daily Sun*, February 7, 1896.
24. "Wheeler Suspected," *Saint John Daily Sun*, January 31, 1896.
25. "A Horrible Murder," *Saint John Daily Sun*, January 29, 1896.
26. "The Bear River Murder," *Saint John Daily Sun*, February 7, 1896.

27. Ibid.
28. Ibid.
29. Ibid.
30. Ibid.
31. "The Bear River Tragedy," *Digby Weekly Courier*, February 14, 1896.
32. "The Bear River Murder," *Saint John Daily Sun*, February 7, 1896.
33. "Bear River Murder," *Saint John Daily Sun*, February 3, 1896.
34. "Only a Circumstantial Case Made Out Against Wheeler," *Saint John Daily Sun*, February 1, 1896.

Additional source: Canada, 1891 Census.

Fifteen — "Don't Kick the Instrument"
1. "Seeking the Slayer," *Saint John Daily Record*, January 29, 1896.
2. Ibid.
3. "Where Murder Was Done," *Saint John Daily Record*, January 30, 1896.
4. Ibid.
5. Ibid.
6. The *Digby Weekly Courier*'s first account of the crime ("Murder at Bear River") was their special edition published January 28, 1896.
7. The *Morning Chronicle*'s first critique of the *Courier*'s errors ran on January 29, 1896.
8. "Is Wheeler the Murderer," *Morning Chronicle*, January 30, 1896.
9. "The Justice of Wheeler's Sentence," *Digby Weekly Courier*, July 3, 1896.
10. "Keeping News Out," *Bridgetown Monitor*, March 18, 1896.

Sixteen — "And a Funeral It Was"
1. "The Bear River Murder: the Coroner's Verdict," *Yarmouth Herald*, February 4, 1896.
2. Ibid.
3. "Is Wheeler the Murderer," *Morning Chronicle*, January 30, 1896.
4. "The Detective's Story," *Morning Chronicle*, February 3, 1896.
5. "The Bear River Murder: the Coroner's Verdict," *Yarmouth Herald*, February 4, 1896.
6. Annie's baptismal record can be found at Nova Scotia, Baptismal Record [Annie Kempton], 1881, Annapolis/Digby County Records (1872-1919), MF 11,195, NSA.
7. "The Bear River Tragedy," *Digby Weekly Courier*, February 7, 1896.
8. Ibid.
9. "Letter to the Editor from J.W. Whitman," *Bridgetown Monitor*, February 5, 1896.
10. "The Bear River Tragedy," *Digby Weekly Courier*, February 5, 1896.
11. Details of Annie's memorial headstone are from "Another Record of the

Crime," *Acadian Recorder*, September 8, 1896; "Wheeler's Execution," *Digby Weekly Courier*, September 8, 1896.

Additional sources: Mount Hope Cemetery, Bear River, Nova Scotia; "The Bear River Tragedy," *Bridgetown Monitor*, February 5, 1896; "Murder at Bear River," *Digby Weekly Courier*, January 31, 1896; "The Bear River Tragedy," *Digby Weekly Courier*, February 7, 1896; "Annie Kempton Memorial," *Digby Weekly Courier*, April 17, 1896; "Special Edition: Peter Wheeler's Execution," *Digby Weekly Courier*, September 8, 1896; "The Bear River Murder: the Coroner's Verdict," *Yarmouth Herald*, February 4, 1896; "The Detective's Story," *Morning Chronicle*, February 3, 1896; "The Execution," *Acadian Recorder*, September 8, 1896.

Seventeen — Echoes of Millman

1. "The Detective's Story," *Morning Chronicle*, February 3, 1896.
2. Details of the Millman case were taken from "Capital case of William Milman [*sic*]," no. 685, Queen v. Millman, as well as from Prince Edward Island, "Queen vs. William Millman."
3. "The Detective's Story," *Morning Chronicle*, February 3, 1896.

Eighteen — Purdy's Purview

1. Ruggles's masthead advertisement can be seen in multiple editions of the *Annapolis Spectator*, for instance, November 4, 1898.
2. Lovett report, Queen v. Wheeler, NSA.
3. "The Bear River Tragedy," *Annapolis Spectator EXTRA*, February 8, 1896, original emphasis.
4. "The Bear River Murder," *Saint John Daily Sun*, February 10, 1896.
5. Ibid.
6. "The Bear River Tragedy," *Digby Weekly Courier*, February 7, 1896.
7. "The Bear River Murder," *Saint John Daily Sun*, February 8, 1896.
8. "The Bear River Tragedy," *Annapolis Spectator EXTRA*, February 8, 1896.
9. Ibid.
10. Ibid.

Additional sources: "Detective Power's Story," *Yarmouth Herald*, February 4, 1896; "The Bear River Tragedy," *Digby Weekly Courier*, February 7, 1896; "The Bear River Tragedy," *Bridgetown Monitor*, February 12, 1896.

Nineteen — Hardy Benson Changes His Tune

1. "The Bear River Murder," *Saint John Daily Sun*, January 30, 1896.
2. "Murder at Bear River," *Digby Weekly Courier*, January 31, 1896.
3. Quoted in "Detective Power's Discovery," *Morning Chronicle*, February 1, 1896.
4. Ibid.

5. "Peter Wheeler to go on Trial," *Morning Chronicle*, January 31, 1896.
6. Ibid, original emphasis.
7. "The Detective's Story," *Morning Chronicle*, February 3, 1896.
8. "To Stand Trial for Murder," *Yarmouth Herald*, February 11, 1896.
9. Ibid.
10. The exchange between Wheeler and Benson was taken from the court transcript, reprinted in ibid.
11. Trial transcript, Queen v. Wheeler, LAC.
Additional sources: Canada, 1891 Census; "The Bear River Murder," *Saint John Daily Sun*, January 30, 1896.

Twenty — Facts Be Damned
1. Payne's contradictions regarding Annie's age were printed in "A Horrible Murder," *Saint John Daily Sun*, January 29, 1896.
2. "The Bear River Tragedy," *Digby Weekly Courier*, February 7, 1896.
3. "The Bear River Murder," *Saint John Daily Sun*, February 10, 1896.
Additional sources: "To Stand Trial for Murder," *Yarmouth Herald*, February 11, 1896; "The Bear River Tragedy," *Digby Weekly Courier*, February 14, 1896.

Twenty-one — An Indictment, of Sorts
1. "The Bear River Tragedy," *Digby Weekly Courier*, February 14, 1896.
2. "The Bear River Tragedy," *Digby Weekly Courier*, February 7, 1896.
3. Ibid.
4. Ibid.
5. Lovett report, Queen v. Wheeler, NSA.
6. "Detective Power's Discovery," *Morning Chronicle*, February 1, 1896.
7. "To Stand Trial for Murder," *Yarmouth Herald*, February 11, 1896.
8. "The Bear River Murder — Very Strong Evidence Against Wheeler," *Saint John Daily Telegraph*, February 3, 1896.
9. "Not a Midnight Murder," *Morning Chronicle*, July 6, 1896.
10. "The Detective's Story," *Morning Chronicle*, February 3, 1896.
Additional sources: Documents relating to Purdy's examination are contained in Wallace A. Purdy, Report of Examination, July 11, 1896, no. 5, Queen v. Wheeler, NSA.

Twenty-two — That Troublesome Timeline
1. "The Bear River Murder: the Coroner's Verdict," *Yarmouth Herald*, February 4, 1896.
2. "To Stand Trial for Murder," *Yarmouth Herald*, February 11, 1896.
3. Ibid.
Additional sources: Canada, Trial transcript, Queen v. Wheeler, LAC;

Environment Canada, Meteorological data from Digby and Yarmouth weather stations for January, 1896, National Climate Data Archives; "Is Wheeler the Murderer," *Morning Chronicle*, January 30, 1896; "Peter Wheeler to go on Trial," *Morning Chronicle*, January 31, 1896; "The Detective's Story," *Morning Chronicle*, February 3, 1896; "Murder at Bear River," *Digby Weekly Courier*, January 31, 1896; "Only a Circumstantial Case Made Out Against Wheeler," *Saint John Daily Sun*, February 1, 1896; "Detective Power's Story," *Yarmouth Herald*, February 4, 1896; "To Stand Trial for Murder," *Yarmouth Herald*, February 11, 1896.

Twenty-three — The Great Divide
1. "Correspondence: The Bear River Tragedy," *Digby Weekly Courier*, February 21, 1896, original emphasis.
2. Ibid.
3. Ibid.
4. "Correspondence: The Bear River Tragedy," *Digby Weekly Courier*, March 6, 1896.
5. Ibid.
6. Ibid.
7. Ibid.

Twenty-four — A Particularly Slow News Day
1. "Wheeler May Not be the Murderer," *Yarmouth Times*, February 24, 1896.
2. Ibid.
3. "The Bear River Tragedy," *Digby Weekly Courier*, February 28, 1896.
4. "An Indian Now Suspected," *Bridgetown Monitor*, March 11, 1896.
5. "The Bear River Tragedy," *Digby Weekly Courier*, February 28, 1896.
6. "Dies in a Few Hours," *Saint John Daily Record*, September 7, 1896.
7. Ibid.
8. It is of interest to note that Joseph Pictou was eventually called to testify during Wheeler's trial (see Trial transcript, Queen v. Wheeler, LAC). During his testimony, he related having seen Annie on the day she died. The newspaper accounts were never mentioned, and at no point was he openly accused of any wrongdoing.

Twenty-five — A Change of Venue
1. Girard, "Townshend, Sir Charles James."
2. Cited in the Motion for a change of venue, in Queen v. Wheeler, NSA. See also "The Venue in the Wheeler Trial," *Digby Weekly Courier*, May 22, 1896.
3. "Dies in a Few Hours," *Saint John Daily Record*, September 7, 1896.
4. "The Venue in the Wheeler Trial," *Digby Weekly Courier*, May 22, 1896.

Additional sources: Judge Townshend's ruling on the Motion for a change of venue, Queen v. Wheeler, NSA; "Motion for Change of Venue in Wheeler Case," *Bridgetown Monitor*, May 13, 1896; Townshend's biography taken from "Creighton Shatford Barristers and Soliciters — Firm History," 2012, accessed October 13, 2012, http://www.csdlaw.ca/history.html; Girard, "Townshend, Sir Charles James"; Rose, *Cyclopædia*.

Twenty-six — The Trial

1. The *Bridgetown Monitor* reported on the grand jury indictment in "A True Bill Against Wheeler," June 10, 1896.
2. "His Life at Stake: Peter Wheeler's Trial Begins at Kentville," *Halifax Daily Echo*, June 26, 1896.
3. At the time of Wheeler's troubles, there were two lawyers named Ruggles working in the region: Henry Dwight Ruggles, aged thirty-five, whose office was in Annapolis Royal, and Edwin Ruggles, aged forty-six, who practised out of Bridgetown. All sources — both official and media — identify Henry Dwight Ruggles as Wheeler's attorney, save one. In the preamble of the trial transcript, where the various parties are identified, "Edwin Ruggles" is listed for the defence (Trial transcript, Queen v. Wheeler, LAC). Throughout the remainder of the transcript, the defence lawyer is identified solely as "Ruggles" or "defense." While it is possible that all other sources are incorrect and it was, in fact, Edwin who defended Peter Wheeler, I have gone with the preponderance of evidence and ascribed Henry Dwight as defence counsel. Interestingly, despite the similarities in surname, profession, and their relative proximity, the two barristers do not appear to be directly related to one another. See Canada, 1881 Census, FHL film 1375809, NAC C-13173, District 16, subdistrict J, pg. 54, family 256 [Ruggles].
4. "His Life at Stake: Peter Wheeler's Trial Begins at Kentville," *Halifax Daily Echo*, June 26, 1896.
5. Ibid.
6. The *Globe*, in "Wheeler Offers No Evidence," questioned Ruggles's refusal to present evidence on June 30, 1896.

Additional sources: A history of the Kentville courthouse and jail is on display at the King's County Museum, viewed June 7, 2012; "Power's Testimony," *Halifax Daily Echo*, June 27, 1896; "Wheeler on Trial for his Life," *Yarmouth Herald*, June 30, 1896; "The Wheeler Murder Trial," *Acadian Recorder*, June 30, 1896; "Wheeler's Life at Stake," *Morning Chronicle*, June 27, 1896; "Detective Power Testifies," *Morning Chronicle*, June 28, 1896.

Twenty-seven — Detective Power Takes the Stand

1. Quoted in "Detective Power's Story," *Yarmouth Herald*, February 4, 1896.

2. Ibid.
3. Ibid.
4. Ibid., see also "Detective Power's Discovery," *Morning Chronicle*, February 1, 1896.
5. Trial transcript, Queen v. Wheeler, LAC.
6. "Detective Power Testifies," *Morning Chronicle*, June 28, 1896.
7. Trial transcript, Queen v. Wheeler, LAC, citing the detective's prior statements in "The Bear River Tragedy," *Bridgetown Monitor*, February 12, 1896.

Additional sources: "The Bear River Tragedy," *Bridgetown Monitor*, February 5, 1896; "Wheeler Suspected," *Saint John Daily Sun*, January 31, 1896; "The Bear River Murder," *Saint John Daily Sun*, February 8, 1896; "Detective Power Testifies," *Morning Chronicle*, June 28, 1896.

Twenty-eight — The Myth of Fingerprints

1. The 1879 Argentine precedent is detailed in Cole, *Suspect Identities*.
2. The first scholarly work on fingerprinting was Faulds, "Skin Furrows."
3. Cited in Northwestern University School of Law, "Wrongful Conviction of Thomas M. Bram."
4. The bloody spoon was marked exhibit T3, according to the trial transcript and exhibits log (transcript of evidence), in Queen v. Wheeler, LAC.
5. "Detective Power's Discovery," *Morning Chronicle*, February 1, 1896.

Additional sources: Twain, *Pudd'nhead Wilson*; Bram v. United States, 168 U.S. 532 (1897); "Murder on the High Seas," *Bridgetown Monitor*, July 29, 1896; "Charged with Triple Murder," *Bridgetown Monitor*, August 5, 1896; "Murder at Bear River," *Digby Weekly Courier*, January 28, 1896; "14-year-old Girl Murdered," *Morning Chronicle*, January 29, 1896.

Twenty-nine — Power, in Hindsight

1. Cited in McGahan, "Detective Nick Power," 52.
2. "New Police Uniforms," *Halifax Herald*, May 25, 1906.
3. Ibid.
4. Power's letter of resignation was published in "Chief of Police Power Resigns after Forty-Three Years Faithful Service," *Morning Herald*, November 4, 1907 and again in "Chief Nicholas Power Resigned from Head of Police Force," *Nova Scotian and Weekly Chronicle*, November 8, 1907.
5. From Power's final application, cited in Templeton, "Police Gallantry."
6. Ibid.
7. Ibid.
8. "Nicholas Power, Colorful Haligonian, Passes to his Reward," *Halifax Chronicle*, October 3, 1938.

Additional sources: Halifax Police Staff Register, 1892-1914, RG 35, 120 series,

16 H, vol. 6, NSA; "Nicholas Power Biography and Obituary," October 3, 1938 MG 100, vol. 209, #31, NSA; Chief's Office Records, 1906-1915, HPD; Halifax Regional Police, "Chiefs of Police — Nicholas Power"; McGahan, "Crime and Policing"; McGahan, "Disciplining the Guardians"; McGahan, "Reorganization"; McGahan, "Detective Nick Power"; "The Sydney Burglar," *Halifax Herald*, December 23, 1903; "Detective Nick Power," *Halifax Herald*, November 21, 1903; [untitled] *Halifax Herald*, December 4, 1905; [untitled report on George Stanley] *Halifax Herald*, February 12, 1906; "Murder on the High Seas," *Bridgetown Monitor*, July 29, 1896; "Charged with Triple Murder," *Bridgetown Monitor*, August 5, 1896; "Eventful Life of Ex-chief Power," *Morning Chronicle*, March 30, 1918; "Nicholas Power, Colorful Haligonian, Passes to his Reward," *Halifax Chronicle*, October 3, 1938.

Thirty — Bad Blood
1. Dr. Jacques's biographical details were taken from JAMA, "Catalogues," 302; as well as his entry in *McAlpine's Nova Scotia Directory for 1896*.
2. Trial transcript, Queen v. Wheeler, LAC.
3. "Trial of Wheeler," *Halifax Daily Echo*, June 29, 1896.
4. Ibid.
5. Trial transcript, Queen v. Wheeler, LAC.
6. "Trial of Wheeler," *Halifax Daily Echo*, June 29, 1896.
7. Ibid.
8. Trial transcript, Queen v. Wheeler, LAC.
9. "Wheeler on Trial for his Life," *Yarmouth Herald*, June 30, 1896.
10. Ibid.
11. "Wheeler Offers No Evidence," *The Globe*, June 30, 1896.

Thirty-one — The Minstrel Show
1. "Power's Testimony," *Halifax Daily Echo*, June 27, 1896.
2. "Wheeler's Trial," *Saint John Daily Sun*, June 29, 1896.
3. For commentary on Ruggles's refusal to offer evidence, see, for example, "Wheeler Offers No Evidence," *The Globe*, June 30, 1896.
4. "Closing the Trial," *Halifax Daily Echo*, June 30, 1896.
Additional sources: "Detective Power Testifies," *Morning Chronicle*, June 28, 1896.

Thirty-two — A Foregone Conclusion
1. "Closing the Trial," *Halifax Daily Echo*, June 30, 1896.
2. "Wheeler Found Guilty," *Morning Chronicle*, July 1, 1896.
3. Ibid.
4. "Peter Wheeler Found Guilty," *Acadian Recorder*, July 1, 1896.

5. "The Wheeler Murder Trial," *Acadian Recorder*, June 30, 1896.
6. Ibid.
7. Ibid.
8. Ibid.
9. "Wheeler Found Guilty," *Morning Chronicle*, July 1, 1896.
10. "Peter Wheeler Found Guilty," *Acadian Recorder*, July 1, 1896.
11. "Wheeler Found Guilty," *Morning Chronicle*, July 1, 1896.
12. "Peter Wheeler Found Guilty," *Acadian Recorder*, July 1, 1896.
13. "Wheeler to Hang," *Saint John Daily Telegraph*, July 1, 1896.
14. "Wheeler Found Guilty," *Morning Chronicle*, July 1, 1896.
15. "Peter Wheeler Found Guilty," *Acadian Recorder*, July 1, 1896.
16. Ibid.
17. "Wheeler Found Guilty," *Morning Chronicle*, July 1, 1896.
18. Psalm 39:4, *Holy Bible*, New International Version, (Colorado Springs, CO: International Bible Society, 1984).

Thirty-three — Poisoned Pens
1. "The Court and Wheeler," *Saint John Daily Sun*, September 9, 1896.
2. "A Yarmouth Man Interviews Peter Wheeler," *Yarmouth Herald*, July 14, 1896.
3. In addition to "Wheeler Found Guilty," *Morning Chronicle*, July 1, 1896, the tale of the poison bottle ran in "Peter Wheeler Found Guilty," *Acadian Recorder*, July 1, 1896; "Wheeler to Hang," *Saint John Daily Telegraph*, July 1, 1896; and "Wheeler Must Die," *The Globe*, July 1, 1896; and in "Wheeler Must Die," *Saint John Daily Record*, July 2, 1896; "Wheeler to Hang," *Toronto Evening Star*, July 2, 1896; as well as numerous other papers using the same wire service.

Thirty-four — No Love Lost
1. "The 100th Year of Service," *Digby Courier*, September 19, 1974.
2. "A Yarmouth Man Interviews Peter Wheeler," *Yarmouth Herald*, July 14, 1896.
3. Wheeler's cell and chains were described in "Wheeler is Ready to Die," *Morning Chronicle*, September 7, 1896.
4. "Peter Wheeler Hanged," *Nova Scotian Weekly Chronicle*, September 12, 1896.
5. Ibid.
6. Ibid.
7. Ibid.
8. "Wheeler's Story," *Morning Chronicle*, July 8, 1896.
9. Ibid.

10. "Peter Wheeler Sentenced," *Digby Weekly Courier*, July 3, 1896.
11. Ibid.

Thirty-five — The Confession(s)
1. "Wheeler's Confessions," *Digby Weekly Courier*, July 10, 1896.
2. "Wheeler has Confessed," *Morning Chronicle*, July 4, 1896.
3. "Wheeler's Confession," *Annapolis Spectator*, July 3, 1896.
4. "Wheeler's Confessions," *Digby Weekly Courier*, July 10, 1896.
5. "Wheeler has Confessed," *Morning Chronicle*, July 4, 1896.
6. "Wheeler's Confession," *Annapolis Spectator*, July 3, 1896.
7. Ibid.
8. Ibid.
9. Ibid.
10. Ibid.
11. Ibid.
12. Ibid.
13. Ibid.
14. Ibid.
15. "Wheeler has Confessed," *Morning Chronicle*, July 4, 1896.
16. "Wheeler's Story," *Morning Chronicle*, July 8, 1896.
17. "Wheeler's Confession," *Morning Chronicle*, July 7, 1896.
18. Ibid.
19. "Peter Wheeler Speaks," *Saint John Daily Telegraph*, July 18, 1896.
20. "Not a Midnight Murder," *Morning Chronicle*, July 6, 1896.
21. "Wheeler's Confession," *Yarmouth Herald*, July 7, 1896.
22. "Not a Midnight Murder," *Morning Chronicle*, July 6, 1896.
23. Ibid.
24. "Wheeler's Story," *Morning Chronicle*, July 8, 1896, emphasis added.
25. Ibid.
26. "Not a Midnight Murder," *Morning Chronicle*, July 6, 1896.
27. Ibid.
28. Ibid.
29. Ibid.
30. Methods of forensic linguistic analysis or idiolect (an individual's characteristic use of vocabulary, spelling, grammar, etc.) are detailed in Olsson, *Forensic Linguistics*; Coulthard, "Author identification"; Grant, "Forensic linguistic analysis"; and Eagleson, "Forensic analysis."
31. "Wheeler's Confession," *Yarmouth Herald*, July 7, 1896.
32. Ibid.
33. Ibid.
34. Ibid.

35. Ibid.
36. Ibid.
37. Ibid.
38. Ibid.
39. "Wheeler has Confessed," *Morning Chronicle*, July 4, 1896.
40. "Peter Wheeler Speaks," *Saint John Daily Telegraph*, July 18, 1896.
41. Ibid.
42. Ibid.
43. There is one possible exception to this. During his trial testimony, Dr. Lovett stated he had Wheeler sign his witness statement after Peter testified at the original coroner's inquest. At that moment, Wheeler was not yet under suspicion, merely one of many witnesses. Under cross, Ruggles challenged the doctor's claim repeatedly, saying Wheeler did not sign the document and demanding the doctor produce it. Lovett could not. Wheeler's statement was included in the documentation sent to the Minister of Justice, prior to Wheeler's execution (retained in Trial transcript, Queen v. Wheeler, LAC). Where the signature should be, Wheeler's name is typed, not written. The only evidence that Peter ever signed anything is Lovett's statement — no surviving document corroborates his claim.
44. "Peter Wheeler Speaks," *Saint John Daily Telegraph*, July 18, 1896.
45. Ibid.
46. Ibid.
47. "Wheeler's Confessions," *Digby Weekly Courier*, July 10, 1896.
48. Ibid.
49. Ibid.
50. "Peter Wheeler's Confession," *Digby Weekly Courier*, August 7, 1896.
51. Ibid.
52. Ibid.
53. "Wheeler's Execution," *Bridgetown Monitor*, September 2, 1896.
54. "Dies in a Few Hours," *Saint John Daily Record*, September 7, 1896.
55. "Peter Wheeler's Confession," *Digby Weekly Courier*, August 14, 1896.

Thirty-six — "But It Had to End"
1. "Wheeler is Ready to Die," *Morning Chronicle*, September 7, 1896.
2. Ibid.
3. Ibid.
4. Ibid.
5. Ibid.
6. Ibid.
7. Ibid.
8. Ibid.

9. Ibid.
10. Ibid.
11. Ibid.
12. Ibid.
13. "Pays the Penalty To-Day!" *Morning Chronicle*, September 8, 1896.
14. "Peter Wheeler Hanged," *Morning Chronicle*, September 9, 1896.
15. "Peter Wheeler's Execution," *Digby Weekly Courier*, September 8, 1896.
16. Ibid.

Thirty-seven — "The Hole in the Floor of the Gallows"
1. "The Bear River Murder," *Saint John Daily Sun*, February 8, 1896.
2. Cited in Patrick Cain, "The Agony of the Executioner," *The Star*, May 20, 2007 .
3. Ibid.
4. The circumstances of Radcliffe's death were taken from Death Certificate — John Radcleve, 1911, Ontario Vital Statistics, Archives of Ontario, MS 935, reel 161, #002173.
5. "Radcliffe will not Hang Wheeler," *Bridgetown Monitor*, August 26, 1896.
6. Ibid.
7. "Murder at Bear River," *Digby Weekly Courier*, January 31, 1896.
Additional sources: Petruk, "Hanging"; Foster, *Hangings*; "Wants to Hang Wheeler," *Bridgetown Monitor*, July 22, 1896; "Radcliffe will not Hang Wheeler," *Bridgetown Monitor*, August 26, 1896.

Thirty-eight — Meeting the Kemptons
1. "A Yarmouth Man Interviews Peter Wheeler," *Yarmouth Herald*, July 14, 1896.
2. Ibid.
3. Ibid.
4. "The Execution!" *Acadian Recorder*, September 8, 1896.
5. "Is Wheeler the Murderer," *Morning Chronicle*, January 30, 1896.
6. *Morning Chronicle* reported that Mary Kempton was working as a maid for her son-in-law — ibid.
7. "The Execution!" *Acadian Recorder*, September 8, 1896.
8. Ibid.
9. Ibid.
10. Ibid.
11. Ibid.
12. "Wheeler is Ready to Die," *Morning Chronicle*, September 7, 1896.
13. "Peter Wheeler's Execution," *Digby Weekly Courier*, September 8, 1896.
14. Ibid.
Additional sources: Nova Scotia, 1871 Census, NSA; Canada, 1881 Census;

Canada, 1891 Census; Death certificate — Mary Kempton, 1935, Death Registry, book 144, page 624, NSA; Death certificate — Isaac Kempton, 1926, Death Registry, book 84, page 1554, NSA; Marriage Registry (Annapolis County) — Isaac Kempton and Mary Parker, 1866, Marriage Registry, book 1801, page 8, no. 58, NSA; Hall, *Heritage Remembered*.

Thirty-nine — Wheeler Gets Religion

1. "Wheeler is Ready to Die," *Morning Chronicle*, September 7, 1896.
2. Ibid.
3. Ibid.
4. "Peter Wheeler Hanged," *Nova Scotian Weekly Chronicle*, September 12, 1896.
5. "Dies in a Few Hours," *Saint John Daily Record*, September 7, 1896.
6. "Wheeler is Ready to Die," *Morning Chronicle*, September 7, 1896.
7. The recipients of Wheeler's last three letters were identified in "The Court and Wheeler," *Saint John Daily Sun*, September 9, 1896.
8. "Pays the Penalty To-Day!" *Morning Chronicle*, September 8, 1896.

Forty — Ottawa Weighs In

1. There are no fewer than eighteen portraits of John Campbell Hamilton-Gordon in London's National Portrait Gallery and he bears the same stern look in all of them.
2. Entry for John Campbell Hamilton-Gordon, in "Earl of Aberdeen," at the Governor General of Canada website.
3. Charles J. Townshend, Letter to Sir Charles Tupper Bart, Secretary of State, July 2, 1896, no. 2631, Queen v. Wheeler, LAC.
4. Joseph Pope, Letter to Charles Townshend, 1896, no. 4118, Queen v. Wheeler, LAC.
5. Remission register, July 9, 1896, no. 4118, 225-296, Queen v. Wheeler, LAC.
6. "Capital Case of Peter Wheeler," no. 4118, Queen v. Wheeler, LAC.
7. Remission register, July 9, 1896, no. 4118, 225-296, Queen v. Wheeler, LAC.
8. Canada, Memorandum to Minister of Justice, August 8, 1869, Queen v. Wheeler, LAC.
9. Biographical details of Oliver Mowat taken from Donald Swainson, "Sir Oliver Mowat," in *The Canadian Encyclopedia*, and from a painting of Mowat circa 1905, housed at LAC, photograph PA-28973.
10. The salaries of all public officials were published in the *Canadian Almanac for 1896*.
11. Benjamin Van Blarcom, Letter to Attorney General, August 17, 1896, Queen v. Wheeler, LAC.
12. Letter from Attorney General [Longley] of Nova Scotia to E.L. Newcombe, Deputy Minister of Justice, August 20, 1896, Queen v. Wheeler, LAC.

13. Memorandum by the Minister of Justice [Oliver Mowat], September 1, 1896, Queen v. Wheeler, LAC.
14. Ibid.

Forty-one — Trouble Brewing

1. "The Court and Wheeler," *Saint John Daily Sun*, September 9, 1896.
2. "Confessed his Crimes," *Toronto Evening Star*, September 8, 1896.
3. "The Digby Hanging," *Saint John Daily Telegraph*, September 8, 1896.
4. Ibid.
5. "Sent Before His Judge — Wheeler Dies in Digby Jail," *Saint John Daily Record*, September 8, 1896.
6. "Dies in a Few Hours," *Saint John Daily Record*, September 7, 1896.
7. The digging of Wheeler's grave was described in "The Digby Hanging," *Saint John Daily Telegraph*, September 8, 1896.
8. The grave is mistaken for the gallows in "Dies in a Few Hours," *Saint John Daily Record*, September 7, 1896.
9. "Letter to the Editor," *Bridgetown Monitor*, February 5, 1896.
10. The reports from across Canada and the United States were noted in "Dies in a Few Hours," *Saint John Daily Record*, September 7, 1896, as well as in many other publications.
11. "The Digby Hanging," *Saint John Daily Telegraph*, September 8, 1896.
12. Ibid.
13. Ibid.
14. "The Execution!" *Acadian Recorder*, September 8, 1896.
15. "Sent Before His Judge — Wheeler Dies in Digby Jail," *Saint John Daily Record*, September 8, 1896.
16. Ibid.

Forty-two — "Lord, I Am Coming"

1. The identity of the witnesses is revealed in a document sent to the Secretary of State following the execution: Declaration of Sheriff and Others, Queen v. Wheeler, LAC. The witnesses were: Benjamin Van Blarcom, William Van Blarcom, Harris Bowles, Rueben Cossaboom (policeman), John Daley (coroner), J. Edgar Jones (prison surgeon), Fred S. Kinsman, W. Morgan, W.A. MacLaren, Elias Allen (captain, Salvation Army), A.D. Daley, and two unnamed members of the medical profession.
2. "Peter Wheeler's Execution," *Digby Weekly Courier*, September 8, 1896.
3. Ibid.
4. Ibid.
5. "Wheeler Executed," *Yarmouth Herald*, September 8, 1896.
6. "The Digby Hanging," *Saint John Daily Telegraph*, September 8, 1896.
7. "The Execution!" *Acadian Recorder*, September 8, 1896.

8. "The Court and Wheeler," *Saint John Daily Sun*, September 9, 1896.
9. "Sent Before His Judge — Wheeler Dies in Digby Jail," *Saint John Daily Record*, September 8, 1896.
10. "The Execution!" *Acadian Recorder*, September 8, 1896.
11. "Peter Wheeler Hanged," *Morning Chronicle*, September 9, 1896.
12. Ibid.
13. Ibid.
14. "Peter Wheeler's Execution," *Digby Weekly Courier*, September 8, 1896.
15. "Pays the Penalty To-Day!" *Morning Chronicle*, September 8, 1896.
16. Ibid.
17. Ibid.
18. "Peter Wheeler's Execution," *Digby Weekly Courier*, September 8, 1896.
19. "Wheeler is to be Hanged at Digby To-Day," *Toronto Evening Star*, September 8, 1896.
20. "The Execution!" *Acadian Recorder*, September 8, 1896.
21. "Peter Wheeler Hanged," *Morning Chronicle*, September 9, 1896.
22. "Peter Wheeler's Execution," *Digby Weekly Courier*, September 8, 1896, original emphasis.
23. "Lord, I am coming" was quoted in "Confessed His Crime," *Toronto Evening Star*, September 8, 1896; "The Execution!"*Acadian Recorder*, September 8, 1896; and Special Edition: Peter Wheeler's Execution, *Digby Weekly Courier*, September 8, 1896. "Jesus, I am coming" was quoted in "Wheeler's Execution," *Yarmouth Herald*, September 8, 1896 and "Pays the Penalty To-day!" *Morning Chronicle*, September 9, 1896.
24. "Peter Wheeler's Execution," *Digby Weekly Courier*, September 8, 1896.
25. "The Execution!" *Acadian Recorder*, September 8, 1896.
26. "Peter Wheeler's Execution," *Digby Weekly Courier*, September 8, 1896.
27. Wheeler's body was left hanging twenty minutes — "Sent Before His Judge — Wheeler Dies in Digby Jail," *Saint John Daily Record*, September 8, 1896; Wheeler's body was left hanging twenty-five minutes — Special Edition: Peter Wheeler's Execution, *Digby Weekly Courier*, September 8, 1896.

Additional source: John Daley, Coroner's report on the death of Peter Wheeler, September 8, 1896, RG 41, series C, vol. 7(b), #13, NSA.

Forty-three — Mob Mentality
1. "Wheeler is to be Hanged at Digby To-Day," *Toronto Evening Star*, September 8, 1896.
2. "The Execution!" *Acadian Recorder*, September 8, 1896.
3. "Wheeler Executed," *Yarmouth Herald*, September 8, 1896.
4. "The Court and Wheeler," *Saint John Daily Sun*, September 9, 1896.
5. "Peter Wheeler Hanged," *Morning Chronicle*, September 9, 1896.

6. Ibid.
7. Ibid.
8. Ibid.
9. Ibid.
10. Ibid.
11. Ibid.
12. From Payson's note to Van Blarcom, quoted in "Peter Wheeler Hanged," *Morning Chronicle*, September 9, 1896.
13. Payson's affidavit is noted in Justice Townshend, Decision regarding Motion for Change of Venue, May 22, 1896, no. 3, Queen v. Wheeler, NSA.
14. From Payson's note to Van Blarcom, quoted in "Wheeler Hanged," *Saint John Daily Telegraph*, September 9, 1896.

Additional sources: Canada, 1891 Census; John Daley, Coroner's report on the death of Peter Wheeler, September 8, 1896, RG 41, series C, vol. 7(b), #13, NSA.

Forty-four — Wheeler's Last Laugh

1. "Peter Wheeler's Execution," *Digby Weekly Courier*, September 8, 1896.
2. Ibid.
3. Ibid.
4. Ibid.
5. Ibid.
6. Ibid.
7. Ibid.

Forty-five — Reclaiming the Moral High Ground

1. "Wheeler's Upcoming Execution," *Windsor Tribune*, September 4, 1896.
2. "Wheeler Executed," *Yarmouth Herald*, September 8, 1896.
3. "The Last of a Disagreeable Affair," *Digby Weekly Courier*, September 11, 1896.

Forty-six — None the Wiser

1. "Peter Wheeler's Execution," *Digby Weekly Courier*, September 8, 1896.

Additional sources: Supreme Court of Canada, Reference re: Milgaard [1992] 1 S.C. R 866, docket # 22732; *CBC News*, "Canada's Wrongful Convictions"; William Grimes, "Donald Marshall Jr., Symbol of Bias, Dies at 55," *New York Times*, August 6, 2009; Ontario, "Kaufman Commission"; MacCullum, "Commission of Inquiry."

Selected Bibliography

Newspapers and Periodicals
Acadian Recorder
Annapolis Spectator
Bridgetown Monitor
Digby Courier
Digby Weekly Courier
Globe [Toronto]
Halifax Chronicle
Halifax Daily Echo
Halifax Herald
Halifax Mail
Kamloops This Week
The Mirror
Morning Chronicle [Halifax]
Morning Herald [Halifax]
The New York Times
Nova Scotian and Weekly Chronicle
Saint John Daily Record
Saint John Daily Sun
Saint John Daily Telegraph
The Star [Toronto]
Summerside Journal and Western Pioneer
Time Magazine
Toronto Evening Star
Windsor Tribune
Yarmouth Herald
Yarmouth Times

Archival Sources
Archives of Ontario
Bear River Historical Society, Oakdene Museum (BRHS)

Halifax Municipal Archives (HMA)
  Halifax Police Department records, City of Halifax Fonds, 102-16C.
  (HPD)
Library and Archives Canada (LAÇ)
  Queen v. Peter Wheeler [1896], RG 13, Vol. 1430, File 278A.
  Queen v. William Millman [1888], RG 13, C-1, vol. 1425.
Nova Scotia Archives (NSA)
  Nova Scotia Supreme Court records [1860-1975], RG 39, D1.
  Queen v. Peter Wheeler [1896], RG39, series C, vol. 17, #761.

Other Primary Sources

Bear River Hotel. Advertisement. BRHS, Box 1, file 5.
Canada. 1881 Census. LAC.
_____. 1891 Census. Accessed June 11, 2012. http://www.collectionscanada.
  gc.ca/databases/census-1891/index-e.html?PHPSESSID=qrin305k9rtg6kqep
  ah1iar391.
_____. Portrait of Sir Oliver Mowat. Library and Archives Canada, photograph
  PA-28973, 1905.
_____. "Service Record and Biography of Lewis Johnstone Lovett." Parliament
  of Canada. Accessed May 25, 2012. http://www.parl.gc.ca/parlinfo/Files/
  Parliamentarian.aspx?Item=c98f70ce-bef0-47c3-9c0c-ac024597b103&Lang
  uage=E&Section=ALL.
Daley, John. Coroner's report on the death of Peter Wheeler. September 8,
  1896. RG 41, series C, volume 7(b), #13. NSA.
Ellison, Robert. Coroner's Inquest of Annie Kempton. January 1896. RG 41,
  series C, volume 7(b), #12. NSA.
Environment Canada. Meteorological data from Digby and Yarmouth weather
  stations for January, 1896. National Climate Data Archives. Accessed June
  14, 2012. http://www.climate.weatheroffice.gc.ca/climateData/dailydata_e.
  html?timeframe=2&Prov=NS&StationID=6515&dlyRan
  ge=1870-12-01|1941-03-31&Year=1896&Month=1&Day=01.
Kempton, Annie. Autograph Book. 1894. BRHS.
Nova Scotia. 1871 Census. NSA.
_____. Baptismal Record [Annie Kempton]. 1881. Annapolis/Digby County
  Records (1872-1919). MF 11,195. NSA.
_____. Halifax Police Staff Register, 1892-1914. RG 35, 120 series, 16 H, vol. 6.
  NSA.
_____. "Nicholas Power Biography and Obituary." October 3, 1938. MG 100
  vol. 209 #31. NSA.
_____. "Nova Scotia Medical Examiner Service — History." 2012. Accessed
  December 8, 2012. http://novascotia.ca/just/cme/.
_____. Portrait of Nicholas Power. Nova Scotia Archives, MG 100 209 #31.

Ontario. "Report of the Kaufman Commission on Proceedings Involving Guy Paul Morin." 2010. Ministry of the Attorney General. Accessed September 29, 2012. http://www.attorneygeneral.jus.gov.on.ca/english/about/pubs/morin/.

Parker, Obadiah. Last Will and Testament. 1910. Nova Scotia Estate Files, Digby County A-1789, Church of Latter Day Saints Family History Department.

Prince Edward Island. "The Queen v. William Millman." Accessed July 1, 2012. http://www.edu.pe.ca/gray/class_pages/rxmacdonald/pei/crime/millman.html.

Supreme Court of Canada. Reference re: Milgaard [1992] 1 S. C. R 866, docket # 22732.

Supreme Court of the United States. Bram v. United States [1897]. 168 US 532.

Secondary Sources

Bear River Tides. "Tour of Historic Houses." January 29, 2012. http://bearrivernovascotia.com/2012/01/29/tour-of-historic-houses/.

Cahill, Barry and Philip Girard. "Longley, James Wilberforce." *Dictionary of Canadian Biography*, vol. 15, University of Toronto, 2003. Accessed June 8, 2013. http://www.biographi.ca/en/bio/longley_james_wilberforce_15E.html.

Camps, F.E. "Establishment of the Time of Death — A Critical Assessment." *Journal of Forensic Sciences* vol. 4, no. 1 (1959): 73-82.

Canadian Almanac (The), 1896. Toronto: The Copp, Clark Company, 1896. LAAC PAAPAY 414 C2. LAC.

CBC News. "Canada's Wrongful Convictions." October 14, 2010. http://www.cbc.ca/news/canada/story/2009/08/06/f-wrongfully-convicted.html.

Cole, Simon A. *Suspect Identities: A History of Fingerprinting and Criminal Identification.* Boston: Harvard University Press, 2001.

Comeau, Louis V. *Historic Kentville.* Halifax: Nimbus Publishing, 2003.

Coulthard, M. "Author identification, idiolect and linguistic uniqueness." *Applied Linguistics* 25, no. 4 (2004): 431-447.

"Creighton Shatford Barristers and Soliciters — Firm History." 2012. Accessed October 13, 2012. http://www.csdlaw.ca/history.html.

Curtis, L. Perry, Jr. *Jack the Ripper and the London Press.* Princeton: Yale University Press, 2001.

Dinn, Alan. "Old Saint Edward Cemetery." August 24, 2005. www.interment.net.

Eagleson, Robert. "Forensic analysis of a personal written text: a case study." In *Language and the Law.* Edited by John Gibbons. London: Longman, 1994, 362-373.

Edmund Rice (1638) Association. *A Genealogical Register of Edmund Rice Descendants.* Rutland, VT: The Charles E. Tuttle Company, 1970.

Faulds, Henry. "On the Skin Furrows of the Hand." *Nature* 22, no. 574 (October 28, 1880): 605.

Foster, Deanna. *A History of Hangings in Nova Scotia*. Lawrencetown, NS: Pottersfield Press, 2007.

Girard, Philip. "Townshend, Sir Charles James," in EN:UNDEF:public_ citation_publication (Dictionary of Canadian Biography) vol. 15 (University of Toronto/Université Laval, 2003–). Accessed October 13, 2012. http://www.biographi.ca/en/bio/townshend_charles_james_15E. html.

Governor General of Canada. "John Campbell Hamilton-Gordon." Governor General of Canada Website – Former Governors General. Accessed June 10, 2013. http://www.gg.ca/document.aspx?id=14615.

Grant, T.D. "Approaching questions in forensic linguistic analysis." In *Dimensions of Forensic Linguistics*. Edited by J. Gibbons and M.T. Turell. Amsterdam: John Benjamins, 2008.

Grimes, William. "Donald Marshall Jr., Symbol of Bias, Dies at 55." *New York Times*. August 6, 2009.

Haliburton, Charles E., ed. *A Biographical History of the Judges of Nova Scotia, 1754-2004*. Kentville, NS: Judges of Nova Scotia Publishers, 2009.

Halifax Regional Police. "Chiefs of Police — Nicholas Power." 2008. Accessed June 12, 2012. http://www.halifax.ca/Police/Chiefs.html.

———. "History." Accessed June 12, 2012. http://www.halifax.ca/Police/ AboutHRP/history.html.

Hall, E. Foster, ed. *Heritage Remembered: The Story of Bear River*. Bear River, NS: New Horizons' Centre, 1981.

Hill, Allan Massie. *Some Chapters in the History of Digby County and its Early Settlers*. Halifax: McAlpine Publishing, 1901.

Hodson, Christopher. *The Acadian Diaspora: An Eighteenth-Century History*. New York: Oxford University Press, 2012.

Hornsby, Stephen J. *Time and Tide: The Transformation of Bear River, Nova Scotia*. Vol. 31. Orono, ME: Northeast Folklore, 1996.

Hustak, Alan. *They Were Hanged*. Toronto: James Lorimer & Company, 1987.

JAMA. "Catalogues of the Graduates and Officers of the Medical Department of the University of the City of New York, 1890." *Journal of the American Medical Association* 60 (1913).

Johnson, J.K. *The Canadian Directory of Parliament, 1867-1967*. Library and Archives Canada, 1968.

Knight, Bernard. "Crowner: Origins of the Office of Coroner." 2007. Accessed December 27, 2012. http://www.britannia.com/history/coroner1.html.

MacCullum, Edward P. "Report on the Commission of Inquiry into the Wrongful Conviction of David Milgaard." 2004. Accessed September 29, 2012. http://www.justice.gov.sk.ca/milgaard/DMfinal.shtml.

McAlpine's Nova Scotia Directory for 1896. Halifax: McAlpine Publishers, 1896.

McGahan, Peter. "Crime and Policing in Late Nineteenth Century Halifax." April 1989. *Atlantic Institute of Criminology, Occasional Papers*, Report # 5. Halifax Municipal Archives, 363.2.M3.

———. *Crime and Policing in Maritime Canada*. Fredericton, NB: Goose Lane Editions, 1988.

———. "Detective Nick Power and the Halifax Police Department, early 1900s." August 1989. *Atlantic Institute of Criminology, Occasional Papers*, Report #8. Halifax Municipal Archives, 363.2.M3.

———. "Disciplining the Guardians: Halifax Police Force 1905-1913." March 1989. *Atlantic Institute of Criminology, Occasional Papers*, Report #6. Halifax Municipal Archives, 363.2.M3.

———. "Halifax Police Department, December 1989. *Atlantic Institute of Criminology, Occasional Papers*, Report #14. Halifax Municipal Archives, 363.2.M3.

———. "The Police Commission and the Halifax 'Guardians,' 1925-1934." November 1989. *Atlantic Institute of Criminology, Occasional Papers*, Report #10. Halifax Municipal Archives, 363.2.M3.

———. "The Reorganization of the Halifax Police Force, 1893." June 1989. *Atlantic Institute of Criminology, Occasional Papers*, Report #7. Halifax Municipal Archives, 363.2.M3.

Newton, Michael. *The Encyclopedia of Serial Killers*, 2nd ed. New York: Checkmark Books, 2006.

Northwestern University School of Law. "Wrongful Conviction of Thomas M. Bram." Accessed July 1, 2012. http://www.law.northwestern.edu/wrongfulconvictions/exonerations/fedBramSummary.html.

Olsson, John. *Forensic Linguistics*, 2nd ed. London: Continuum, 2008.

Parker, Mike. *Historic Annapolis Valley: Rural Life Remembered*. Halifax, NS: Nimbus Publishing, 2006.

———. *Historic Digby: Images of our Past*. Halifax, NS: Nimbus Publishing, 2000.

Petruk, Tim. "Hanging: Canada's Hangmen Lived Dark but Colorful Lives." *Kamloops This Week*, March 19, 2012. Accessed August 11, 2012. http://www.bclocalnews.com/news/143410946.html?mobile=true.

Rose, George Maclean. *A Cyclopædia of Canadian Biography*. Toronto, ON: Rose Publishing Company, 1886.

Shpayer-Makov, Haia. *The Ascent of the Detective: Police Sleuths in Victorian and Edwardian England*. Oxford, England: Oxford University Press, 2011.

Spitz, Werner U. *Spitz and Fisher's Medicolegal Investigation of Death: Guidelines for the Application of Pathology to Crime Investigation*, 4th ed. Springfield, IL: Charles C. Thomas, 2006.

Sugden, Philip. *The Complete History of Jack the Ripper.* New York: Carroll & Graf Publishers, 1994.

Swainson, Donald. "Sir Oliver Mowat." *The Canadian Encyclopedia,* 2012. Accessed June 8, 2013. http://www.thecanadianencyclopedia.com/articles/ sir-oliver-mowat.

Templeton, Jack. "Police Gallantry — the King's Police Medal." March 28, 2007. Accessed June 12, 2012. http://winnipeg.ca/police/History/story37.stm.

Thurston, Arthur. *Poor Annie Kempton — She's in Heaven Above.* Yarmouth, NS: A. Thurston Publications, 1987.

Twain, Mark. *Pudd'nhead Wilson.* 1894. Reprint, Mineola, NY: Dover Thrift Editions, 1999.

Van Den Oever, R. "A Review of the Literature as to the Present Possibilities and Limitations in Estimating the Time of Death." *Medicine, Science and Law* 16, no. 4 (1976): 269-276.

Wade, Lennie D. *Historic Glimpses of Picturesque Bear River.* Bear River, NS: Self-published, 1908.

Wagner, E.J. *The Science of Sherlock Holmes: The Real Forensics behind the Great Detective's Greatest Cases.* Hoboken, NJ: John Wiley and Sons, 2006.

Whitfield, Harvey. *Blacks on the Border: The Black Refugees in British North America, 1815-1860.* Lebanon, NH: University of Vermont Press, 2006.

Wilson, Isaiah W. *A Geography and History of the County of Digby, Nova Scotia.* Belleville, ON: Mika Publishing Company, 1985.

Woodman, Harold. "Lovett Family Active for Generations." *The Mirror.* December 1, 1982.

Illustration credits

Page 14 Map illustrated by author.

Page 21 Illustration of Annie Kempton, from the *Halifax Morning Chronicle*, September 9, 1896. The drawing is based on the only known photo of Annie Kempton, copies of which are on public display at the Admiral Digby and the Bear River Museums.

Page 23 Bear River, Nova Scotia (Digby County side), circa 1908. Nova Scotia Archives, Edgar McKay Collection, 1992-450 no. 51.

Page 23 Bear River, Nova Scotia (Annapolis County side), circa 1910. Nova Scotia Archives, Edgar McKay Collection, 1992-450 no. 52.

Page 34 Portrait of Nicholas Power, ex-chief of police on his seventy-fifth birthday, 1917. Photographer: C.H. Climo. Nova Scotia Archives, C.H. Climo Collection, 1987-72 no. 5.

Page 36 "Police Force, City of Halifax," September 15, 1894. Nova Scotia Archives, Tom Connors Collection, 1987-218 no. 675.

Page 43 Dr. Lewis Johnstone Lovett in his Bear River surgery, circa 1900. Photo courtesy of the New Horizons' Centre.

Page 53 The original map drawn by Bernard Parker for the coroner's inquest. "Plan Showing Kempton House . . ." Nova Scotia Archives, *Queen v. Wheeler*, RG 39, Series C, Digby County, vol. 17, #761.

Page 55 Bernard Parker's second and revised map, introduced at the coroner's inquest. "Plan showing Kempton House, roads and rivers in Bear River area." Nova Scotia Archives, *Queen v. Wheeler*, RG 39, Series C, Digby County, vol. 17, #761.

Page 70 Photograph of Peter Wheeler, taken in the Digby jail on August 7, 1896. Admiral Digby Museum.

Page 84 Illustration of Mrs. Mary Kempton from the *Digby Weekly Courier*, September 8, 1896.

Page 91 Illustration of Peter Wheeler from the *Morning Chronicle*, September 7, 1896.

Page 95 Illustration of Annie Kempton from the *Digby Weekly Courier*, September 8, 1896.

Page 97 Illustration of Annie Kempton from the *Acadian Recorder*, September 8, 1896.

Page 101 Illustration of Peter Wheeler from the *Saint John Daily Sun*, February 8, 1896.

Page 110 Headstone marking Annie Kempton's actual resting place in the Bear River Mount Hope Cemetery. Photo by author.

Page 110 Kempton family headstone identifying the family plot in the Mount Hope Cemetery. Photo by author.

Page 111 The Annie Kempton memorial in the Mount Hope Cemetery. Photo by author.

Page 116 Sketch of Mary P. Tuplin from the *Summerside Journal and Western Pioneer*, Thursday April 12, 1888, 2. Public Archives and Records Office of Prince Edward Island.

Page 116 Sketch of William Millman from the *Summerside Journal and Western Pioneer*, Thursday April 12, 1888, 2. Public Archives and Records Office of Prince Edward Island.

Page 162 Portrait of the "Honorable Sir Charles James Townshend, Chief Justice of the Nova Scotia Supreme Court, 1907-1915." Artist: Grier. Nova Scotia Archives, NSA Photograph Collection: People: Townshend, Sir Charles.

Page 171 Kentville, Nova Scotia, circa 1900. Photographer: A.L. Hardy. From the private collection of Louis V. Comeau.

Page 195 Detective Nicholas Power at his home, 119 Dresden Row, April 1935. Photographer: Allen Fraser. Nova Scotia Archives, NSA Photograph Collection: People, Power, Nicholas.

Page 225 Illustration of Peter Wheeler from the *Nova Scotian*, September 12, 1896.

Page 228 Illustration of Police Officer Harris W. Bowles from the *Digby Weekly Courier*, September 8, 1896.

Page 242 The press office of the *Digby Weekly Courier*, circa 1900. Admiral Digby Museum.

Page 258 Illustration of Isaac Kempton from the *Digby Weekly Courier*, September 8, 1896.

Page 286 Illustration of the Digby Jail from the *Morning Chronicle*, September 9, 1896.

Page 296 The purported signature of Peter Wheeler, taken from his alleged confession in the *Digby Weekly Courier*, September 8, 1896.

Index

Royal Navy 36, 253
Ruggles, Edwin 321
Ruggles, Henry Dwight 135, 136, 181,
    182, 185, 186, 201, 207, 208, 216,
    235, 321, 326

S

Sadler, James 31
Saint John NB 14, 93, 109
Saint John Daily Record 20, 48, 61, 90,
    103, 106, 161, 166, 243, 266, 276,
    278, 279, 284, 329
Saint John Daily Sun 81, 82, 93, 94,
    96, 99, 100, 101, 139, 155, 185, 205,
    213, 254, 275, 291
Saint John Daily Telegraph 235, 238,
    240, 241, 275, 276, 278, 294
Salvation Army 227, 250, 266, 281,
    283, 329
Seeley, "Kid" 189
Simpson, O.J. 91, 302
Southwest River PE 114, 118
Stanice Brothers 109
Stanley, George (a.k.a. John Ryan) 191
Stewart, W.B. 77
Stride, Elizabeth 29
*Summerside Journal and Western
    Pioneer* 116
Supreme Court (Nova Scotia) 122,
    123, 143, 164, 190
Supreme Court (Prince Edward
    Island) 118
Supreme Court (United States) 184,
    190
Sydney Burglar 189

T

Thompson, Sir John 254, 269
Thompson's Point PE 118
Thurston, Arthur 12
time of death 59, 60
Titanic 43

Toronto Evening Star 20, 275, 286,
    289
Toronto Star 255
Townshend, Reverend Canon 164
Townshend, Sir Charles J. 162-167,
    170, 171, 208, 212-217, 227, 270,
    271, 292, 340
Townshend, J. Medley 164
Townshend, Lady Margaret
    (MacFarland) 166
Trask, Charles 249, 250, 267
Truscott, Steven 301
Tuplin, Mary Pickering 114-118, 120,
    340
Tupper, Sir Charles 269
Twain, Mark 182-184

U

Unger, Kyle 301

V

Van Blarcom, Sheriff Benjamin 227,
    246, 249, 256, 257, 259, 262, 272,
    273, 293, 329
Van Blarcom, William Elmer 223,
    281, 285, 288, 329
Victoria, Queen 306

W

Wallace, W.B. 171, 214
Westerberg, Justus Leopold (Charlie
    Brown) 184, 185, 190
Wheeler, Captain David Stevenson
    24
Wheeler, Emily 24
Wheeler, Louis 24
Whitechapel UK 27-30
Whitman, J.W. 109, 276
Wickwire, H. 172, 173
Windsor NS 164, 243, 297
Windsor Tribune 297, 298
Wolfville NS 41

Debra Komar has worked as a forensic anthropologist in the US, UK, and Canada for over twenty years. She has investigated human-rights violations resulting in violent deaths for the United Nations and Physicians for Human Rights, testified as an expert witness in The Hague and across North America, and authored the authoritative *Forensic Anthropology: Contemporary Theory and Practice* for Oxford University Press. *The Lynching of Peter Wheeler* is her second book on historic crimes. Her first, *The Ballad of Jacob Peck*, was published in 2013 and was met with considerable critical acclaim.